The Shattering of the Self

)( )(

The Shattering

of the

Self

Violence, Subjectivity, and Early Modern Texts

CYNTHIA MARSHALL

THE JOHNS HOPKINS UNIVERSITY PRESS
Baltimore & London

© 2002 The Johns Hopkins University Press
All rights reserved. Published 2002
Printed in the United States of America on acid-free paper

2 4 6 8 9 7 5 3 1

The Johns Hopkins University Press
2715 North Charles Street
Baltimore, Maryland 21218-4363
www.press.jhu.edu

Library of Congress Cataloging-in-Publication Data

Marshall, Cynthia.
The shattering of the self : violence, subjectivity, and early modern texts /
Cynthia Marshall.
p. cm.
Includes bibliographical references and index.
ISBN 0-8018-6778-9
1. English literature—Early modern, 1500–1700—History and criticism.
2. English drama (Tragedy)—History and criticism.   3. Subjectivity in literature.
4. Renaissance—England.   5. Violence in literature.   6. Self in literature.   7. Catharsis.
I. Title.
PR428.S82 M37   2002
822'.051209353—dc21
2001004068

A catalog record for this book is available from the British Library.

In memory of Susan Snyder (1934–2001)

) (

Contents

List of Illustrations   ix
Acknowledgments   xi

Introduction   1

1. *Violence, Subjectivity, and Paradoxes of Pleasure*   13

2. *"To Speak of Love" in the Language of Petrarchanism*   56

3. *Foxe and the Jouissance of Martyrology*   85

4. *The Pornographic Economy of* Titus Andronicus   106

5. *Form, Characters, Viewers, and Ford's* The Broken Heart   138

Conclusion   159

Notes   163
Bibliography   193
Index   209

)(

Illustrations

Figure 1. The martyrdom of William Gardiner   86

Figure 2. Three martyrs   117

Figure 3. The roasting of martyrs   119

Figure 4. The severing of martyrs   120

Figure 5. The removal of breasts, teeth, and tongue from martyrs   132

)(

Acknowledgments

I AM HAPPY TO ACKNOWLEDGE the institutional support of Rhodes College, which provided the sabbatical leave in 1999 during which I wrote most of this book. I am especially grateful to John Planchon, then dean of academic affairs, who went out of his way to advance what must have seemed a rather peculiar project. I benefited from the generosity shown to Rhodes College by Connie and Dunbar Abston. The Folger Shakespeare Library granted me a short-term fellowship in 1999 that proved extremely valuable. I am grateful to the Folger Shakespeare Library for permission to reproduce the illustrations and to Dean Robert Llewellyn at Rhodes College for funds allowing their appearance here. Parts of the work were presented at the Modern Language Association conference in 2001, at the International Conference on Narrative at Dartmouth College in 1999, in seminars at meetings of the Shakespeare Association of America in 1999 and 2000, and at the World Shakespeare Congress in 1996. My thanks to the sponsors and audiences of these events.

It is a pleasure to thank other individuals who helped this book come to fruition. My colleagues in the English department at Rhodes College have provided a congenial and stimulating environment; special thanks to Bob Entzminger, a longtime supportor of my work. Early in the project, exchanges with Barbara Baines and Sara Eaton prompted my thinking about early modern pornography and violence, and Lisa S. Starks inspired my emerging ideas about the literature of sadomasochism. David McCarthy offered concepts and materials that proved important for chapter 4. For their support and guidance, I am grateful to Bruce Smith, Martha Ronk, and

Christy Desmet. Mary Marshall answered my questions about human physiology, some of them quite extreme, with impressive equanimity and thoroughness. Ellen Armour, Gordon Bigelow, Bob Entzminger, and Gail Kern Paster read portions of the manuscript and provided helpful comments. Amy Hollywood enabled this project in all kinds of crucial ways: she challenged me to write about Foxe, advised my understandings of Lacan, read the entire manuscript with her usual penetrating insight, and guided the book to its completion; her contribution, and my thanks, would be difficult to overstate. For his support, incisive suggestions, and intellectual generosity, I owe a profound debt to Jonathan Crewe. I am grateful as well to an anonymous reader for Johns Hopkins University Press whose acute insights and sympathetic criticism helped me improve the book. My thanks to my editor Maura Burnett for her skill, efficiency, and imagination and to Linda Forlifer for guiding the book into print. As for my family, the poise and intensity with which they pursue their own work has inspired me, while their attitude of tolerant interest toward this book has aided me in writing it. Among her other gifts, Anna Traverse proved remarkably adept at sorting out the details of martyrologies. John Traverse contributed to the project at every stage, with characteristic generosity.

The Shattering of the Self

) (

Introduction

$\mathcal{A}$T LEAST SINCE SAMUEL JOHNSON RECORDED his anguished response to Cordelia's death, critics have struggled with the awesome power of *King Lear* to unsettle its audiences. How to explain the aesthetic goal or moral purpose of a work that so determinedly wrenches readers or viewers past the bounds of emotional comfort, past even the certainty of physical safety? The blinding of Gloucester, Cordelia's unanticipated death, and the formal and structural excessiveness of the play's design have led some to speculate that Shakespeare was purposefully tormenting his audience. Stephen Booth, apparently troping on A. C. Bradley's remark that *Lear* was Shakespeare's greatest achievement but not his greatest play, called *King Lear* an *audience's* greatest achievement, shifting the focus from a formalist concern with design to a phenomenological one with reception. Performance critics such as Michael Goldman have also emphasized the emotional experience of viewers or readers as the site of meaning.[1] These were productive moves, but still the problem persists, for what sort of explanation can it be to assert that Shakespeare's viewers willfully chose to endure an emotionally devastating few hours? Such a claim runs counter to generally held ideas that great art is pleasurable or recreative and that it conforms with affirmative moral, religious, and/or aesthetic designs.

King Lear presents an extreme example of an emotionally demanding text, yet it was hardly anomalous within its own culture in purposefully shattering the repose of viewers or readers. In this book I show that an astonishing range of texts offered to late-sixteenth- and early-seventeenth-century English audiences an experience of psychic fracture or undoing. So multifarious was this element in early modern English texts that its exploration takes us from the religious propaganda of John Foxe's *Acts and Monuments* to the lovesick sonneteers of Petrarchan tradition, from the rough spectacle of the public theater to the coterie drama at Blackfriars. In these various settings, we find works that ratchet up emotional energies in what was evidently a carefully contrived effort to dismantle the composure of those who read, watched, or listened. The impulse resulted from the uneasy consolidation of early modern subjectivity: in the face of forces that were shaping a liberal, autonomous subject, there existed a well-established notion of individuality as both morally and ontologically suspect. This older understanding was manifest in multiple ways: in the established sense, derived from humoralism, of the human body as fluid and changeable and of the emotional self as highly volatile; in a religious tradition dubious of claims of individual self-importance; in a textual aesthetic of excess and extension; and in cultural practices that encouraged public display of emotion and shared catharsis. The contrast between these existing elements of early modern English society and the emerging idea of subjectivity demonstrates why and in some ways how an aesthetic of shattering or self-negation took hold: it constituted a counterforce to the nascent ethos of individualism.

The historicist model recently dominant in literary studies has overlooked or suppressed the tendency of early modern texts to shatter rather than to affirm selfhood. Stephen Greenblatt's influential concept of "self-fashioning" effectively recuperated the humanist narrative of the birth of individualism in the Renaissance, giving new impetus to a paradigm equating subjectivity with power and control. Although the investigations of materialist critics into political ideologies and economic and social conditions have added immensely to available knowledge of the period, they have too often maintained an unexamined sense of the congruency between history and literature. Moreover, the new historicist idea that texts do the work of culture and manifest power within it collapses textuality into culture, denying the imaginative space of writing. The force of textuality itself has gone largely unremarked, and the dialectical relation of texts to the culture within which they arise—the way writing arises from within a culture but exists at a self-conscious remove from it—has been neglected. What a culture in its official versions of itself is suturing together and publicly solidifying—such as the outlines of the individual subject in early modern England—texts designed for entertainment or meditation might be busily undoing. Our modern culture's entertainment industry, of course, largely operates on this model.

To understand some of the fixations of our culture, we can return to the question of the appeal in early modern England of textual violence. In the case of *King Lear*, for instance, we should ponder the way Shakespeare seeks out exactly those elements within available traditions that were most likely to promote a sense of undoing or loss of control. The apocalyptic elements that Frank Kermode identified structurally and thematically and that others have put into historical and political context are part of this effect, but I refer here to aspects of the play that would register in more immediate phenomenological ways, with compelling physical and emotional resonance for viewers.[2] These are the spectacle of Gloucester's mutilation, the way it calls attention to viewers' own vulnerable, observing eyes, and Gloucester's continued mutilated presence on stage; reiterated references to an unruly body understood in humoral terms as threatening to betray the speaker's control (e.g., Lear's *"histerica passio,"* his "rising heart," and his willingness to risk that heart breaking "into a hundred thousand flaws" rather than to weep [2.2.226, 285, 450]);[3] the effective martyrdom of Cordelia, sacrificed to her father's cause, and like most martyrdoms, calling up difficult questions even as it inspires sympathetic admiration; the play's determined refusal of closure, its structural excess matched only by its emotional demands, leading to an exhaustion so profound that it is remarked upon within the final scene ("Is this the promised end?" [5.3.237]). The play offers its viewers models for catharsis in Gloucester, whose "flawed heart . . . 'Twixt two extremes of passion, joy and grief" bursts "smilingly" (5.3.187–90), and in Lear himself, whose death presumably effects the heartbreak for which Kent calls. This list contains nothing new; commentators have explored each of these aspects of *King Lear*. What has gone unacknowledged, and my reason for beginning with this brief discussion of *King Lear*, is the way the play draws together early modern culture's available terms for dissolving the self. *King Lear* achieves its power by offering a compendium of Renaissance modes of self-shattering.

Although in many eras extreme forms of art have offered what Nietzsche theorized as Dionysian release, a conjunction of forces led to the proliferation of such works in England during the Renaissance. An emergent sense of the autonomous self, individually operative as never before in the spheres of politics, religion, and commerce, existed in tension with an established popular sense of the self as fluid, unstable, and volatile. Because the narrative terms in which we have understood the so-called birth of subjectivity invest value in the emergent self, we have overemphasized its early dominance, for a surprising variety of popular texts indicate the considerable pleasure afforded to early modern audiences by experiences of shattering or dissolution. These were moments of allowable reversion to the unstable and poorly defined idea of selfhood familiar from humoral psychology, underlying the antitheatricalists' idea of emotional contagion, and granted theological license in the form of imagined identification with suffering martyrs. If in one sense texts affording self-shattering served as counterforces to the development of modern subjectivity, in a longer view they enabled its continued growth by offering temporary respite from the accumulating pressures of individual selfhood. As a result, we inherit from the Renaissance not only a violent literary culture but also a notion of subjective identity partly molded through interaction with textual forms that cast pleasure in terms of dominance and submission, assertion and dissolution.

In the essays that follow, I approach, through two related arguments, the Renaissance impulse to negate selfhood. First and more polemically, I engage with recursive attempts by critics and theorists to plot the emergence of subjectivity in early texts. Second and more straightforwardly, I examine the historical conditions shaping the early modern experience of selfhood, emotion, and response to literature and drama. First, we need to isolate the idea or model of human existence operative in early literature, since to understand the transitive force of violence, we need to understand what it is violence *against*. Although recent work on the early modern subject has emphasized its ideological complexity and resulting distance from the coherent structure of identity projected by humanism, in practice a reversion to traditional models has limited analysis of the fundamentally paradoxical way in which individual identity is established in many early modern texts. Accordingly, where recent cultural historicist work has found in the "early modern" period the evidence of nascent modernism (the traces, that is, of our own self-image), I will be more inclined to emphasize historical differences between the earlier period and our own. This is less the result of an effort to demonstrate the alterity of the past than to show the ways in which a Renaissance literature of self-shattering appealed to its audiences by drawing on available terms for psychic dispersion. Even as significant discourses were effecting the emergence of the modern autonomous self, an alternative textual tradition made available another way of thinking about subjectivity.

I deviate from the cultural historicist approach for another reason: its dominant emphasis on the way texts do cultural work has eclipsed the dimension of pleasure and enjoyment from consideration. In breaking decisively with an earlier ahistorical formalism that understood violent episodes or images as motifs contained within an encompassing and usually affirming aesthetic design,[4] cultural historicism has paid inadequate attention to elements of formal structure and often has overlooked the question of audience or reader reception. Understanding violent entertainment to emerge, express, or reflect the culture within which it appears, cultural historians neglect the dimension of how and why viewers or readers (presumably) enjoyed it. Entertaining an audience is part of any text's goal, but it is for semiotic rather than intentionalist reasons that we need to consider this issue: the site at which texts take on meaning is that of the reader or viewer, and this dimension is accordingly crucial to discerning how and why violent entertainments signified. We need a way to account for an audience's pleasure in projected suffering such as that portrayed in violent Renaissance literature. A focus on pleasure is far from a denial of literature's seriousness: providing pleasure may well be the most subversive of tactics. In turning to the elusive question of readers' or viewers' responses to violent literature, my goal is to establish the discursive terrain within which something we call *pleasure* would have been experienced in the early modern period and thus to reinsert into a workable critical model consideration of the formal, aesthetic grounds of textual pleasure.[5]

Considering the way narrative poems about rape and popular stage plays featuring dismemberment and gory death proliferated in the early modern period, it seems obvious that early modern codes of textual pleasure depended upon a significant charge of violence. However, rather than attempting to demonstrate the pervasiveness of self-shattering throughout the period's texts, I have chosen to focus upon a representative variety of works from several genres. I have selected particularly striking examples of texts that undo or negate the self, and by the standards of established literary tradition, these works are distinctly marginal. The sonnets I discuss are by the lesser lights among English Petrarchanists; the "Book of Martyrs" has exerted its considerable influence without being considered a readable text; *Titus Andronicus* was long deemed one of Shakespeare's bastard children; and *The Broken Heart* ranks as a sensationalistic work by a somewhat bizarre minor writer. Their compromised status may seem to undermine my claim that an impulse toward self-shattering existed widely within early modern texts—perhaps leading to the suspicion that odd or bad texts simply pursue peculiar aims or achieve unpleasant effects. But the matter is not so simple.

Most of the works I consider were, in their own day, distinctly popular. Although no firm basis exists for determining the success of individual sonneteers, their work was part of a Petrarchan boom in the 1590s. The *Acts and Monuments* was reissued repeatedly throughout the late sixteenth and early seventeenth centuries, and other texts throughout the period make frequent references to it. Judging from the interest it attracted in its day (three quartos published in Shakespeare's lifetime, the Peacham drawing, the sneering reference by Ben Jonson in the Induction to *Bartholomew Fair*), *Titus Andronicus* seems to have been among Shakespeare's most successful works in the early theater. Only in the case of *The Broken Heart* is there no evidence of early popularity. We can account for the negative critical assessment of these works once we acknowledge that our literary culture has valued texts confirming the dominant model of heroic or autonomous selfhood. Works instead illustrative of the impulse toward self-shattering have been, for this very reason, considered inferior and even detrimental to readers. The history of strenuous but inevitably insufficient critical efforts to account for *King Lear* by placing it within a framework such as Christian allegory or political critique illustrates the challenge presented by a canonical text that fails to affirm the emergent model of selfhood.

Canon building is one example of the developmental, reconstructive, and structural paradigms within which critics approach the texts of earlier eras and impose congruency on our relation to the past. By contrast, the model of paradoxical subject formation I discuss effectively unsettles such narratives, both on the level of the individual subject (where it suggests the regressive element of pleasure) and in terms of a broader genealogy (where it upends cultural meliorism). Given the necessity of reading history "retroactively," in Slavoj Žižek's term,[6] an important concern in this book will be discovering the reasons why an erotics of violence tended to emerge in the literary expressions of the early modern period. Exploring the early modern literature of self-shattering involves not only recovery of a type of textual expression prior to or innocent of theory, but also tracing of the movement of that early textuality *into* theoretical self-consciousness. In other words, because the modes of self-shattering examined here are so intimately bound up with the development of subjectivity as a textual form, my argument proceeds diachronically as well as applying the terms of a modern theoretical discourse synchronically. I use modern terminology and the insights of its discourse not to pathologize the desires of the Renaissance but to bring them into focus and demonstrate their historical contingency.

As I investigate why readers and viewers would seek out texts and forms of entertainment that repackage the inequities and horrors of everyday life, psychoanalytic theory provides some crucial tools for engaging relevant issues of subjectivity, identity, and modes of personal interaction. Since audience response is notoriously difficult to index or explain—a difficulty compounded by the absence of sustained early modern reflections on the pleasures of reading about or viewing violence—I proceed dialectically, setting Renaissance denunciations of theatrical involvement beside insights from modern phenomenology into the dynamics of viewer response, early modern theories of the passions next to Freudian, Lacanian, and post-Lacanian theories, and Reformation models of sacrifice and self-loss against contemporary understandings of subjectivity and identity.

The theoretical concept of sadomasochism proves particularly helpful in understanding a desire for violence in textuality and in uncovering the early modern impulse to undo or negate the emergent self. Whereas the ego psychology familiar to many American academic readers asserts essentialist notions of subjective identity, the theoretical construct of sadomasochism, like the practice itself according to its practitioners, determinedly and disconcertingly works against established models of subjectivity. From Freud's early struggles with the concept onward, sadomasochism has been the barbarian within the gates of psychoanalysis, troubling established models by confirming what they imply but have rarely embraced: the contradictory, self-canceling nature of subjectivity. The discourses of psychoanalytic theory can be useful to the extent that we understand how they recapitulate the textual advances of earlier literature; as Joel Fineman put it, "contemporary speculation about subjectivity repeats in a theoretical mode . . . what literature accomplishes toward the end of the Renaissance."[7] Contemporary terms such as *sadomasochism* and *jouissance* can be shown to coincide in reference with an earlier language of catharsis, heartbreak, and passion. Psychoanalysis in fact evolved from traditional discourses emphasizing the complexity and instability of the subject—including, not least, Shakespearean drama. By contrast, cultural historicist paradigms follow the conceptual terms defining the political subject, and hence their limitation in the matter of understanding textual encounters; historicist models have proven particularly impoverished when it comes to exploring the pleasures many texts evoke as either a means or an end.

Moreover, contemporary psychoanalytic theory is scarcely divorced from politics. In particular, masochism, which has recently been defined as a set of strategies for collapsing socially sanctioned identities,[8] has profound political and historical dimensions. In sadomasochistic attitudes and behaviors, the disciplines (notably those of gender, class, and race) ordering normalized subjectivity are subversively turned to the uses of pleasure. Considering the way sadomasochistic practices contest these ordering codes, it is not surprising that sadomasochism seems to have developed in Western culture simultaneously with a modern subjectivity. Roy F. Baumeister reports that, beginning with "isolated cases around 1500, it [masochism] began to spread during the 1600s, and it became a widespread and familiar feature of the sexual landscape during the 1700s," although only in the nineteenth century were sadism and masochism isolated as identifiable perversions.[9] As society was perfecting the means to regulate subjective experience, pleasure in subverting those codes and effecting the subject's temporary disappearance seems to have proliferated. Provocative as these ideas are, however, this book does not search for evidence of overtly sadomasochistic erotic practices in the Renaissance. While it will be central to my point that aesthetic and erotic pleasure were and are bound up with experiences of physical and psychic pain, and while lines like Cleopatra's reference to "a lover's pinch, Which hurts and is desired" (*Antony and Cleopatra*, 5.2.286–87) and Isabella's eagerness to wear "th' impression of keen whips" as "rubies" (*Measure for Measure*, 2.4.101) attest to the presence of an erotics of pain in the Renaissance, my argument proceeds in a different direction, investigating an aesthetic of masochism—that is, a dynamic of textual interaction. Because imaginative literature occupies an oblique position in relation to a culture's public image, the literary texts of any given period do not simply or even primarily reflect established historical practices; instead, they embody the desires, often otherwise unexpressed, of writers and their projected audiences.[10]

Precisely because of the necessary and complex relation between desire and ethical thought, we need a means to analyze desire in order to take account of individual action within a culture, no matter how determinative the culture's forms. At the start of *The Ethics of Psychoanalysis*, Jacques Lacan, hardly known as a champion of individualism, proposes that it is fundamental to the task of ethical consideration. He suggests that psychology sometimes substitutes for moral critique, although it problematically offers only "a mask" or "alibi" to stand in for the necessary "effort to focus on the problem of our own action—something that is the essence and very foundation of all ethical reflection" (*Seminar VII*, 19). Rather than signaling capitulation to his critics' position, Lacan's remarks announce his effort in *The Ethics of Psychoanalysis* (and later texts) to move away from an earlier structuralist paradigm toward more direct involvement with the problems of social existence. He embarks on this course through consideration of the writings of the Marquis de Sade, recognizing in Sade's work an extreme example of how individual pleasure and social harmony seem to be antithetical and how textuality offers a complicated mediation of this conflict. Lacan demonstrates how a psychoanalytic discourse that promotes consideration of the terms and conditions of pleasure assumed in early texts can enable ethical reflection on our own relations to textuality and pleasure.

IN CHAPTER 1, I SET EARLY MODERN and psychoanalytic models of subjectivity into relation with one another and consider the implications of each for theorizing aesthetic pleasure. I begin by demonstrating how the discourses of humoralism, passion theory, antitheatricalism, and theology in their various ways attest to an early modern experience of the self as fluid, volatile, and vulnerable to outside influence. The picture of self-experience painted in these texts is strongly at odds with the type of autonomous subjectivity that cultural materialist and new historicist critics discover as emergent within early modern texts. Still under the sway of Jacob Burckhardt's celebration of the autonomy of Renaissance man, historicist critics have problematized the degree to which individuals were able to succeed in shaping their own destinies, but the central premise of an unbroken quest or drive for individuality has for the most part gone unexamined. Freud, by contrast, while sharing several of Burckhardt's assumptions, basically undid the humanist model of the self with the idea of the unconscious. Yet the concept of sadomasochism presented so strong a challenge—essentially a deconstruction of the humanist subject—that Freud struggled with it throughout his career. An examination of his evolving thought on this issue shows how Freud's position came eventually to correspond with that of early modern theorists on the passions by affirming the fundamentally paradoxical nature of pleasure. Much as Freud's own discovery of a primary masochism destabilized his notion of the libido-driven subject, so attention to the destructive passions evidenced in Renaissance literature shakes the putatively composed and forward-moving self of liberal ideology.

After placing the mythical birth of the subject into dialogue with early modern texts on the dispersive self and putting the triumphal humanist narrative into dialogue with Freud's concept of primary masochism, I move, in the final section of chapter 1, to suggest another sort of dialogue, this one between a moralistic understanding of violence in literature and an "esthetics of masochism," such as that outlined by Leo Bersani, that foregrounds the importance of viewers' pleasure in emotional release (*Freudian Body*, 107). Drawing from Jean Laplanche's reading of Freud, Bersani outlines a concept of the ego or sense of self as formed in response to a wish for its own dissolution and constituted through that wish. The type of masochism Bersani is interested in "has nothing to do with self-punishment"; it is instead an adaptive mechanism through which people, from infancy onward, seek "shattering of . . . psychic stability as a source of pleasure."[11] Historicized in relation to the early modern period, when new possibilities for subject formation involved corresponding desires for dissolution, Bersani's largely formalist model takes on further dimensionality. However, because the formal pleasures of a masochistic aesthetic are embodied in language, they are themselves subject to slippage. As a strategy for subverting culturally ascribed roles and their accompanying possibilities of pleasure, sadomasochism troubles the norms of representation and the position of authority on which language depend. Lacan's attention to the specifically linguistic implications of masochism is therefore relevant. In particular, his insight into how language compensates for loss or pain secures the relation between the violent literature of the early modern era and the historically coinciding emergence of a sense of self.

In subsequent chapters I examine early modern self-shattering as it was manifested in different discourses and textual traditions within the culture. Chapter 2 explores the fundamental paradox of speaking of love through a language of violence and shows how the studied prolongation of this dynamic in Petrarchan poetry dissolves purported oppositions between self and other, pleasure and pain, masculine and feminine, mastery and submission. Drawing examples from neglected sonnet sequences by William Percy, William Smith, Samuel Daniel, Michael Drayton, Barnaby Barnes, and the anonymous *Zepheria*, I show how poets turn formal excess to peculiar aesthetic purpose, breaking down symbolic structures to enable masochistic jouissance. I relate the Petrarchanists' pleasure in pain to the described experience of lovesickness in the Renaissance, which indicates a cultural predisposition to view love as an eroding force.

Petrarchan poets have frequently been called masochistic in their determination to be martyrs to love. When it comes to the real martyrs whose histories John Foxe recorded, the terms of debate are clearly different, yet the fascination that the immensely popular *Acts and Monuments of the Christian Martyrs* afforded its readers has never been adequately explained. In chapter 3 I show how the neglected question of readerly engagement is critical to understanding the influence of Foxe's work on subsequent debate. Lacan's meditation on Sade points the way toward an understanding of Foxe's appeal: rather than providing "pleasure" in the ordinary sense, martyrologies offer the more extreme, paradoxical, dispersive experience of jouissance.

Chapters 4 and 5 examine stage plays that invite viewer identification with spectacles of violence designed to effectively destroy a sense of self. Because theater not only entails multiple viewpoints but is the occasion for viewers to identify with various characters, it involves a fluidity of emotions and subjective positions.[12] In the case of *Titus Andronicus*, an audaciously physical recreation of martyrdom on stage challenges viewers in a more immediate way than do illustrated texts like Foxe's or Gallonio's. Since Shakespeare overtly sexualizes martyrdom through the plot device of Lavinia's rape and through the insistent focus on her body, *Titus Andronicus* delivers the early modern equivalent of hard-core pornography, pushing the erotics of pain, suffering, and dominance to new limits.

Like *Titus Andronicus*, John Ford's *The Broken Heart* exhibits a breakdown of structure, with the formal integrity of the play sacrificed to the cause of spectacular violence. But where the plot of Shakespeare's play from the 1590s proliferates occasions for violent action, Ford's play, written around 1629, is characterized by a virtually disabling restraint in terms of plot that is mirrored in the passive forms of suffering (starving, bleeding to death) that eventually are so stunningly represented. This shift from overt to passive suffering suggests the increased internalization of violent desires. It points to a future in which what exists in Renaissance literature as an outgrowth of the development of subjectivity came eventually to be played out mainly in ritualized subcultures and distinctively marked texts. The explosion of violent texts and entertainment in our own postmodern culture indicates a new age of tension between established and emergent understandings of subjectivity.

The literature of self-shattering that I examine reveals a deep, constitutive impulse within the early modern subject, an undertow that pulls against the drive Greenblatt identified as "self-fashioning." Our own culture's Emersonian ethos renders "self-fashioning"—almost a contemporary version of "self-reliance"—more appealing, at least in a traditional moral sense, than attention to its opposing force. Indeed, a recent work of cultural criticism raises the specter of a sadomasochistic culture as a terrifying tendency in contemporary America if we fail to correct our "Gothic drives."[13] *The Shattering of the Self* argues that we might better understand our current cultural moment by taking full account of a similar one four hundred years ago. Ted Hughes, writing on Shakespeare's affinity with Ovid's *Metamorphoses*, notes the two writers' "common taste for a tortured subjectivity and catastrophic extremes of passion that border on the grotesque." Hughes does not emphasize the individual tastes of Ovid and Shakespeare but instead sees them as products of similar times to which they give vivid expression. The *Metamorphoses*, Hughes writes, "establish . . . what it feels like to live in the psychological gulf that opens at the end of an era."[14] If Shakespeare's corresponding moment at the end of the medieval era and the beginning of early modernity produced an exuberant outpouring of energy, creativity, and self-determination, it also created a "psychological gulf" in the experience of many people. I show how a literature of self-shattering—including works by our greatest writers, although not limited to them—appealed to this mood and gave it aesthetic expression.

) (

Violence, Subjectivity, and Paradoxes of Pleasure

THAT A NEW IDEA OR AWARENESS OF THE SELF EMERGED in the Renaissance has become a simple statement to make but a complex one to qualify. In the past twenty years, new historicist and cultural materialist literary critics have repeatedly asserted that the human subject as known today—variously labeled as "liberal," "humanist," or "bourgeois"—began to emerge during the early seventeenth century.[1] Although the breadth of these claims has recently been quite appropriately questioned,[2] it is indisputable that developments in several areas complicated and extended the ways in which people in early modern Europe thought about their own existence. The advent of the printing press and the growth of literacy made it possible to read and internalize privately the words of other people; the Protestant Reformation emphasized the spiritual life of the individual; the growth of commerce presented a new array of items for personal consumption and display; the spread of the arts brought new images and perspectives on life before the populace. "What is striking is the way in which such a monumental change in self-understanding is fed from a multitude of sources," Charles Taylor observes in his authoritative historical survey *Sources of the Self*.[3] No one would seriously suggest that human beings underwent some cognitive change around 1600, but available evidence both supports the notion that a new idea of the self came into existence and accounts to some extent for why it did so.

A relevant question follows: what sort of self was it? The humanist movement, encouraging a delight in the human being as the glory of creation, and the growth of rationalism, culminating (at least in the standard historical narrative) in the Cartesian *cogito*, together fostered a sense of the conscious, self-determining individual as the one sure point in the universe. But while such was the emerging ideal, any number of signs indicate an experiential slippage from it. The violence accompanying the establishment of new forms of religious and state authority gives vivid testimony to the uneasiness or even terror with which many people in the early modern era confronted their autonomous existence. A focus on the individual self was morally suspect within a Christian ideology that encouraged selflessness and humility. Moreover, the ideas of personal autonomy and individuality presented ontological difficulties, challenging established patterns of cognition through which people were accustomed to thinking of themselves as unstable in some very fundamental ways. Indeed, various discourses give evidence to a concept of the self in late-sixteenth- and early-seventeenth-century England as not merely volatile but paradoxically affirmed in its moments of self-canceling or shattering. The degree to which early modern subjects were conflicted in their emergent selfhood, not just unstable structurally but dynamically and often simultaneously pulled toward opposite extremes of dissolution and coherence, has been downplayed by humanism's developmental emphasis. In fact, the contradiction between autonomy and instability *defined* the emerging subject.

In the early modern period, dominant psychological and physiological models, derived from Galenic humoralism, fostered a concept of the human person as literally fluid, since the body was understood as porous, volatile, and highly susceptible to outside influences. Gail Kern Paster's important work on early modern humoralism has suggested the extent to which the drama of the period refers to a leaky body and a tumultuous set of emotions, indicating a popular self-understanding radically at odds with the upstanding subject of moral discourse.[4] Humoral theory emphasized the invisible but ineradicable differences within a person. The physician Timothy Bright explains that, "although to the outward viewe" bodily nourishment may appear "uniforme," it actually "consisteth of diversitie of partes," refined through the digestive processes. Likewise, "the bloud which seemeth in all parts like it selfe, no egge liker one to another, is preserved distinct in all partes," actually consisting of four "partes," or humors, with variable functions and effects. Physical and mental health depended on the proper balance of these humoral fluids, yet individual bodies seem rarely to have enjoyed equilibrium. Women especially were understood to be unstable in their fluidity. If a strongly dualistic conception of the self had held sway, the body's volatility would have been less important, but in this pre-Cartesian era what we now consider the psychological correlates of the self—the emotions (or passions, as they were called) along with the general state of mind and intellectual function that they influence—were understood to be determined by physiology. Even Bright's twinning pronouns express the compounding of physical and psychological when he proposes to explain "the familiaritie . . . betwixt mind and bodie" by noting "how it affecteth it, and how it is affected of it againe."[5]

For humoral theorists, the passions in fact provided linkage between body and soul. Nicolas Coeffeteau's *Table of Humane Passions,* translated into English in 1621, follows Aquinas in explaining how the sensitive soul mediates between its rational and appetitive counterparts. By Coeffeteau's account, sensory data are judged and effectively labeled in terms of two opposing "powers"—one desirous or "concupiscible," the other oppositional or "irascible"—which in various mixtures compose the body's passional response. As a result of movement of these two powers,

> the heart and liver beeing thus troubled in their naturall dispositions, the whole body feeles it selfe mooved, not onely inwardly, but also outwardly, according to the nature of that passion which doth trouble it. For in motions of joy and desire, the heart melts with gladnesse. In those of sorrow and trouble, it shrinks up and freezeth with griefe. In those of choler and resolution, it is inflamed and all on fire. In those of feare, it growes pale and trembling. A Lovers words are sweete and pleasing, and those of a cholerick man are sharpe and rough: Finally, there riseth no passion in the soule, which leaveth not some visible trace of her agitation, upon the body of man.[6]

For Coeffeteau, the existence of two powers explains "the diversity of passions in man, the contrary motions & desires, wherewith his soule is tost" and why "many times we have a desire of that which wee strive against, and resist with vehemency." Rather than assuming a dualism of body and soul, then, he indicates subjective complexity in terms of contradictory emotions, felt as physical effects, sometimes in quite deleterious ways: "those things which delight the senses, cause a sensible alteration in the body. As in joy wee feele our heart open and dilate it selfe; especially if this joy proceede from an unexpected thing which concernes us much, it may be so mooved and agitated, as death may follow. As it happened in those women of Carthage, who having newes that their sonnes had beene slaine in battaile, when as they saw them living before their eyes: this joy happening contrary to their hopes, they dyed suddainely."[7]

For other theorists as well, a chief danger of the passions was their capacity to pull in different directions. Thomas Wright laments the "internall Combate and spirituall Contradiction" a person might suffer because "inordinate Passions, will he, nill he, cease not almost hourely to rise up against Reason, and so molest him, troubling the rest and quietnesse of his Soule." Part of the problem, in Wright's view, is what he calls "contrarietie of Passions," the way "one Passion fighteth with an other":

> The cholericke Cavaliere would with death revenge an injurie, but feare of killing or hanging opposeth it selfe against this Passion. Gluttonie would have dainties, but Covetousnesse prescribeth parsimonie. Lecherie would raigne and dominier, but dreadfulnesse of infamie, and feare of diseases draw in the raynes of this inordinate Affection. By which opposition we may easily perceive, how unquiet is the heart of a passionate man, tossed like the Sea with contrary windes, even at the same time and moment.[8]

The problem is not only with negative emotions such as gluttony, covetousness, and lechery; simple desire for pleasure was, to Wright's mind, a solvent of the self. Having "dayly and hourely discovered, an insatiable desire of delight," he finds it remarkable "how men affected with pleasure are chaunged and metamorphosed from themselves, untroubled with such an inordinat passion." Similarly, Robert Burton writes of the danger that excessive emotion might cause one to be "torne in pieces" by the passions, "as so many wild horses." Although he is describing what he calls "diseases of the minde," Burton's book makes clear the extent to which physical as well as emotional dispersal threatens those who fall prey to the ravages of passion and counsels physical as well as (indeed more than) intellectual or spiritual remedies. Even when Edward Reynoldes proposes that a "dissipation and scattering" of excessive passion may be effected by a "mutuall confounding of them amongst themselves," his notion of admitting "some further perturbation . . . and so distracting the forces of the former" assumes, homeopathically, that disruption can best be cured by further disruption.[9]

People so vulnerable to the effects of the passions would seem to put themselves in real danger by attending stage plays designed to arouse emotional response. So the antitheatrical writers thought, at any rate, without offering a developed explanation for why people sought out and were willing to pay for the agitations of theater. The antitheatricalists give further evidence of a concept of the self as "pliable, completely manipulable, like a . . . fluid that took its shape according to the kind of container in which it was put," as Laura Levine has shown. Imagining the self as fundamentally unsound, Stephen Gosson fears that exposure to mimed emotion will dissolve an established identity; actors can "wounde the conscience" of a viewer and "effeminate the minde, as prickes unto vice." William Prynne describes how an actor "degenerate[s] into a woman."[10] For Levine, the antitheatricalists testify to the fragility of a masculinity in peril of collapsing. As her analysis implies, of course, something about this incipient collapse must have been pleasurable, or theatergoers would never have sought it out.

That the passions were understood to be highly contagious supplies further evidence of the permeable boundaries of the early modern self. Virtually all the antitheatricalists refer to the effects of the stage as "infectious," as William Rankins does in the subtitle to his *A Mirrour of Monsters:* "Wherein is plainely described the manifold vices, & spotted enormities, that are caused by the infectious sight of Playes, with the description of the subtile slights of Sathan, making them his instruments." How exactly did the infection spread? For Phillip Stubbes, the vulnerable eyes were to blame: "For such is our grosse and dull nature, that what thing we see opposite before our eyes, to pearce further, and printe deeper in our harts and minds, than that thing, which is hard onely with the eares." Gosson suggests how theatrical "spectacles effeminate, & soften the hearts of men, vice is learned in beholding, sense is tickled, desire pricked, and those impressions of mind are secretly conveyed over to the gazers, which the players do counterfeit on stage." The effects of poetic verse were also involved: "because the Poets send theire verses to the Stage upon such feete as continually are rowled up in rime at the fingers endes, which is plaucible to the barbarous, and carrieth a stinge into the eares of the common people." Earlier he had described how poetic speeches entering "by the privie entries of the eare slip downe into the hart and with gunshotte of affection gaule the minde." Anthony Munday maintains that theater has a special power to implicate its viewers, for where "Al other evils pollute the doers onlie, not the beholders, or the hearers," theater makes participants of its audience, "For while they saie nought, but gladlie looke on, they al by sight and assent be actors. . . . So that in that representation of whoredome, al the people in mind plaie the whores. And such as happilie came chaste unto showes, returne adulterers from plaies. For they plaie the harlots . . . ."[11] For Munday, viewers' emotional participation in the enacted scene renders them "actors" themselves.

If we read through the moral outrage inspiring these writers, we find a notion of the self as highly wrought by emotions and a view of the emotions themselves as aspects of physicality. The self accordingly is mutable, so far from being immune to the physical effects of emotionality that we can understand, as writers on the passions like Coeffeteau make clear, the passions to foster the link between the higher, rational portion of the self and the lower, appetitive part. By arousing the emotions, theater exercised this link, bringing viewers' rigidly upright selves into contact or conjunction with their physical or appetitive natures. Although Prynne does not suppose Cupid's dart to work literally when he describes how theater's power to inflict love could effectively "devirginate" maidens in the audience, he gives a powerful statement of the force of emotional identification: "You neede goe no other where than to the theatre . . . . if you will learne to cogge, lie and falsifie . . . to pollute your selfe, to devirginate maides, to deflowre wives, or to ravish widdowes."[12] In a particularly revealing example, John Rainoldes tells of theatergoers in the city of Adbera who caught an "ague" that mutates into, or carries with it as symptom, the "phrensie" of speaking tragic verse:

> at midsummer, in very hott weather, *Andromeda* (a Tragedie of *Euripides*) being played, manie brought home a burning ague from the theater: about the seventh day folowing, they were ridde thereof, some by much bleeding, some by sweating, but all, as soone as they were abroade out of their beddes, did fall into a strange distemper and passion of a light phrensie. The which exciting them to say & cry aloude such things as were sticking freshly in their memorie, and had affected most their minde, they grewe all to Tragedie-playing, and full lustilie they sounded out *Iambicall speeches:* their toungs harping chieflie on *Euripides, Andromeda,* and the melodious woords of *Perseus*

touching love. So that the whole citie was full of pale and thinne folke, pronouncing like stage-players, and braying with a loude voice . . . untill at length the winter and colde, waxing great, asswaged their distemper, and eased them of their frantike follie.[13]

Rainoldes ambiguously suggests that the "passion" inspired by those "things as were sticking freshly in their memorie" may have caused the "ague" rather than vice versa. Since existing theories of contagion mandated the closure of the public theaters in early modern London during times of plague,[14] the association between the infectiousness of plague and another sort of theatrical infectiousness involving the passions was perhaps inevitable; Prynne cited classical precedent for the plague striking as divine punishment for stage plays.[15] All this suggests that early modern theatergoers did not simply seek a few hours of entertainment but put themselves in several ways at risk—and yet evidently enjoyed doing so.

The antitheatricalists indeed understand better than some modern commentators that theatrical pleasures may be distinctly paradoxical. From their moral standpoint, this contributes to the unpredictable danger of theatrical involvement: not only are things on stage not what they seem to be, but viewers' responses may not correspond to what they seem or are expected to be. Thus, Gosson observes how enacted or remembered sorrow may beget delight, even though the two ordinarily are contraries, and Rankins holds that those who seek to alleviate melancholy by attending the theater will find that "pleasure doth increase the same, and Playes rather enflame the fury therof, then quench the flame by any rest." Rainoldes goes even further, arguing not only that emotions may cause, or turn into, their opposites, but that viewers may hold contradictory responses at the same time. Rainoldes refutes its defenders' argument that theater teaches moral themes by allowing that viewers may recognize enacted virtue without unequivocally admiring it. Virtue may in fact arouse lust, so that men will "not wish them selves as chast" as a moral exemplar or maidens be "contented to become unchast in yeelding" to an attractive figure. If the appearance of chastity roused no desire, "Happy would Lucretia then have thought her selfe. For shee was not inferiour in chastitie to *Penelope*: and when *Tarquin* saw her, he saw her employed as a most vertuous woman. Yet, for all the wonderment he had of her vertue: he was more inflamed with love of her beautie. Yea, the very sight of her chast behaviour stirred up his wicked lust."[16] It is precisely because of what he understands as the waywardness of desire that theater, to Rainoldes, presents a danger. Pleasure, he well understands, is neither simple nor predictable, and it does not necessarily work in the subject's best interests. Rainoldes instead correlates pleasure with the violence of desire and with the desire for violence, both of which are seen as unsettling the self, and he anxiously acknowledges that audiences seek out such pleasures.

Both humoral theorists and antitheatricalists conceive of a fearfully unstable subjectivity and invoke the principles of Christian theology to guide and uphold the wayward subject. Yet by a peculiar paradox that bears investigation, the idea of dissolving or destroying selfhood was a desirable goal within orthodox religious discourse. We can glimpse this concept in the writings of humoral theorists, as when Edward Reynoldes claims that the passion of love is regulated by "the Master-Wheele" of divine love, "whereby the Soule being ravished with the apprehension of his infinite Goodnesse, is earnestly drawne and called out." For Reynoldes, a disruptive or dissolving passion is cured through the more complete disruption of divine "ravish[ment]." A weak form of the paradox appears when a moralist like Pierre de la Primaudaye observes that the conjunction in humankind of immortal soul with mortal body could best be "maintained by agreeing discords," achieving a "harmonie" "through their continuall striving." In its strongest form, dissolving the self through submission to God is actually constitutive of identity. For instance, when Coeffeteau recommends "contemplation of the first truth" as a remedy against grief, he notes how "some Martyres have given a thousand testimonies of joy in the midst of their torments: And Some marching barefooted upon burning coales, have protested constantly and truly, that they thought they trod upon Roses." Not only are grief and pain transformed into glory, but the martyrs achieve their identity through this paradoxical act of submission. As Jonathan Sawday reminds us, the concept of "self" carried a distinctly negative valence in the early modern era; "selfhood . . . was a token of the spiritually unregenerate individual."[17] We need to keep in mind the extent to which religious discourse shaped ideas about the body and the self in the early modern era and how regularly both Protestant and Catholic churches encouraged individual humility, submission to authority, and incorporation within the community. As I will discuss in chapter 3, the martyrologist John Foxe encouraged readers to identify with martyrs in their acts of personal dissolution, as a strategic means to redefine identity in terms of religious devotion.

In contrast to popular Western conceptions today, authenticity or good-ness in early modern England was not a matter of asserting one's "self" (or, in the odd popular phrase, one's "real self") but of accomplishing acts of submission to one's social superiors, to political authorities, and ultimately to God. Holding onto one's autonomy suggested sinful pride. To convey the undesirability of self-assertion, both Catholics and Protestants used the bodily image of a hard or stony heart as an emblem of spiritual deadness. John Donne's familiar line "Batter my heart, three-person'd God . . . breake, blowe, burn and make me new" or his prayerful plea to "thinke mee worth thine anger, punish mee, Burne off my rusts" registers the antipathy felt to-ward an assured, confident selfhood, which was understood to impede the requisite humility of faith. The purpose of battering or shattering the heart was not to obliterate it, but to render it soft and pliable, yet where the soft-ened heart was viewed by Gosson as a sign of, or a route to, moral decline, it signifies differently within the theological context, as a soul capable of yield-ing spiritual love for God. "With love / Stonie hearts will bleed," writes George Herbert approvingly.[18] The rhetoric of mainstream religious poets such as Herbert and Donne, as well as the theological opinions cited by moral philosophers such as Pierre de la Primaudaye, allow us access to the way religious constructions shaped individual self-understanding in the early modern period. Like the way scientific discourse determines the dominant worldview in the West today, theology in Renaissance England provided the accepted terms for considerations of essence and existence. One need not have been particularly devout to draw on religious terminology; it was sim-ply the available language for investigating questions on topics ranging from the functioning of the human body to social interaction to the politics of pleasure. Religion, along with the discourses of humoral psychology and antitheatricality, will be a recurrent site of historical positioning in this book. These may seem like odd partners, since religious and secular dis-courses have until recently been segregated in much historical and critical scholarship on the early modern period, but the modes of spiritual and bodily self-understanding actually were in many ways congruent.[19]

As we have seen, the subject theorized in the Renaissance was viewed as either dangerously unstable or worrisomely self-enclosed; it was thus necessarily contradictory, its moments of pleasurable balance at best elusive and fleeting. To bring together the various strands of discussion presented thus far, I will follow other writers on the birth of the subject by briefly turning to Hamlet as paradigmatic. Typically, Hamlet's reference to "that within which passeth show" (1.2.85) has been read as evidence for a dimension of internal awareness, and certainly Hamlet's interiority seems indisputable, if less than remarkable. That he understands this interiority in simultaneously physical and psychological terms is evidenced by his use of living metaphors, such as his references to "a kind of fighting" in his heart (5.2.4) and "all here about" it (5.2.150), which compound bodily symptomatology with consciousness.[20] Hamlet shares with the antitheatricalists a deep respect for the power of theater to affect its viewers, and he assumes that theatrical promptings will be uncontrollable, so that Claudius will spill his secret.[21] Indeed, Hamlet himself twice responds with passionate intensity to theatrical moments—the player's recitation of Hecuba's grief moves him to a guilty rage, and the *Mousetrap* (and ensuing events) set him into a frenzy.

What particularly bears notice, however, is how the discourses of subjective instability pressure the emerging sense of an autonomous self: how the most vividly developed and memorable character in this period's literature is obsessed with *not being.* "Oh that this too too solid flesh" (1.2.129), "to be, or not to be" (3.1.58), "conscience does make cowards of us all" (3.1.85), "we fat ourselves for maggots" (4.3.23)—over the course of the play, many of Hamlet's best known statements reiterate his wish to dissolve. Although the narrative plot of the play moves Hamlet into action and decision, as a character or literary subject his existence is achieved through his expressed desire to shake off the cares of living. Merely to focus on how his particular cares provoke weariness with life is to overlook the paradox through which he is constituted: Hamlet's recurrent wish *not to be* effectively deconstructs his character. Hamlet exemplifies how the masochistic self comes into being, is actually constituted, by a paradoxical longing *not to* be separate and autonomous. In this sense, regression is its original name, and textual interactions are accordingly most powerful when they appeal to the disintegrative urges embedded in this sort of subjectivity—as typically occurs with violent forms of literature. Further, since the established tradition of critical focus on Hamlet's character assumes an audience's identification with him, his constitutive self-dissolution is extended to those who watch or read. Hamlet eventually achieves heroic action, but for the long course of the play he displays doubt, uncertainty, anger, moral upheaval—experiences that fracture autonomy rather than confirm it.

The complexity of Hamlet's much-studied subjectivity has scarcely been overlooked, although the extent to which he is a self-canceling subject has been. One reason is the resilient influence of enlightenment humanism, which has continued to shape both the historical narrative and the model of subjectivity adopted by literary critics. As Levine suggests, even critics who reject liberal humanism per se have adopted its narrative of the triumphant emergence of subjectivity.[22] In an important corrective argument, David Aers observes that "the 'history of the subject' produced by cultural materialists and new historicists seems committed to reproducing aspects of the ideology which gave us the term 'Renaissance.'"[23] The self-regarding aspect of all scholarship of the Renaissance, but perhaps especially that concerned with tracing an emergent subjectivity, is striking: critics seem condemned to discovering their own self-image in those remote ancestors. A historicism focused on social relations of power and hierarchy has been particularly vulnerable to this habit, however, because of its tendency to flatten the literary text into a mirror reflecting the society within which it has been produced, a society that frequently exhibits patterns and problems similar to those of the critic's own.

The sort of critical narcissism that characterizes recent historical work can be attributed to two problematic tendencies. First, much of this work is built on an edifice that inadequately theorizes its own historiographic project, sometimes assuming an illusory objectivity, sometimes creating a dialogue among nonequals, as with Stephen Greenblatt's effort to "speak with the dead."[24] Second, attending to the intellectual and cultural context in which early texts were conceived, historicists can overlook the formal complexity of the texts themselves. This is problematic not simply in terms of aesthetic valuations but also because formal density shapes reception and hence helps to determine a text's function and meaning within its society. Too often historical readings proceed by flattening the text into a reflective surface lacking the density to alter impressions left upon it or to produce complex readerly interactions. For instance, an eclipsing of psychic experience has frequently led historicist critics to affirm the goals of early moralists who counseled rational, ethical self-direction rather than to pay adequate heed to their anxious accounts of what they fight against.[25]

Rather than seeing a picture of Renaissance culture revealed by historical texts per se, this book examines the space of fantasy, the zone or margin between the culture's official versions of subjectivity and the vagaries of the individual subject in his or her interaction with cultural ideologies. I take from new historicism a method of eclecticism, reading early modern texts from a variety of discourses: here medical, religious, political, antitheatrical, poetic, and dramatic texts are placed in conjunction. But where historicists emphasize the way the early modern texts shed light on one another and together reveal the world in which they were created, my work will also explore texts through their intersections with later theoretical conceptualizations. I join in this project with other recent critics who have worked to extend Joel Fineman's insight that contemporary psychoanalytic theory recapitulates what Renaissaince literature achieved in a different mode.

In the following section I examine relations between history, historiography, and aesthetics, beginning with consideration of the ideological function of the new historicist account of subjectivity, a topic that has been discussed quite a bit in the past decade. I return to it here to demonstrate the tension between a literary historical project that discerns a growth or development of modes of being and a literary critical project focused on the reading and reception of the text as a formal event. In recent years, this tension has manifested itself in debates between historicist and psychoanalytic approaches to Renaissance texts.

Self-Reliance, Self-Fashioning, Self-Shattering

The project of literary historicism presupposes a narrative structure, often a teleological one. The developmental model producing the "birth" of the subject, the spatial one enabling the "emergence" of capitalism and other modern forms of being, the sheer temporality of the "early modern" instance the design of an unfolding story, leading ineluctably to the writer's own moment. In many traditional models of literary study, this diachronic structure was complemented by a formalist criticism focusing on the text in its synchronic dimensionality. The assumption of a prevailing humanism, whereby themes and meanings passed smoothly from one era to the next, enabled the continued functioning of a complementary historical formalism. When structural and poststructural theories threatened to dissolve the humanist synthesis altogether, one powerfully successful response was the realignment of traditional historicism and criticism into the design of "new historicism." By this method, texts deriving from any discourse might be shown to shed light on the "cultural poetics" of a historical moment; the cultural moment itself was now the object of formal scrutiny. If new historicism in one sense emphasized the alterity of the past by seeking to uncover documents that would shed light on the peculiarities of other contemporaneous texts, in another sense the method collapsed the chronological division by encouraging critics to enter into dialogue with the scrutinized past, to inscribe themselves in their writings as interlocutors with their historical subjects.

In contrast to the established linearity characteristic of historicism, psychoanalytic theory posits an inevitably retrospective quality in all knowledge of the past—which is to say, at least in regard to the humanities, in all knowledge. As Elizabeth Bellamy has carefully argued, the psychoanalytic model of identity formation shares with the idea of the Renaissance a conscious interplay of before and after, whereby progress and development are a matter of remembering and repeating—and, sometimes, of working through.[26] From a psychoanalytic perspective, all forward movement in the human sphere is subject to what Bellamy terms the "temporal illogic" of recursivity.[27] But where a pragmatic, melioristic historicism attempts to shake the dust of the past from its boots and move forward, an approach based on psychoanalysis calls for an effort to assess and work through an entanglement with the past, toward the goal of greater understanding. However, no prescribed model for doing so exists, and informed critics seek different sorts of rapprochement between historicist and psychoanalytic models. For instance, in *The Story of All Things*, Marshall Grossman traces a progression in Renaissance narratization of the self, while in *The Tears of Narcissus*, Lynn Enterline resists "cultural genealogy" to focus on moments of textual disruption that encode the complex task of expressing loss.[28] Bellamy's acute diagnosis of new historicism's "premature foreclosing on the unconscious" suggests the extent to which the method failed to take the measure of its own position. In her insightful account of new historicist practice, "psychic experience disappears in the gaps of the subject's dispersal in the discursive formations of ideology."[29]

To put the matter another way and to begin to trace the ideological implication of new historicism, the notion of the subject's autonomy is recuperated by the very process that posits its vulnerability to shaping social forces. In the classic and influential new historicist text, *Renaissance Self-fashioning*, Stephen Greenblatt seemed to counter the humanist synthesis by documenting the elusiveness of a personal identity inescapably subject to cultural forces. And yet, by emphasizing a heightened Renaissance interest in the self and by writing about figures who were, for whatever reason, confident of their ability to fashion themselves,[30] Greenblatt in effect recapitulated the humanist credo, echoing for an American audience Emerson's "Self-reliance," with its affirmation of individualism.[31] In terms of function as well as content, Greenblatt's work shared something with Emerson's. As critics of new historicism have regularly pointed out, some of its dominant practitioners were concerned to fashion *themselves* as theory-smart but pragmatically historicist academics,[32] and in this way they resembled the sixteenth-century figures they studied, employing power in Greenblattian terms as "the ability to impose one's fictions upon the world" (*Self-fashioning*, 13). Both as critical thematic and as careerist opportunity, the concept of "self-fashioning" provided a late-twentieth-century academic version of self-reliance, rhetorically ensuring the autonomous subject against the incursions of poststructuralist theories that had threatened to dissolve the concept of self altogether.

Revisionists have problematized the historical model outlined in *Renaissance Self-fashioning*, pointing out how Burckhardt's master narrative of hierarchical medieval culture disrupted by powerful Renaissance forces remains intact in the book.[33] Less fully acknowledged is the way Greenblatt's book also reproduces Burckhardt's outline of the Renaissance individual and his humanist model of the triumphal emergence of subjectivity.[34] According to Greenblatt's frequently cited formulation, "there is in the early modern period a change in the intellectual, social, psychological, and aesthetic structures that govern the generation of identities" (*Self-fashioning*, 1). Placing strong emphasis on an individuality defined through negotiations of power, Greenblatt writes of an embattled self, pressured by shaping cultural codes. But if in Greenblatt's formulation the subject is beset with challenges from without, it nevertheless remains secure in its position as the unquestioned foundation of experience. Precisely because Greenblatt assumes that individuals exist prior to and outside of their encounters with culture's shaping codes, *Renaissance Self-fashioning* stops short of delivering on its strong claim that individuals are ideological products. That is, although Greenblatt sees the subject as challenged and even imperiled by the existence of shaping forces, he does not adequately problematize the *idea* of individuality, but rather assumes, Burckhardt-like, that it is the compelling goal of human existence.[35] As Levine points out, "the notion of a self abides even in the very attempt to get rid of it."[36]

Acknowledging that he owes to Burckhardt the "crucial perception . . . that the political upheavals in Italy in the later Middle Ages . . . fostered a radical change in consciousness," Greenblatt also attributes to his predecessor the theme of his own book: the new Renaissance men "were cut off from established forms of identity and forced by their relation to power to fashion a new sense of themselves and their world." Where he differs from Burckhardt is in the latter's view that Renaissance men "emerged at last as free individuals." Instead, says Greenblatt, the old feudal restrictions disintegrated, but "men created new models . . . as a way of containing and channeling the energies which had been released" (*Self-fashioning*, 161–62, 162). Greenblatt envisions a human subject born free yet everywhere in chains. His notion of released energies bespeaks an originary subject behind or beyond the law, whose drives are channeled by social restriction and whose vital essence laments being "unfree." He undermines, that is, the radical force of his own argument that the human subject is itself "the ideological product" of power relations by assuming that subject's prior existence. Even the Greenblattian discovery of a "'real' self" (*Self-fashioning*, 32) within the composite layers of the subjects he examines replicates Burckhardt's idea of powerful individuals "inwardly emancipated" from subjection when they realize the relative claims of state or judicial authority.[37] In psychoanalytic terms, Greenblatt adopts an oedipal construction whereby themes and their moralistic burden are passed from tradition (the Burckhardtian father) to the present (the Greenblattian son) through the body of the text (the mother).

I invoke these Freudian terms because Greenblatt's unresolved attitude toward psychoanalytic theory would prove indicative of the new historicist view of subjectivity. Although the work of Freud and Lacan is cited several times in *Renaissance Self-fashioning*, a few years later, in the essay "Psychoanalysis and Renaissance Culture," Greenblatt disavowed the theory's relevance, declaring psychoanalytic interpretation of early modern texts to be "marginal or belated."[38] In her powerful critique, Bellamy points out "Greenblatt's almost Oedipal ambivalence toward Freud" and notes that Greenblatt "at times . . . seems actually to be supporting the claims of psychoanalysis," not least by directing attention toward Renaissance "selves."[39] Yet his project depends on emptying the psychological implications of the terms he adopts from psychoanalytic discourse; he employs the theory without seriously grappling with its implications. For instance, Greenblatt explains the violence provoked by the Bower of Bliss in Spenser's *Faerie Queene* in terms of the framing idea of *Civilization and Its Discontents:* "'Civilization is built up upon a renunciation of instinct.'" Guyon's violence against Acrasia enacts a sublimation; it works as an alternative to sensual indulgence and in gratifying service to the higher goal of civilization. But as Greenblatt inhabits Freud's idea, its psychological meaning evaporates. Cultural violence—the English struggle with Ireland, Reformation iconoclasm—becomes the "reiteration" of the attack on sensuality in Spenser's Bower of Bliss (*Self-fashioning,* 179). For Freud, the success of civilized groups is in jeopardy for the same reason that individual contentment within civilization is compromised: because sexuality is the barbarian *within* the subject. Freud, that is, posits an inherently conflicted subject who creates a conflicted society; Greenblatt adopts the social thesis but largely passes over its underlying psychological basis. Consequently, Greenblatt normalizes the aggressive subject and rejects the route toward revealing its pathology.[40] In lieu of problematizing the relation between civilization and what it opposes, he posits violence as a necessary outcome of the advance of Western culture.

Although from the culturalist perspective *Civilization and Its Discontents* is taken to record Freud's general dismay about civilization, the text's pessimism is rooted more particularly in his structural sense of a misfit between social life and the human psyche in its sexual dimension. This idea, later developed by Lacan in relation to the writings of the Marquis de Sade, will figure importantly below. For Freud, the problem of civilization turns out to be the problem of human sexuality, especially its constitution in relation to aggressivity (*Freudian Body,* 18–19). Freud uneasily notes that "it is not only the pressure of civilization but something in the nature of the [sexual] function itself which denies us full satisfaction and urges us along other paths. This may be wrong; it is hard to decide."[41] When Greenblatt borrows the idea that people subjugate their own sexuality to correspond with his major thematic of power relations, he leaves behind Freud's supporting notion of a complex, internally riven subjectivity, presumably because for Greenblatt psychoanalysis is irrelevant to Renaissance literature. But like many great works, *Civilization and Its Discontents* encompasses the conflict over its interpretation, for readers typically emphasize *either* the pleasure-seeking subject's inevitable frustration *or* the tensions inherent in civilized society, when the work seeks to explore *both* in their doomed interrelation. The political stakes in any reading are high, for the very possibility of equitable and satisfying social behavior is at issue. Readings such as Greenblatt's that locate an entrenched conflict between the desires of the individual and the compromises necessary for group existence are the norm. As I have suggested, this reading enables the Burckhardtian thesis of the great man.[42] Yet Freud does not actually posit society per se as the culprit, but rather a structural complexity within the human constitution.

When Greenblatt turns to the sexual violence of *Othello*, the argument is similarly pushed in a culturalist direction, blunting its acuity. Finding in the play "a manifestation of the colonial power of Christian doctrine over sexuality," Greenblatt attributes Othello's murder of Desdemona to the Moor's sexual anxiety, awakened by her "frank acceptance of pleasure" (*Self-fashioning*, 242, 250). By killing his wife, Othello combats his own troubling sexuality. But how and why does this exchange—her life for his trouble—take place? Once again the psychological force of Freud's argument is sacrificed to the effort to locate overt social consequences of anxiety. Since it is acknowledged that Othello's own powerful feelings of erotic love present the fundamental threat to his established sense of an autonomous self, it would seem more germane to employ a dynamic model, such as the one Freud outlines at the start of *Civilization and Its Discontents*, where he finds the appearance of an "autonomous and unitary" ego "deceptive" and notes the erosion effected within the self by the unconscious and the dissolution of external boundaries experienced in love (*Civilization*, 66).

Nevertheless, in terms of the exercise of power, it is not especially difficult to understand why men kill their wives or why a white man would attempt to dupe a successful black man in a racist culture. The harder questions raised by *Othello*, and at least partially approachable in the Freudian terms Greenblatt adopts, concern the conjunctions of violence with erotic and aesthetic appeal: why does Iago find it sexually exciting to mislead Othello? and why is pleasure derived from watching Othello stifle his wife in her bed?[43] Because of its cultural emphasis, the historicist approach largely neglects the question of why sadistic spectacles of this sort appeal to audiences, and this is its real poverty as a critical method.[44] Although, as David Kastan notes, questions of pleasure and response receive more and more attention as Greenblatt's argument proceeds, it was his notion of shaping social codes that exercised a dominant influence on literary criticism.[45] In keeping with the views outlined in the essay "Psychoanalysis and Renaissance Culture," the evolved historicist model became one in which psychological complexity was a matter of social negotiation and literary expression occupied an empirical, political sphere.

In some ways this is an ironic outcome of the book's influence, because Greenblatt himself is an extraordinarily sensitive reader, and perhaps the deepest insight in *Renaissance Self-fashioning* is the recognition of a recurring dream of self-annihilation, the revelation that "self-fashioning always involves . . . some loss of self" (*Self-fashioning*, 9). More seeks "the dream of a cancellation of identity itself"; his *Utopia* offers the "pleasing reassurance that the fantasy of self-annihilation may be indulged in playfully without real loss." Wyatt's "goal . . . is to *lose* the body," whose "centrality" is "unbearable." Spenser's Bower of Bliss offers "absor[ption] into a world in which the normal conceptual boundaries are blurred" (*Self-fashioning*, 32, 54, 123, 172). Not precisely a suicidal wish, this longing typically evinces the deepest moment of self-revelation for Greenblatt's subjects. Paradoxically, the self reveals itself in its wish not to be. His own responsiveness as a reader produces this insight, although Greenblatt for the most part puts it into the service of his main argument, using the wish for subjective escape as evidence for the alienating pressure of the codes that mold the social self, an indication of the burden of living within a world of ideological forces. But the recurring dream of canceling identity shows something fundamental about the subjectivity of the Renaissance figures Greenblatt studies: for them, the having of a self is a burden from which they seek escape. More wishes to retreat into monastic anonymity, Wyatt in spiritual cancellation, Iago dissolves himself in order to inhabit his victims (*Self-fashioning*, 236). If these Renaissance subjects sought to model or fashion themselves, their efforts proceeded in the face of a fundamental wish to escape the burdens of selfhood. Their "loss of self" reveals a deep, constitutive impulse within the early modern subject, an undertow that pulls against the drive Greenblatt identified and offered to late twentieth-century scholars as "self-fashioning."

To understand the appeal of Renaissance texts to their audiences, we need to take better account of this paradoxical wish for escape or self-negation rather than merely accommodating it to the forward drive of self-fashioning. By colonizing psychoanalytic concepts, Greenblatt launched a historicism that was preoccupied with social and political negotiations of power and often inattentive to desires lurking beneath the textual surface. The method flattened its own analytical edge by insisting on a spuriously available cultural realism.

Moreover, historicism (old and new) tends to collapse the complexities of textual production, performance, and response into the large outlines of its chronological project. Even if we credit a developmental account of subjectivity, tracing in the centuries between the early modern period and our own what Lacan calls "the historical era of the 'ego,'" it is a mistake to assimilate modes of textuality to this forward curve and to assume a parallel progression in modes of textual interaction.[46] That is, individual readers or viewers in any era may respond not only variously but obliquely to texts whose content represents or enacts the organization and growth of modern subjectivity. Criticism employing a cultural studies model tends to assume an easy mimetic relation between literary or dramatic texts and historical ways of being in the world. Greenblatt, for instance, treats historical subjects and fictional figures as alike exemplary of Renaissance self-fashioning. Too often the moment or event of textual response is evacuated, and meanings based upon the phenomenology of reading or viewing are eclipsed.

Although historicist approaches have served for the past twenty years as what Carla Mazzio and Douglas Trevor call the "default mode" of critical practice, recently there have been ample signs of the mode's exhaustion.[47] One indication is the latest round of oedipal struggle, in which Greenblatt functions as disavowed father to a new generation of critical offspring (and in which I have participated by reciting grievances with new historicism and its signal text). The reiteration of this pattern certainly tells us something about the ingrained habits of Renaissance scholars. But I think it can more productively be understood as a resistance against the shaping ego traditionally conferred by the father—the sort of putatively autonomous identity Greenblatt observed Renaissance figures ambivalently seeking and resisting. With an acknowledgment that the ego imposes an alienating unity that fails to contain all aspects or levels of the subject's experience and knowledge, we can better understand why early modern texts focus so regularly on shattered selves, fragmented bodies, and perverse desires. A historicized post-Freudian model of subjectivity, one that is alert to the gaps within the subject caused by the misfit between ego constructions and unruly desires, has begun to enable a more decisive break with the humanist narrative and its recent avatar, new historicism.

Indeed, in the fifteen years since Greenblatt diagnosed the necessary "bafflement of psychoanalytic interpretation by Renaissance culture" and asserted the superiority of a historicism whose "multiple, complex, refractory" character successfully countered theory's "totalizing vision," the picture in early modern studies has changed considerably.[48] Some critics have taken up Greenblatt's gauntlet and proceeded to historicize psychoanalytic theory in relation to Renaissance texts, in the process showing the usefulness and relevance of each discourse to the other.[49] In extending questions of power and gender into those of desire and specularity, theoretically minded historicists have shifted the focus away from mimetic character and toward the interaction between readers or viewers and the performed or received text. The result has been greater attention to the phenomenology of reading and viewing and a more nuanced sense of how textual meaning is created and conveyed.

For Greenblatt, the claims of psychoanalysis were eroded by a chronology that rendered it anachronistic in relation to the Renaissance and thus doomed it to repeat rather than to analyze what had gone before. However, this model has been significantly problematized by those attending to the work of Jaques Lacan. The crucial move here is the insertion of the Lacanian "third term," or attention to language as the enabling factor in human negotiation with the unconscious and its powerful forces. Lacan's positioning of language in the center of psychoanalytic theory reveals a limitation of conceptualizations of a subject or a historiography that do not take account of the symbolic structures themselves and of the slippages, gaps, and displacements that render the claims of positivism deeply suspect. The nuancing of psychoanalytic theory accomplished by Lacan and by those who have followed him, including Julia Kristeva, Jean Laplanche, Mikkel Borch-Jacobson, and Slavoj Žižek, has made an enormous difference in the availability and applicability of psychoanalytic models to Renaissance texts. Simply put, it is no longer strictly possible to set a historical and political reading of early texts against a psychoanalytic one because claims made in the name of ideology and through language have been shown to enact psychoanalytic constructions.[50]

Moreover, the call for renewed attention to the formal and aesthetic dimensions of texts indicates a weariness with a historicism that too quickly or too thoroughly mapped complex texts onto their cultural contexts.[51] Greenblatt's move to turn the texts of Spenser and Shakespeare outward, for instance, made understanding of early modern culture a central objective of literary study; in the hands of less subtle critics, revealing a society's discursive networks became the only goal of textual analysis. For culturally minded critics today, the point of literary study is "to challenge the status quo and effect positive social change." Whatever one makes of this goal, an approach that collapses literature into a society's symbolic and discursive systems has effectively denied the grounds for meaningful political critique. As Michael P. Clark argues, "Literature as such simply disappears against a general background of material action or symbolic determination, and with the disappearance of literature . . . the possibility of productive independence, individual autonomy, effective resistance, and difference itself disappears as well." Revived attention to formal and aesthetic dimensions of textuality is desirable not as a counter to the social and political orientation of historicism and not as a nostalgic return to a New Critical sensibility, in which texts were seen as isolated from the vagaries of history. Rather, literature's distinctively literary qualities have begun once again to demand attention because the density and uniqueness of powerful writing demonstrate what Clark terms the "dialectical relation between work and world," the complex relation between the order of language (given undue emphasis by formalists) and the social and material reality of history (the goal of recent historicist and culturalist study).[52]

Although Lacanian psychoanalysis is often criticized for its structuralist models that seem to erase any space for individual voices, we will see that Lacan's work, because it addresses the misfit between the subject and the symbolic order, can aid analysis of the literature's form and function, and particularly of violence and aggression translated into textuality. Objecting that hisoricism has reached the point that "we have been left with no limit, internal or external, to the political, no space to reflect upon the specific forms that resistance should take," Tracey Sedinger finds such a space within psychoanalysis. The "discovery of the unconscious warps a positivist epistemology in which representations correspond to external objects." Such warping is not a denial of reality (as some opponents would insist), but the condition of the subject's connection to the social order. For Sedinger, attending to this "disjunction between the subject and the social" opens the way for political critique. Bellamy, too, has argued that psychoanalysis holds the potential to enable the critique of ideology, although she cautions that "a kind of discursive 'acting out'"—deploying psychoanalytic paradigms as analogies—frequently replaces a meaningful "working through."[53] Building on these points, I argue, more specifically, that a psychoanalytic focus on textual violence opens up the space of fantasy and thus points toward the textual density that often seems to evaporate under historicism. But first I trace the development of psychoanalytic ideas about the relationship between violence, fantasy, and pleasure as fundamental determinants of a subjectivity that remains always to some extent in doubt or under question.

Masochism and the Deconstruction of the Humanist Subject

The ideological character of Greenblatt's Burckhardtian thesis becomes even more clear when it is contrasted with the psychoanalytic account of the subject's formation. Placing the Freudian model in dialogue with early modern discourses demonstrates the recurrence of a fundamentally paradoxical configuration of subjectivity. Through comparison of the two accounts of subjectivity, we can appreciate how the humanist narrative of the subject's emergence tells only part of the complex story of the interrelation among textuality, violence, and subjectivity. Not only was a drive toward autonomy and individuality inscribed within humanistic texts, but a regressive pleasure in emotional dispersal was invited by a range of popular texts, though increasingly these were marginalized by humanist tradition.

Burckhardt's *Die Cultur der Renaissance in Italien; Ein Versuch* was first published in 1860. The historical text that would prove so formative for twentieth-century views of the Renaissance is not cited directly in the *Standard Edition* of Freud's work, although Burckhardt twice receives mention: in "The Moses of Michelangelo," reference is made to his *Der Cicerone*, and in "Leonardo Da Vinci and a Memory of His Childhood," reference is made to Burckhardt's words as quoted by Konstantinowa (1907).[54] We can gauge the influence of the historian's work on Freud and the culture in which he wrote by these references. Freud in many respects shared Burckhardt's nineteenth-century German worldview: both men embarked on ambitious projects scrutinizing the processes and meaning of human society, both evinced a Hegelian sense that the roots of dissolution were inextricable from the foundation of a civilized group, both emphasized the role of individuals and devoted much of their work to the scrutiny of particular people. If Freud's deep attachment to Rome did not necessarily testify to a Burckhardtian dimension in his imagination, his famous analogy between the Eternal City and the human mind—remnants of earlier stages of development survive in each—recalls Burckhardt's work not only in its archeological content but also in the humanist idea of the past's continuing influence. Burckhardt's understanding of the Renaissance individual, in its broad outlines, is congruent with the Freudian subject: formed in reference to earlier models, honed through conflict with powerful adversaries (who are at times allies), driven by violent passions.

But where Greenblatt more than a century later adopts Burckhardt's model virtually intact, Freud over the course of his long career unravels it. Burckhardt notes dialectically that "the fundamental vice of this [Renaissance] character was at the same time a condition of its greatness—namely, excessive individualism." Yet his Renaissance subject never loses a confident, self-identical autonomy: "In face of all objective facts, of laws and restraints of whatever kind, he retains the feeling of his own sovereignty."[55] Freud will label as "deceptive" this sort of belief in individual autonomy and radically revise the humanist outline of the subject, maintaining that "even the feeling of our own ego is subject to disturbances and the boundaries of the ego are not constant" (*Civilization*, 66). The dramas that Burckhardt sees occurring between powerful princes in Renaissance states are moved by Freud inside the subject, where the dominant superego strives to establish and maintain its rule. Freud's modification of the Burckhardtian subject radically unsettles the humanist model, reconceiving the subject's conflicts with forces in the external world as structural, essential, and unavoidable.

Nothing preys on the humanist model of the self-identical subject, however, like the concept of masochism. Where the existence of the unconscious introduces a structural inconstancy in the subject, masochism entails a dynamic one—a more truly paradoxical, because essentially active, movement of the self against the self, rather than the merely static existence of an elusive, internal otherness. Freud initially resisted a fully extended conception of masochism, approaching it instead as a perversion and a secondary development, but gradually it came to occupy a central position in his theory—even to become constitutive of the Freudian understanding of sexuality, in the assessment of some readers. Masochism presented a problem for Freud because it conflicted fundamentally with his view of a pleasure-seeking subject. To allow it into his theory meant a radical revision, essentially a deconstruction, of his model of the self. Sadism, on the other hand, initially presented little explanatory difficulty, since it was largely consistent with Freud's view that "the sexuality of most male human beings" contains "an element of *aggressiveness*," as he put it in his first discussion of the concept, in "The Three Essays on the Theory of Sexuality" (1905) (*Three Essays*, 157; his emphasis). In fact, understanding the relationship between sadism and masochism was the real challenge for Freud, as for many later writers on the subject. His discussions are central here because they have prompted ongoing consideration of the relationality of subjects in a contract combining pleasure and unpleasure. Moreover, because Freud saw masochism as a matter both of interaction and of representation, it presented for him "a problem of language."[56] Freud's evolving work on masochism points us not just toward an understanding of torturing and suffering subjects inscribed in literary fiction, but toward an explication of the reader's position in connection to such works. At the same time, because Freud's efforts to theorize the rupture in the humanist model of the self that masochism evidences are never entirely successsful, a review of his work helps us to appreciate masochism's powerfully disruptive theoretical potential.

At this point in the development of psychoanalytic and postpsychoanalytic discourse, masochism has a history of its own. Because of its sexually marked character, the concept usually elicits strong fixed opinions. While granting the irretrievability of a "pure" concept of masochism (even assuming such a thing ever existed), I want nevertheless to propose the similarity between it and the early moderns' simultaneous desire for and fear of self-undoing. In each case, extreme experience grants a temporary release from the ordering structures of identity. What the early moderns knew in various configurations as lovesickness, martyrological jouissance, or heartbreak, Freud theorized as sadomasochism. This is not to assert universal categories of experience: as I have begun to show, the modes of self-undoing in the early modern period were quite historically specific. Rather, I am arguing that Freud's theoretical framework allows recognition and articulation of phenomena obscured by the myth of the humanist subject. To the extent that early modern concepts shape our culture, we can understand pyscho-analysis as belatedly manifesting the earlier ideas.

In the "Three Essays," Freud comes close to seeing sadism and masoch-ism as congruent, arguing that these "most common and most significant of all the perversions" involve "the desire to inflict pain upon the sexual object, and its reverse." Sadism's "roots" are explicable because of the aggressive ele-ment in sexuality, but Freud doubts that masochism "can ever occur as a pri-mary phenomenon" (*Three Essays*, 157, 158). As Freud muses over what he calls "the most remarkable feature of this perversion," we glimpse the direction his argument on the subject will later take; he notes that "its active and pas-sive forms are habitually found to occur together in the same individuals. . . . A sadist is always at the same time a masochist" (*Three Essays*, 157, 159). With this observation, the distinction between the two forms, and hence the prior-ity given to sadism, begins to erode. Furthermore, the theory of the "Three Essays" labors under a wider, structural burden. Freud makes the odd move of beginning a systematic study of sexuality by examining the "sexual aberra-tions." Approaching the normal by way of the abnormal, the argument seems to acknowledge something out of kilter, something dysfunctional, about sexuality itself. As Bersani shows, in each of the "Three Essays" Freud confronts a problem inherent in his understanding of sexuality: how to rec-oncile the derivation of pleasure from an unpleasurable feeling of tension (*Freudian Body*, 34).

The inquiry into "what sort of relation exists between pleasure and unpleasure" continues in "Instincts and Their Vicissitudes" (1914), in which Freud once again denies the primacy of masochism (*Instincts*, 121). The essay theorizes the mobility of instincts, which may undergo reversal, "turning round on the self" (i.e., reflexivity), repression, or sublimation. This allows the explanation that "masochism is actually sadism turned round upon the subject's own ego," and Freud outlines three steps in this process: sadism proper, in which pain is inflicted on an external object (another person); the replacement of this object by the self; the recruitment of another, an "extra-neous person," to play "the role of the subject" (*Instincts*, 127). The confusion of grammar that occurs here requires a footnote in the *Standard Edition,* and no wonder. Freud has split the subject, cast one part in the role of object (to the sadistic self), and then replaced the other (actively sadistic) part with a role-playing "extraneous person." This tendentious argument manages technically to avoid positing a masochism that does not originate in sadism, but as Jean Laplanche perceives, Freud's special pleading gives his cause away.[57] Freud goes so far as to posit that sadists identify with their victims, which leads to the admission that "the enjoyment of pain would thus be an aim which was originally masochistic," yet with the apparently contradictory qualification that such an original masochism "can only become an instinctual aim in someone who was originally sadistic" (*Instincts,* 129). He works himself into a logical deadlock with the effort to maintain both that sadism and masochism are separate phenomena *and* that only the former has primacy. The underlying assumption is the same as that of the Renaissance antitheatricalists: a dangerous sort of pleasure resides in the force of psychic identification, a potential to dissolve the self altogether.

The dynamic, shifting positionality theorized in "Instincts and Their Vicissitudes" develops into a full-blown fantasy sequence in "A Child Is Being Beaten" (1919). Here Freud actually constructs a hidden masochism to account for his patients' beating fantasies, in the process acknowledging the shifting ground of fantasy, the logical necessity of masochism, and the odd status of masochism as both fantasy and emotional truth. Once again he grounds the masochistic scenario in something like sadism: he claims to uncover an initial phase in which the patient imagines "my father is beating the child whom I hate." But the fantasy is not exactly sadistic, Freud says, because "the child producing the phantasy is never doing the beating herself" (*Child,* 185). Indeed, it may not even be a fantasy proper, but rather a set of memories of witnessed events or of fleeting desires. To solder this (pseudo) fantasy into the patient's emotional life and to attach a sexual charge to it, Freud constructs a second "momentous" phase, "of an unmistakably masochistic character": now the patent imagines "I am being beaten by my father." As "a construction of analysis," this phase "is never remembered, it has never succeeded in becoming conscious" (*Child,* 185). However, in Freud's account it is logically necessary in order to account for the pleasure derived from the third, objective phase of the fantasy: "a child is being beaten." The pleasure depends on a hidden masochism, which takes on a motive force and priority not previously granted in Freud's formulations. He makes a further move toward acknowledging a paradoxical basis for pleasure by admitting that "unpleasure" has a part in masochism as well as "passivity," although he still maintains that masochism "originates from sadism which has been turned round upon the self" (*Child*, 194). "A Child Is Being Beaten" furthers the transitive emphasis of "Instincts and Their Vicissitudes," with the aim itself maintained while both its object and its subject shift.

"After 1920"—or after "Beyond the Pleasure Principle"—"what is considered as the initial stage is the reflexive, masochistic moment: to make oneself suffer or to destroy oneself" (*Life and Death*, 88). With this move, "The Economic Problem of Masochism" (1924) can account for what was previously inexplicable by positing a conjunction of the death instinct with the libido to produce several kinds of masochism. Here Freud distinguishes three forms: erotogenic "pleasure in pain," which is said to underlie the other two forms as well; feminine masochism, in which men fantasize about or seek out the submissive role in sexual play; and moral masochism, manifested in a "sense of guilt" that Freud finds entirely comprehensible. The incommensurability of these designations is striking. Erotogenic masochism is not really a separate category, since it provides the basis for the other types. Moral masochism has "loosened its connection with what we recognize as sexuality" (*EPM*, 165), and while Freud works to resecure that connection by attributing moral masochism to the fusion of the death and erotic instincts, his own account acknowledges the lack of specificity in this type of masochism (which corresponds to current usage of the term in a descriptive sense with no explicit overtones of erotic practice). Feminine masochism, which in a clinical sense interests Freud the most, introduces its own set of puzzles, since its name persists in the equation of femininity with passivity. Yet one notices that a specifically *female* form of masochism receives no designation in this essay, and this fact, together with Freud's acknowledgement of the role-playing that is crucial to the feminine masochist's pleasures, loosens the stability of gender differentiations. As John Noyes argues, Freud's theory of primary masochism "disqualifies a biologically founded distinction between male and female sexual behavior."[58] Indeed, later theorists, notably Margaret Mahler, would understand masochism to arise from preoedipal psychodynamics, before identity or gender has been constituted.[59] Of course, to Freud undifferentiated gender would be coded as "feminine," so in a sense he anticipates his preoedipal revisers by gendering "feminine masochism."

The turning point in Freud's considerations of masochism occurs in "Beyond the Pleasure Principle," where he admits for the first time that the pursuit of pleasure does not tell the whole story of human psychology. The biologistic argument for "the *conservative* nature of living substance" locates an "inertia," a wish "to restore an earlier state of things," inherent within nature. According to this principle and the evolutionary logic that "inanimate things existed before living ones," Freud finds a developmental tension whereby "what had hitherto been an inanimate substance endeavor[s] to cancel itself out" (*BPP*, 36, 38). The genesis of life itself is accompanied by a wish for dissolution. Freud makes an effort to save the sexual instincts, at least, from the pull of death by suggesting a dualism whereby the ego instincts pressure the subject toward death while the sexual instincts exert a countertug toward life. But since, by his own account, the "ego is the true and original reservoir of libido," the attempted separation of ego instincts from sexual ones breaks down (*BPP*, 51). This leads to the further step of allowing that "there *might* be such a thing as primary masochism." The death instinct, directed outward, would account for sadism, but the new focus on the movement toward dissolution within the subject means that masochism now seems to be the prior state. After all, the pleasure of sexuality "is associated with a momentary extinction," so pleasure now appears to Freud to be paradoxical at its very core.[60]

Freud's long struggle to incorporate a primary masochism into his understanding of the human subject points toward four relevant conclusions. First, he unsettles the triumphal narrative of humanism and many of its central, cherished distinctions. By locating (a self-directed) aggressivity within the subject, he disrupts the contest between civilization and barbarism, whereby the former supposedly defeats the violence of the latter. By showing the sadomasochistic sequence to shift in terms of subject and object, he undoes the stable link between cultural categories of identity (gender, race, class) and erotic positionality. As Laplanche indicates, "the *exception*—i.e. the perversion [that is, sadomasochism]—ends up by *taking the rule along with it*. . . . undermining and destroying the very notion of a biological norm."[61]

Second, Freud derives a model of the subject that is neither autonomous nor self-identical. Rather than placing the subject in endless quest of an individuality that is denied by social forces (the culturalist view, as exemplified above by Greenblatt), Freud posits a more radically paradoxical birth of the subject. In Bersani's words, "*the first psychic totality would thus be constituted by a desire to shatter totality.* The ego, at its origin, would be nothing more than a kind of passionate inference necessitated by the anticipated pleasure of its own dismantling." As masochism enters into this understanding of subjectivity, it "has nothing to do with self-punishment"; it is instead about the *formation* of the self.[62] Yet the formation and the dissolution of the self are locked in a profoundly paradoxical tension, and this paradoxical account of subjectivity has implications for aesthetic theory. Because art can perpetuate, elaborate, and interpret the pleasurable tensions of violence, Bersani posits an "esthetics of masochism."[63] For some, this will seem a dangerously self-indulgent and (in the term of early Freud) perverse relationship between art and literature. But as Bersani, drawing on Laplanche, understands the human situation, the choice is not really between violent and nonviolent forms of entertainment. "If . . . human sexuality is grounded in masochism, we are, ontologically, implicated in violence almost from the beginning; our choice is not between violence and nonviolence, but is rather between the psychic dislocations of mobile desire and a destructive fixation on anecdotal violence" (*Freudian Body*, 70). Whereas in current popular debate forms of entertainment that "glorify" violence are set against forms that stringently avoid it, Bersani regards it as given that people will be drawn to violence in the arts. For him, the useful contrast is between narrative or anecdotal violence, which is privileged and repeated for its own sake, and formally complex uses of violence that subordinate the actions of particular subjects, problematize simple repetition, and throw established identities into question (*Freudian Body*, 70–75).

Recent theoretical discussions of masochism have been highly politicized, with considerable disagreement registered about both the plausability and the desirability of masochism's unsettling of established norms of gender and power. Kaja Silverman, arguing that a dissolved subject is inherently superior to a unified one, sees masochism as a subversive tool against mastery and established power. In her analysis, the male masochist "deploys the diversionary tactics of demonstration, suspense, and impersonation against the phallic 'truth' or 'right,' substituting perversion for the *père-version* of exemplary male subjectivity." Suzanne Stewart, by contrast, argues that male masochism has historically served to recuperate masculinity; in Stewart's view, masochism, through its apparent marginalization, functions rhetorically to ensure male hegemony.[64] Clearly, the argument goes to basic issues in postmodern theory, having to do with the possibility of a viable political subject in a realm that does not perpetuate structures of power that are inevitably unequal. Bersani himself rejects utopian claims for masochism, while maintaining that his model is a dynamic one. "A pleasure in losing or dissolving the self . . . is in no way equated with loss," since the subject is initially formed through a dissolution or shattering "but comes rather through rediscovering the self outside the self." An aesthetics of masochism involves self-shattering that is also "self-accretion," the "effect of reaching toward one's own 'form' elsewhere."[65] Thus, it involves neither an overturning nor a recuperation of established power relations, but a movement toward renegotiation of the terms of power themselves. For Bersani, an aesthetics of masochism would not be a matter of simply theatricalizing or repeating scenarios of domination and subordination (as, arguably, occurs in sado-masochistic sex acts), but of delivering a pleasure in relinquishing control, so that power's preeminence in structuring the subject is loosened.[66] From one angle, of course, this sounds decidedly utopian, and from Stewart's feminist perspective Bersani disavows and "de-Oedialize[s]" the father to effect his return in place of the traumatically seductive mother.[67]

Third, as Stewart's critique of Bersani indicates, dissolution of identity carries implications for gender. Freud's interpreters have developed these implications in several directions. For Mahler, as noted above, masochism is rooted in infantile symbiosis with the mother,[68] and the preoedipal paradigm illuminates the flexible role-playing, ambivalences, and aversion to closure that formally characterize masochistic scenarios. Gilles Deleuze also points to the potency of the mother figure in what he sees as a regressive masochistic embrace of the oral mother of infantile fantasy (*Coldness*, 57–68). Deleuze's view is compromised in that the mother is precisely *not identified* by the infant until after the (oedipal) fact; the pleasure of infantile symbiosis is largely that of undifferentiated identities.[69] The wish for self-shattering includes, or may actually center upon, an impulse to negate gender identity, and both men and women manifest such a wish. Nevertheless, the forms in which the wish is expressed—the ways it shapes behavior and the ways in which lived experiences motivate and structure it—are profoundly subject to gender difference. As we will see, the self-shattering inscribed in early modern texts is primarily presented for masculine pleasure. Where women are offered up as martyrs in Foxe or as spectacular victims like Lavinia in *Titus Andronicus* or as exemplars of self-destructive energy like Calantha in *The Broken Heart*, their position as feminine would heighten the masochistic dissolution available to identifying male viewers or readers. For female audience members, accustomed as women traditionally were to taking the male experience as universal, images of masculine suffering would have been more likely to promote imaginative self-shattering, while the spectacle of feminine dissolution might have been more likely to register as heroic. Because women were culturally defined as less firmly fixed than men in their identity structures—more vulnerable to passion, more fluid in their bodily economy, more susceptible to familial and social controls—they were unlikely to have experienced the same crisis of imposed autonomy that men did. Instead, women may well have taken pride and subversive pleasure in the heroic deeds performed by female characters, even when the deeds led to punishment or self-destruction.

In both a structural and a historical sense, the potential Bersani uncovers in the psychoanalytic concept of masochism as "a powerful weapon in the struggle against the disciplinarian constraints of identity" takes us back to the established early modern concept of the fluid, undefined self.[70] The Freudian idea of pleasure recapitulates in another key what the antitheatricalists feared—a dissolution of identity—and hence the usefulness of the theoretical concept as a way to recognize the psychological tendencies of early texts. Moreover, I am proposing that an "aesthetics of masochism" arises in response to the specifically historical development of subjectivity in culture, and not as the inevitable correlate of individual subject formation.

To begin to imagine the pleasures and benefits of a dissolved identity and (if Bersani is right) the accompanying "self-accretion" in an era of newly exploding possibilities for thinking about the self such as the Renaissance pushes us toward the fourth implication of Freud's endorsement of a primary masochism. Laplanche points out that Freud specifically forgoes the most available explanation for masochism—that of the *"internalization of the entire scene,"* whereby the subject, divided against itself, would cause pain with one part or agency of the self in order to produce pleasure for another.[71] Although Freud comes close to producing this solution in the paradigm for the production of masochism in "Instincts and Their Vicissi-tudes," his long-term avoidance of it—even though it would seem to follow readily upon the basic psychoanalytic insight of the split subject—indicates the truly radical nature of his conception of masochism. Rather than ac-commodating masochism to his established model, Freud acknowledges that it introduces a fundamental wrinkle into the forward-moving, plea-sure-seeking, humanist self. In Laplanche's words: "The subject is masoch-istic only insofar as he derives enjoyment *precisely there where* he suffers, and not insofar as he suffers in one place in order to derive enjoyment in an-other. . . . This may also be formulated as follows: the subject suffers *in order to* derive enjoyment and not only *in order to be able* to derive enjoyment (or to pay the 'tax' for enjoyment)" (*Life and Death*, 104; emphasis in original). Rather than resolving the problem of masochism by imposing a structural or temporal model, Freud conceives a thoroughly paradoxical masochism. Where the death drive is frequently supposed to involve an originary, outer-directed aggressivity, Laplanche articulates primary masochism along different lines, those of reflexivity: "The essential dimension of the affirma-tion of a death drive lies neither in the discovery of aggressiveness, nor in its theorization. . . . It is in the idea that the aggressiveness is first of all directed against the subject and, as it were, stagnant within him, before being deflected toward the outside." Moreover, Laplanche suggests that sexuality only exists to the extent that such a reflexivity occurs, "so that, within *the field of sexuality*, masochism is already considered as primary" (*Life and Death*, 86, 89; emphasis in original).

In Laplanche's lucid account of psychoanalytic theory, human sexuality itself develops as a kind of perversion, initiated in "a *deviation from instinct*," specifically the instinct toward self-preservation. Building on Freud's work in the "Three Essays," Laplanche refutes the existence of a sexual instinct per se and finds the "very notion of a biological norm" subverted (*Life and Death*, 23; emphasis in original). In this reading, sexuality is not the ground of subjective or gendered identity, but instead is part of the warping of the drive toward preservation effected by the infant's dependency. Life is main-tained by means of reliance on the object, but through a process of "prop-ping," new, highly charged objects and associations are introduced into the equation. In Freud's own words, "we are thus warned to loosen the bond that exists in our thoughts between instinct and object" (*Three Essays*, 148).

Laplanche not only problematizes the biologistic concept of a sexual drive but also outlines a theory of sexuality as "*essentially traumatic*" and as occasioning a field of creative fantasy. Because an incipient sexuality "*metaphorizes its aim, displaces and internalizes its object, and concentrates its source on . . . the erotogenic zone,*" it constitutes a swerving from instinct proper and initiates a principle of vicissitude into the subject's quest for enjoyment (*Life and Death*, 105, 23; emphasis in original). The "*actual* emergence of sexuality" occurs when the original object is lost and "replaced by a fantasy, by an object *reflected* within the subject." Sexuality emerges, in short, as a reflexive turn from the object toward the self. Laplanche in fact calls sexuality a "principle of 'un-binding' or unfettering (*Entbindung*)," associating it with the death drive and differentiating it from Eros, which "seeks to maintain, preserve, and even augment the cohesion" of the ego structure (*Life and Death*, 88, 123; emphasis in original). Sexuality thus is at odds with egoic structures—a formulation that we will find illustrated in Petrarchan poetry—and, when deployed through proffered sites of identification, might well be expected to provoke the shattering rather than the confirmation of the subject.

As a consequence of Laplanche's derivation of sexuality from an early *anaclisis* or "propping" upon the object, the subject itself is eclipsed or evaded, for the object (not the subject) functions as the anchor of this process. Yet the translation or "metaphorization" of the aim occasions a swerve away from the body as ground and from the drive to preserve life as fundamental: the initial object is lost in the movement into sexuality, such that henceforth "the finding of an object is in fact a re-finding of it."[72] The resulting emphasis on function or process supports the appearance of a repetition compulsion, or the "drive" of sexuality itself. However, Laplanche avoids asserting a structural necessity for sexuality or a purely regressive model with his emphasis on cultural fantasy. The intervention of shaping fantasies causes a slippage from the original object, so that "the object which has been lost *is not the same* as that which is to be rediscovered."[73] The subject's initial self-evasions are internalized, "*conflict itself* substantialized" through fantasy, which in turn provides what Christopher Pye calls "the space within which the subject is suspended and multiply inscribed."[74] Fantasy, in other words, functions as the field on which "the subject's life as a whole" is "shaped and ordered," through a process not merely "thematic" but "dynamic" and "constantly drawing in new material."[75] Laplanche, in sum, argues that the shifting scenes of fantasy are the subject's way of incorporating and staging for itself the "unbinding" energies of masochism.

If we understand literary and dramatic texts to engage the subject by offering fresh scripts for fantasy, Laplanche's formulation helps us to see how violent scenes appeal to the reading or viewing subject by conforming with an internalized death drive. Central to Laplanche's concept of fantasy is its complexity and irreducibility: fantasies are "scripts" in which the subject is generally present, but the "sequence" rather than the proximity of a particular object is what carries the charge of meaning. We might compare Linda Williams's argument that viewers of violent entertainment take on various and often shifting identifications.[76] It would seem, in fact, that violent spectacles are provocative to the extent that they challenge viewers to explore subjective identities different from their own. Since sadism and masochism, together and apart, trouble the boundaries of subjective identity and how it is negotiated, questioned, adapted, and broken down, a term suggesting variability and plurality is appropriate. For this reason, although I agree with Noyes and Laplanche that masochism, the primary term in Freud's ultimate theorization, absorbs and contains sadism in an analytical sense, I continue to use the term *sadomasochism* to suggest the multiple positionality that is so important in understanding viewer response, even while I retain the terms *sadism* and *masochism* to refer to separate aspects or positions within the dynamic.

In retaining the term *sadomasochism*, I deviate from Deleuze's influential view of the word as a "semiological howler" that forces two quite distinct sexual identities into unlikley conjunction (*Coldness*, 134). Deleuze's analysis strongly privileges the eponymous authors Leopold von Sacher-Masoch and the Marquis de Sade, equating the content of each work with the writer's fantasy rather than acknowledging authorial and narrative strategies that influence and shape a reader's experience. In fact, Deleuze overlooks the role of the reader or consumer altogether. He maintains his paradigmatic separation of masochism and sadism even in the face of evidence to the contrary from the texts in question. Masoch's narrator in "Venus in Furs" eventually rejects the position of "anvil" to become himself the "hammer."[77] Sade's texts involve contracts and theatrical episodes, both of which Deleuze cites as characteristics of masochism, and Sade includes characters who express masochistic sexual preferences. Sade's efforts to specify, control, and proliferate violent sexual encounters bespeak his aestheticism, another quality

Deleuze would eliminate from sadism but attach to masochism (*Coldness,* 134). Deleuze, like Freud at certain moments, attempts to bring sadomasochism under control by separating it into discrete identities. Toward this end, he is committed to the chronological sequencing of pain and then pleasure (*Coldness,* 71, 89, 118), rather than allowing the fully paradoxical union of pleasure and pain, pleasure *in* pain, that Laplanche uncovers: "*precisely there where* he suffers" the masochist derives pleasure.[78]

Paying Pleasure

The insertion of theories of masochism into consideration of early modern texts helps us to rediscover the dimension of pleasure in readers' or theatrical viewers' experience. The sociological and political frameworks of recent historicism have occasioned a neglect of the aesthetic and sometimes an active denigration of it as a bourgeois construction. Yet as Feste says, "pleasure will be paid, one time or another" (*Twelfth Night,* 2.4.69–70). As an original aim of textual production and the force behind particular texts' continued visibility and relevance in cultural debate, pleasure is a central, if nebulous, component of textual analysis as well as an inherently political one.

The two main routes to theorizing the pleasure afforded by violent forms of art and literature correspond to the divergent arguments of Deleuze and Laplanche. Presumably a reader or viewer is shaken from a comfortable complacency by acts or images of violence: either the experience is endured *in order to be able* to derive enjoyment, or it is (paradoxically) pleasurable in and of itself. Freud's late theory of the subject points toward the latter position, which contradicts the classic understanding of catharsis and formalist theories of art, both of which assume that unpleasurable aspects of art are endured only because of the reward offered by the total experience. Given deeper consideration, however, the Aristotelian model of catharsis actually accords with the psychoanalytic one I am presenting. Aristotle acknowledges how theatrical mimesis involves a fundamental paradox of pleasure when he observes that "we enjoy looking at accurate likenesses of things which are themselves painful to see, obscene beasts, for instance, and corpses."[79] Aristotle has generally been understood to have believed that an audience's experience of strong emotion purges them in a way that is either socially beneficial or pleasant for the individual, or perhaps both. In contrast to to-day's moralistic critics, he did not think audiences needed positive role models: "The unbalanced, manic audience is not given a model of sanity to identify with, but by way of inoculation and immunization is presented with madness to exhaust them: terrifying plots, and characters driven to insanity by the gods. . . . The unbalancing of the emotions is thus a sine qua non of good narrative art, and has a therapeutic effect on emotional disturbances endemic in the audience."[80]

On the other hand, the metaphor of purgation (or even of "cleaning," as the Greek *katharsis* might be more simply translated)[81] strongly indicates that the process of emotional involvement may produce happy results but is not, in itself, a pleasurable experience. Certainly the metaphor is normative, presupposing a state of balance to which audiences will be redelivered after their purgative encounter with art. Most interpreters understand catharsis to be "a matter of plot, not character," invoking the "drama of recognition, exploration, and reintegration."[82] Since a plot must be completed to offer the possibility of "reintegration," the excitement and pleasure afforded by a work in its entirety—before its conclusion is reached—remain incompletely explained by this reading of catharsis. So do the responses of readers or viewers who do not start from, aim toward, or happily arrive at a condition of personal balance and integration. Since, as we have seen, early modern models of subjectivity did not theorize the self as stable and contained, familiar interpretations of catharsis bear at best an elliptical relation to Renaissance literary interactions. Nevertheless, Aristotle's idea that emotion was physical—something that could be purged—corresponds to humoral models and therefore helps us understand the dynamics of Renaissance aesthetic form, as I will discuss in chapter 5. Moreover, English Renaissance dramatists (unlike their counterparts on the continent) implicitly rejected any social utilitarian claims for the emotional purgation.[83] Instead, their practice largely supports the antitheatricalists' charge that drama excited, perpetuated, and affirmed the passions rather than working to cleanse or expel them.

In his provocative book *Why Does Tragedy Give Pleasure?*, A. D. Nuttall proposes a modification of Aristotelian catharsis, which in his opinion conceives of the viewer as overly passive. Nuttall's more active spectator enjoys tragedy because it provides "a kind of psychic exercise," "a game in which the muscles of psychic response, fear and pity, are exercised and made ready," a means "to practice for crises." Nuttall appropriately emphasizes viewers' emotional involvement, and his attention to form is salutary. Yet he resists the extension of his ideas to violent entertainments such as horror films (where "the notion of a facing of the worst, the cognitive element, is only half-present") or public executions ("A snuff tragedy is not a tragedy"), preferring to maintain a focus on dramatic tragedy as traditionally defined.[84] For Nuttall, tragedy is valued for its capacity to prepare viewers for personal tragedy by chastening the will, stocking the intellect, and exercising the emotions. Given this analysis, one wonders if tragedy actually gives pleasure after all.

Nuttall's revision of "pleasure"—which he rewrites as cognitive or moral gain—is no doubt related to his understanding of the Freudian pleasure principle. Acknowledging in Freudian theory a duality between the realistic pleasures enjoyed by the conscious mind and the darker pleasures of the unconscious, Nuttall oversimplifies the relation between the two. Nuttall treats the Freudian subject as preconstituted; the contradictory desires that form the subject are taken to be entrenched positions. So, for instance, he writes that "the Freudian Death Instinct is not primarily a wish for one's own death but a desire to inflict death on others."[85] Although Freud writes that "sadism . . . [offers] the clearest insight into [the death instinct's] nature and its relation to Eros," his point is that in sadism "the death instinct twists the erotic aim in its own sense and yet at the same time fully satisfies the erotic urge." Sadism, that is, evinces one form of the peculiarly vexing "struggle between Eros and Death" that "all life essentially consists of" (*Civilization*, 121, 122). Freud's inquiry into the paradoxical relation between Eros and Death explores the resolutely peculiar nature of human pleasure, and it is a long way from the simple aggression of wishing "to inflict death on others" that Nuttall suggests. We might recall further how, in "Beyond the Pleasure Principle," Freud's attempt to maintain a division in instinctual life—differentiating the ego-instincts, which pressure toward death, and the sexual-instincts, which impel in the direction of life—breaks down. Since Freud believes the "ego is the true and original reservoir of libido," ego-instincts share a common origin with sexual ones; moreover, the priority of the ego means that the death instinct was initially directed toward that "original reservoir of libido" (*BPP*, 49–55, esp. 51). In other words, masochism seems to be the prior state in emotional life, with sadism—or in Nuttall's version, "a desire to inflict death on others"—a vicissitude of this arrangement, not a primary wish.

Nuttall proposes a moralistic approach to the pleasure afforded by trag-edy: he admits that the simple pleasure of emotional arousal plays a not in-considerable part but insists that "in tragedy the irresponsible pleasure of arousal is joined with bonds of iron to the responsibilities of probable knowledge and intellectual assent."[86] This familiar theory of the sugar-coated pill accounts for the way a culture might license or promote works that are considered to have redeeming value and thus for the way a viewer might feel, at the end of *Macbeth* and perhaps even of *King Lear*, though pre-sumably not of *Titus Andronicus*, that the experience has been worthwhile. But cordoning off as "irresponsible" and temporary the pleasure viewers enjoy while actually watching the play does not explain why tragedy gives pleasure.

By building on Nuttall's theory, we can see that aesthetic pleasure in-volves some fundamental paradoxes. In the pursuit of pleasure, the subject, in other respects so eager to build up and maintain conscious control, seeks a dissolution of boundaries. Because sexuality affords, in Freud's words, the "greatest pleasure attainable" (*BPP*, 62), it presents the clearest example of this paradoxical wish for self-shattering. But other experiences that effect self-distancing follow the same model: losing oneself through imaginative involvement with literature or drama is typically experienced as highly plea-surable. Identification with a character, for instance, temporarily realigns one's ego boundaries, and for a time the familiar self disappears. Since ordi-nary experiences of literary pleasure are related in this sense to masochistic pleasure, it follows that violent or extreme images and situations carry heightened possibilities for enjoyment. But a further important link that has thus far been implicit in this discussion remains to be explored: how do plea-sure and masochism come to be linguistic or literary affairs?

Freud's most memorable writing on the conjunction of pain and pleasure is the notorious *Fort/Da* formulation in "Beyond the Pleasure Principle." Freud presented as an example of psychic compensation the game played by his young grandson, who repeatedly pitched a spool away (*Fort* ["gone"]) only to drag it back (*Da* ["there"]) by its string. Freud was able to explain in part why the child would repeat a painful experience of loss by noting the mastery achieved in the game, a symbolic mastery, since the child supposedly "compensated himself" for the absence of his mother by converting a pas-sive situation (being abandoned) into an active one (throwing away and re-trieving his toys) (*BPP*, 15). But Freud noticed that the first ("*Fort*") part of the game "was staged as a game in itself and far more frequently than the episode in its entirety, with its pleasurable ending" (*BPP*, 16). Freud had to conclude that the repetition, or the staging of the game, was pleasurable in itself; and, as we have seen, by the end of "Beyond the Pleasure Principle" he proposes both a death instinct and primary masochism.[87]

Reflecting on the *Fort/Da* formulation, Lacan suggests that Freud over-looks the step of converting actual loss (the mother's departure) into sym-bolic loss (casting away the toy and assigning words to the enactment).[88] Reading the two as equivalent, Freud proposes a mechanical repetition of emotions on the part of the little boy. Lacan extends the paradigm by plac-ing the crucial step in the movement to symbolize loss, since the positions of absence and presence are reversed through "the introduction of the symbol." "Don't forget," Lacan writes, "when he says *Fort*, it is because the object is here, and when he says *Da* the object is absent." Language effects not a sim-ple repetition, but an inversion, so that "absence is evoked in presence, and presence in absence." Far from understanding this as accident or coinci-dence, Lacan labels it the essence of human discourse; the introduction of the symbol "opens up the world of negativity, which constitutes both the discourse of the human subject and the reality of his world in so far as it is human" (*Seminar I*, 173–74). Where the mechanistic reading of the *Fort/Da* scenario finds only compulsion to repeat and master, Lacan sees a symbolic conversion that "opens up a world of negativity," a linguistic reality in which "the thing" accords imperfectly with "the symbol." If under this order noth-ing is ever quite what it seems, if reality is displaced by language, a world is nevertheless "opened up" by the symbolic process. As Lacan puts it, "the subject does not just in this master his privation . . . but he also raises his de-sire to a second power" (*Seminar I*, 173).

Throughout his work, Lacan insists upon an idea often misinterpreted in readings of Freud: the death drive, or primary masochism, is directed against the alienating structure of the ego, not the biological organism of self or of other. I have traced above the notion of a subject inaugurated in its moment of becoming conscious of its separateness, using terms derived from La-planche and Bersani; behind these theorists lies Lacan's massive rereading of Freud. At this point my argument traces back directly to Lacan, who secures the crucial link (implicit in Freud) between language and masochism. Lacan's recognition of language as a fundamental third term of psychic reality complicates the idea of primary masochism: it occurs "at the juncture between the imaginary and the symbolic," where the subject enters the world of symbolism including, most fundamentally, the alienating structure of the ego. Primary masochism features here as the necessary condition of "this life we're captive of, this essentially alienated life" (*Seminar I*, 172; *Seminar II*, 233); it is a matter of the paradoxical losses and gains of language acquisition. Because the ego offers incomplete form to the subject, there is "a drive toward difference over unity, fragmentation over wholeness, heterogeneity over any principle of sameness [which] is identifiable with a drive to signification."[89] In Lacan's terms, "life is only caught up in the symbolic piece-meal, decomposed. The human being himself is in part outside life, he partakes of the death instinct."[90]

Lacan goes on to link "primal masochism" with the movement into language, "this initial negativation . . . this original murder of the thing" (*Seminar I*, 174). The possibility of intersubjective relations depends upon acceptance of the symbolic bargain, the substitution of words for things:

> Intersubjectivity is given in the manipulation of the symbol, and this is the case right from the beginning. Everything begins with the possibility of naming, which is both destructive of the thing and allows the passage of the thing onto the symbolic plane, thanks to which the truly human register comes into its own. It is from that point on that, in a more and more complicated manner, the embodiment of the symbolic within imaginary experience takes place. The symbolic will shape all those inflections which, in the life of the adult, the imaginary commitment, the original captation, can take on. (*Seminar I*, 219)

The subject who refuses to release "the thing" and enter fully into language will be, at best, melancholic, and melancholic fixation of this sort seems relevant to Petrarchan poetry. Even more strikingly, the unbinding, fragmentation, and dehiscence of the ego that Lacan associates with the death drive are likewise indicators of jouissance.

We have followed the way that Freud, who began by labeling sadism and masochism "perversions," came eventually to suggest that all human pleasure might involve masochism. Lacan, in his turn, broadens the scope of masochism, essentially suggesting that it lies at the heart of human discourse.

Laplanche allows us to begin to refine this widening gyre with the further, radical proposal that masochism may be fundamental to fantasy itself.[91] This suggestion takes us from a structural link between language and primary masochism to a creative one, whereby not only the artist's imaginative act but the audience's ability to participate in it are proliferations of sadomasochism. Hence, it becomes the case that literary pleasure, at least as we have come to know it since the Renaissance, is bound up with a conjunction of pleasure and pain. Standard literary devices, such as formal repetition, replacement through tropes, and redefinition of people and experiences, come into new focus in the light of this analysis as the conventions necessary to deliver pleasure. So, too, with the enjoyment afforded by the description of violent acts or their enactment in the theater: through imaginary immersion in these events, the subject is pleasurably shattered, lost to him- or herself. The shattering goals of sadomasochism were enabled by developments in the entertainment industry: technical innovations in the field of printing and social innovations such as the growth of public theaters created new systems for creating the desired pleasure in being shattered.

These sorts of creations and pleasures are densely clustered in the Renaissance, a time of proliferating systems of language and self-expression: printing presses and the spread of literacy; the Reformation, with its emphasis on the individual in matters of faith; the growth of cities, with the complex interactions they enabled; developments in commerce and trade that made available a wider array of consumer goods; and the establishment of popular theaters. Together and separately, these changes brought an increased complexity to the available sense of the self as a *linguistic* event. Although people were obviously fully conscious before the early modern era, the explosion of available symbolic systems created an exponential increase in typical experiences of self-awareness. Renaissance texts support (as, viewed from a different angle, they gave rise to) the psychoanalytic view of the self as paradoxically constituted in a wish for its own dissolution. In various formations through the range of English Renaissance texts, one meets the masochistic longing for dissolution or the vicissitude of this wish, the sadistic destruction of others. Far from being gratuitous, these images offered their audiences the complex pleasure of shucking off a newly acquired sense of an autonomous self.

In proposing that the Renaissance literature of self-shattering has a complexly historical as well as a thematic relevance, I mean to emphasize how these works show the instability of the emergent subject. Attention to the suffering consciousness of viewers and readers may seem to effect a premature affirmation of the bourgeois subject, but my intention in showing how a literary tradition grew up as a means of counteracting that subject is to call into question its purportedly fixed and self-contained contours. While not overtly contradicting the view that cathartic literature enabled the smoothly regulated functioning of a populace, my argument pushes further to suggest how the violent pleasures of Renaissance literature denote a selfhood fundamentally challenged by the call to autonomy and by the terms that necessarily structure that autonomy in social interactions.

In the chapters that follow, I examine a variety of texts spanning more than fifty years: Petrarchan sonnet sequences, a polemical religious history, a popular work from the public theater, and a coterie drama from the tail end of the Renaissance period. This variety demonstrates the broad existence of the motif I identify, how it appears in discourses usually considered remote from one another and describes a fundamental aspect of the period's aesthetic and textual interactions. I have selected suggestive works rather than attempting to exhaust the application of my argument, with the hope that readers will see connections between these texts and others. The modes of response detailed in these essays—sharing a lovesick rejection through Petrarchan poetry, identifying with martyrs' jouissance in the *Acts and Monuments*, troubled eclipsing of autonomous positionality in *Titus Andronicus*, and experiencing cathartic pleasure in shattering in *The Broken Heart*—are not exclusive to the particular works under discussion but might be understood as potential responses of audiences to many other works from the period. In each chapter, I identify available counterdiscourses that competed with dominant humanist themes.

The book's course follows the movement through which self-shattering was institutionalized in popular entertainment in England. The logical initial step in this process, if not the first chronologically, was the inscription of violence into a language of love. Chapter 2 examines Petrarchanism's conversion of overwhelming emotion into poetry; by elaborating the trope equating desire with suffering, poets took a decisive step toward ensuring that the subjectivity "invented" in their lyrics (in Fineman's term) was founded on an embrace of pain. If Petrarchanism strikes today's readers as effete, elitist, and of little consequence to pressing ideological and historical developments in the period, chapter 3 shows that shattering the self could be politically expedient. John Foxe invites readers' contemplation of martyrdom in order to undo identities that could then be recuperated for the Protestant cause. Foxe offers the image of martyrdom as a heroic drama and, considering the way he positions his readerly audience, pushes my argument toward an actual theatrical dynamic. Chapter 4 examines the problematic of viewer positionality in relation to *Titus Andronicus.* Where Foxe is a pragmatic polemicist, urging readerly dissolution to garner further followers in the faith, Shakespeare more radically appropriates the imagery of martyrdom for the commercial theater. Rather than recuperating shattered subjects to a stable position, Shakespeare and other dramatists sought to excite a taste for the paradoxical pleasures of shattering entertainment. Chapter 5 returns to issues of form and expression, showing how *The Broken Heart*'s sensationalism is provoked by its carefully restrained structure. *The Broken Heart* has been labeled "decadent" by literary critics, but the play's abundant correspondences to today's popular films and television dramas suggest that we might better label Ford's aesthetic precocious than decayed. One of the lessons our culture evidently learned from Renaissance literature was the pleasure of imaginative involvement with violence. *The Shattering of the Self* aims to bring that pleasure into fuller consciousness.

CHAPTER TWO

"To Speak of Love" in the Language of Petrarchanism

For Love is a perpetuall flux, *angor animi*, a warfare, *militat omnis amans*, . . .
a grievous wound is love still, and a Lovers heart is *Cupids* quiver, a consuming
fire . . . an inextinguible fire. . . . This continuall paine and torture
makes them forget themselves.
—Robert Burton, *Anatomy of Melancholy* (3.2.3.1)

LOVESICK. Few things tell us so much about the attitudes toward pleasure and the erotic economies of people in early modern England as their capacity for and even established habit of considering love a sickness. In his *Table of the Human Passions* (1621), Nicholas Coeffeteau wrote approvingly of what he called the "first effect" of love, its "uniting vertue." But though love could bring together, it could also rend apart: Coeffeteau notes a "second effect" that was literally unsettling, for in this case love "causeth the soule of him that loves, to bee more where it loves, than where it lives." Echoing the moralist and historian Plutarch, who wrote that "the soul of a lover lived in another body, and not in his own," Coeffeteau indicates the passion's capacity to disrupt personal autonomy. No wonder he notes a further degree of "very violent" love that causes "languishings, extasies, and amazements." Nor is it a long step from here to Robert Burton's casual claim that "it is so well knowne in every village, how many have either died for love or voluntary made away themselves, that I need not much labor to prove it . . . Death is the common *Catastrophe* to such persons."[1]

Oddly, given the claims of such writers on the passions as Coeffeteau and Burton that people actually did suffer dangerous and even fatal effects of lovesickness, the poetic genre corresponding to this malady—Petrarchan poetry—has typically been construed as emotionally bankrupt. Critics consider the flush of sonnet sequences composed in England in the 1590s to be a stylish form of experimentation and self-promotion. In the view of most modern readers, the Petrarchan code that shapes the sequences—suffering lover, scornful beloved, oxymoronic passions, obsessive complaint—registers their distance from actual emotional experience. Poetic fame rather than erotic fulfillment is taken to be the scarcely hidden goal.[2] This perception of Petrarchanism as an artificial genre, false either in the poets' declarations of love or in their analysis of the experience (or both), is built on the assumption that love has an essential, transhistorical truth, and presumably a happy one, to which the sonneteers' suffering extremes correlate poorly. But the vogue of Petrarchanism together with early modern concerns about lovesickness document the currency in the Renaissance of a conception of love involving loss of self, an emotional economy acknowledging, however painfully, an undercurrent of desire for suffering in the erotic experience.

Probing the connection between the psychology of lovesickness and the rhetoric of Petrarchanism provides historical contextualization to an understanding of love as it figures in Renaissance poetry. Nevertheless, my argument assumes that love—as emotion, experience, and trope—remains for several reasons structurally resistant to analysis. Partly this is the result of the displacement noted above, the way love decenters the subject by involving emotional investment in another person and perhaps identification with that other.[3] Moreover, love presents an extreme instance of the capacity of language both to constitute and to alienate the subject, as seen when lovers, frustrated by the inadequacy of shopworn words, attempt to create original expression that will somehow be more true to their particular passion—thereby investing and dealing in an alienating currency. The complex resonance of masochism in Petrarchan ideology, although frequently judged extreme or perverse, nevertheless contributes significantly to prevailing humanist conceptions of love and romantic experience. Exposing that resonance allows us to recognize how Petrarchanism effects a link between early modern self-shattering and the proliferating narratives of masochism in the modern era.

Deeming themselves martyrs to love, the English Petrarchanists charged their language with a secular form of the jouissance at play in martyrologies such as the *Acts and Monuments*. As Thomas Lodge presents the trope of martyrdom, fire and ice occasion an endless near-death, or actually "two united deathes" whose paradoxical union forestalls mortality.

> *As where two raging venomes are united,*
> *(Which of themselves dissevered life would sever;)*
> *The sickly wretch of sicknesse is acquited,*
> *Which else should die, or pine in torments ever.*
> 　*So fire, and frost, that holde my heart in seasure,*
> *Restore those ruines which themselves have wrought,*
> *Where if a part they both had had their pleasure,*
> *The earth long since, hir fatall claime had cought.*
> 　*Thus two united deathes, keepe me from dying,*
> *I burne in Ice, and quake amidst the fire:*
> *No hope midest these exteames or favour spyinge,*
> *Thus love makes me a Martir in his yre.*
> 　*So that both colde and heate do rather feed,*
> 　*My ceaslesse paines, then any comfort breede.*[4]

In Lodge's descriptive enactment of erotic martyrdom, the lover is at once destroyed and defined by his suffering. In this chapter I focus on such linguistic aspects of the historical process through which eroticism annexed martyrology's rhetoric and emotion. I call attention to the degree that language, for Petrarchan poets, registers and enacts the experience of love, or lovesickness. Although the argument privileges the power of rhetoric, it deviates from the constructionist conclusion that experience is shaped by cultural codes. Instead I highlight a significant complication of constructionism: since love offers the most intensely personal of experiences and yet finds form and expression in the terms of a shared and recycled language, a gap opens between the individual subject and the world of words. Petrarchanist poetry is situated in this gap.

In directing attention to poetry as the mediating point between emotion and expression, I am building on the work of those who have in recent years analyzed the position of the Petrarchan speaking subject, complicating the traditional sense of Petrarch's early humanism and precocious modernity. Petrarch's invention of what John Freccero calls a "poetry whose real subject matter is its own act and whose creation is its own author" fostered a distinctly reflexive form of humanism.[5] The idolatrous love for Laura, created within the space of poetry, does not effect the subject's transcendence of self; instead, the poet's devotion to the lady furthers his own self-portrait. This inherent circularity in Petrarch's rhetorical act contributes to the fracturing of the speaker's subjectivity. While the poetic text serves as "the ground for the constitution of the self," writes Giuseppe Mazzotta, Petrarch nevertheless "seems to call into question in the *Canzoniere* . . . precisely the myth of the center and of the centrality of the self." Furthering these accounts by supplying a psychoanalytic framework for the functioning of language, Lynn Enterline has lucidly traced the way Petrarch's rhetoric displaces the self as it gives utterance to subjectivity, noting in particular the latent violence in the poet's expressions of desire.[6]

Moreover, Joel Fineman was building on an appreciation of Petrarch's self-fracturing rhetoricity when he argued that within Shakespeare's sonnets a new form of subjectivity was invented, an "identity of ruptured identification." In Fineman's account, it was Shakespeare's achievement to revive a "tired" tradition by focusing on the "hollowness of a fractured verbal self."[7] However, Fineman may have overemphasized the degree to which Shakespeare's sonnets differed from those of his contemporaries. The sheer density of language as a medium for presenting subjective experience, or what Fineman calls "languageness" of language, features in many poems of the period and, as it does in Shakespeare's sonnets, this sort of language functions as much to embed or entrap the self as to express it.[8]

My interest (in this chapter, at any rate) is less on poetic subjectivity per se than on masochism as the structural outcome of the representation of desire through language. Traditionally, the masochism of Petrarchan poets has been conceived as thematic, as an adopted pose or expressive trope, an idea that has contributed to a heuristic opposition between reality and rhetoric. But it is a false opposition: Petrarchanism actually delivers jouissance *through* language, or more specifically through linguistic failure. In the traditional critical terms of debate, the problem was seen as one of audience, or "two audiences" in Hallett Smith's formulation: is the poet primarily communicating love to the mistress or recording and analyzing it for the sake of other readers?[9] Later critics saw Petrarchan poetry as serving to compensate or substitute for an impossible love.[10] In a provocative advance on the argument about sincerity, C. S. Lewis suggested that "a good sonnet . . . was like a good public prayer," designed not for the sonneteers "to tell their own love stories," but rather to provide voice to "us others, the inarticulate lovers."[11] While presented in the binary terms of the rhetoric/reality debate, Lewis's comments point in a radical direction if we take the comparison to "public prayer" seriously, assuming (as Lewis in his mode of Christian apologist would have us do) that prayer is more than mere rhetoric, that it effects a link between the individual and a larger power. Prayer in this strong sense comes close to being an analogue within Christian humanist tradition to language as it functions within Lacanian psychoanalysis as a third term or level of psychic reality.

Because Lacan sees the human subject as enabled and in a sense created by language but also as inevitably and irretrievably alienated by it, the terms of Lacanian psycholinguistics usefully complicate the critical opposition between reality and rhetoric. In Lacan's triangulated formulation, the Symbolic order of language constitutes the privileged aspect of a subject's experience; it speaks for or actually determines meanings. At the level of what Lacan calls the Imaginary, the subject takes the symbolic forms for truth, thanks largely to ideological manipulation. People ordinarily live on the level of the Imaginary, disregarding the unconscious and assuming the reality of the symbolic order. But while the Symbolic can effectively encompass the Imaginary, a certain excess or remainder inevitably resists symbolization, and this Lacan terms the Real. Rather than a simple opposition between rhetoric and reality, Lacan offers a three-part structural model, with the Symbolic (corresponding here to Petrarchanism's shaping codes) capable of encompassing within its terms the Imaginary (a poetic speaker's ordinary experience), although the two orders do not exactly coincide. The third level, that of the Real, is neither explained by the Symbolic nor accounted for within the Imaginary, yet it is here that the subject finds its jouissance. Petrarchan poetry and the described experience of lovesickness converge, I argue, on the level of the Real. This is the point of language undoing itself, of the subject exposing its own faultline.

Lacan offers not only an architectural scheme but an account of the emergence of fantasy as the subject's way of mediating between the symbolic order and reality. As Slavoj Žižek explains: "Our experience of reality is always-already structured by the symbolic order. . . . It is never given in its pure pre-symbolic 'innocence' (since as such it would be the experience not of *reality* but of the impossible Real). . . . Fantasy [is] strictly correlative to the inconsistency, 'faultiness', of the big Other, the symbolic order." Fantasy, occurring at the threshold of the symbolic order and the subject's temporal existence, occasions (imagined) resistance to the established order. Moreover, because fantasy is a product of the inconsistency or failure of the symbolic order, it involves more individual variation than does the Lacanian Imaginary, or what Žižek calls "ideological fantasy": "What [people] overlook, what they misrecognize, is not the reality but the illusion which is structuring their reality, their real social activity."[12] For Lacan, the ego is the fundamental construct of the Imaginary.

Although deconstructive practice alone might allow us to break down a critical dualism between rhetoric and reality, probing Petrarchanism through the psychoanalytic terms of the human subject "born into language" opens the further door to an understanding of the violence characterizing Petrarchanist fantasy (*Écrits*, 103). For Lacan, the subject's entry into the Symbolic universe coincides with primal masochism or the death instinct: "The masochistic outcome . . . is located at the juncture between the imaginary and the symbolic. . . . That is also where one must locate what is usually called the death instinct" (*Seminar I*, 172). Entering the linguistic universe, the subject gains the ability to use words, but in the process, by becoming subject to language, he or she suffers division or self-alienation. Movement into the symbolic exposes the subject to an awareness that the ego itself is an imaginary construction and as such is necessarily partial.[13] Masochism features here as a fantasy of fragmentation or undoing of the challenged conscious ego. The exchange involved in entry into the symbolic order may be necessary, but the moment entails masochism and eventuates a masochistic outcome because "the subject is not simply mastering his privation by assuming it, but . . . raising his desire to a second power" (*Écrits*, 103). The subject gives up in order to get or, more precisely, gets through the act of giving up. Thus for Lacan "the symbol manifests itself . . . as the murder of the thing" (*Écrits*, 104) and language initiates its users into a tolerance and even love for the violent substitution of words for things, or "the thing." Lacan formulates these ideas in a discussion of Freud's account of the *Fort/Da* scene, in which the "thing" that is symbolically replaced is the child's mother—a point that holds its own relevancy for Petrarchanism, as we will see.

Lacan's connection between language and the violence of loss can help explain a poetry of disappointed love. From a structural viewpoint, denial in love is constitutive of the Petrarchan experience, not merely the frustration of its erotic goal, such as a surface reading would suggest. But how to account for the sheer proliferation of this mode in England in the 1590s, the evident indulgence of poets and their readers in scenarios of painfully unrequited affection, willful cruelty, fantasized revenge, and personal disintegration? What sort of delight or pleasure did these poems offer their readers? My analysis focuses, with only one exception, on poems from the lesser-known sequences because they are more purely symptomatic of the vogue and less the achievements of particularly accomplished individuals. The formal excess of the poems I treat—their sheer susceptibility to parody—is indicative of their peculiar aesthetic function.[14] The oxymoronic rhetoric, unreasonable demands, self-canceling reflection, and recoiling violence effect a breakdown of symbolic structure that allows or causes the emergence of the Real, which Lacan links with jouissance. That is, the capacity of Petrarchan love poems to deliver the overwhelming sense of pleasure/pain Lacan calls jouissance seems paradoxically to be ensured by their dense structures of rhetorical impossibility. This was a jouissance not of achieved romantic love or of sexual fulfillment, but of masochistic fantasy. As such it partakes both of the structural masochism that occurs at the subject's juncture with the symbolic and of the experiential masochism of lovesickness, a symptomatic eruption of the Real.

Because lovesickness itself constitutes an emergence of the Real—defying coherent symbolization, requiring oxymoronic descriptors, involving the body in its states of extremity, terrifying or overwhelming the sufferer—it correlates imperfectly with Petrarchanism, if that term is understood to name a rhetorical convention instancing the symbolic order. Yet Petrarchanism has the odd quality of being at once more than, and other than, itself. Like the Lacanian split subject, it resists unification. From the start the tradition displays an "unease at its core," with Petrarch himself questioning the conventions he employs.[15] Further, a quality of belatedness inheres in the tradition;

as Roland Greene suggests, following Petrarch means questioning and revising Petrarch. Developing these perceptions, Heather Dubrow shows how the discourses of anti-Petrarchanism are laced throughout the achievements of English Petrarchan poets.[16] The Lacanian framework for analyzing subjective experience helps us understand how Petrarchanism could function in the Renaissance as a symbolic order at once fervently declaimed, exposed as transparent, and somehow most compelling in its moments of collapse.

WHEN SILVIUS, THE LOVESTRUCK SHEPHERD of *As You Like It*, warbles "O, Phoebe, Phoebe, Phoebe!" (2.4.38), his speaking ability is reduced to bird song, instancing the linguistic crisis thought to characterize lovesickness. In the early modern period, speech was considered a function of reason, and reason an enemy of passion, so that one who fell prey to lovesickness departed from the domain of reasonable speech altogether. In Burton's estimate, "the sensitive faculty most part over-rules reason, the Soule is carried hood-winked, and the understanding captive like a beast."[17] Rather than coherent discourse, the lovesick person uttered the sort of "vain bibble-babble" (4.2.89) Malvolio is accused of in *Twelfth Night*. Whereas other forms of melancholy could potentially aid in linguistic achievements, erotomania disrupted a person's relationship to truth, thereby launching semiotic crisis. So while Burton freely admits that he embarks on the project of writing the *Anatomy* as therapy for his own tendency to melancholia, when it comes to lovesickness he disclaims personal authority: "I confesse I am but a novice, a Contemplator only . . . I have a tincture, for why should I lye, dissemble or excuse it, yet *homo sum, etc.* not altogether inexpert in this subject, *non sum praeceptor amandi*, and what I say, is meerely reading, *ex aliorum forsan ineptiis*, by mine owne observation, and others relation."[18]

Given this presumed incompatibility of lovesickness and linguistic proficiency, poets would seem to be at a decided disadvantage in writing about the experience of suffering love. Petrarchanism eschews the approach of reminiscing about love from a temporal distance; the aim is to express the white heat of passion and also to comment on or analyze the experience at the same time. Aware of the nested challenges of their task—to write when deprived by love of reason, to convey love to an unwilling ear, and to comment provocatively on this situation—poets frequently make language itself their subject. For instance, William Percy concludes his *Sonnets to the Fairest Coelia* by offering the poems as the imprint of his body:

> *Receave these writs, my sweet and deerest frend,*
> *The livelie patterns of my livelesse bodie,*
> *Where thou shalt find in Hebon pictures pend,*
> *How I was meeke, but thou extreamlie blodie.*
> *I'le walke forlorne along the willow shades,*
> *Alone complaining of a ruthlesse dame;*
> *Where ere I passe, the rocks, the hilles, the glades,*
> *In pittious yelles shall sound her cruell name.*
> *There I will waile the lot which fortune sent me,*
> *And make my mones unto the savage eares,*
> *The remnant of the daies which nature lent me,*
> *Ile spend them all, conceald, in ceaselesse teares.*
> *Since unkind fates permit me not t'enjoy her,*
> *No more, burst eyes, I meane for to annoy her.*[19]

His "writs" are for Percy a perfect language of the body, conveying "in Hebon pictures" the story of his painful love. The sense of his poetry as presymbolic is furthered by Percy's references to "yelles," "mones," and "teares," aspects of what Julia Kristeva would call semiotic communication.[20] By rendering the vitality of his "livelesse body" into the "livelie patterns" of the verse she will receive, Percy can claim to demonstrate the beloved's cruelty: he conscripts her into a position of receiving his energy, his very life. Thus, the poem enacts an aggression toward the beloved that is openly declared in the last line ("I meane for to annoy her!") even as it sounds a self-pitying complaint. The ostensible crisis of love becomes the occasion for a witty reinvention of poetic language as the body's speech. But by writing the poem the speaker finally does convey into symbolic form the "imprint" of his experience, resolving his struggle with language by directing his anger toward the beloved.

The anonymous author of *Zepheria* does something similar in his concluding poem:

> [But i]f she shall attend what fortunes sequeld
> [The n]aufrage of my poore afflicted barke,

> [T]hen tell, but tell in words unsillabled,
> [I]n sighs untuned accents move her to harke
> Unto the tenor of thy sadder processe:
> [S]ay then his teares (his hearts intelligencers)
> [D]id intimate the grieves did him possesse,
> [Cry]ing, Zepheria unto thee these messengers
> I send, oh these my loves my faith shall witnesse:
> Oh these shall record loves and faith unfayned,
> Looke how my soule bathes in their innocencie,
> Whose dying confidence him designes unstayned
> Of guiltie blush note of impuritie,
> Oh death high way to life, when love is disdayned.
> > This sayd, if cruell she no grace voutsafe,
> > Dead, may her graves stone be her Epitaph.[21]

As in Percy's poem, symbolic language is rejected in favor of the purportedly truer communication afforded by "teares," "sighs," and "words unsillabled." But in this complex web of messages, the poet translates the message destined to be told in those sighs and unsyllabled words. As in Kristeva's demonstration of the relation between semiotic and symbolic realms, the two forms of communication depend upon and interanimate one another in an ongoing process.[22] Here, the scripted text refers back to the lover's tears, conveying the meaning of "these messengers." The effect is that of a closed circuit, with words and bodily language, or symbolic and semiotic, pointing reflexively toward one another, denying a fixed perspective from which meaning can be secured. The preeminence of the beloved's name registers its heightened significance for the lover; as Burton observes, "there is some secret power and vertue in names."[23] As typically among the Petrarchan poets, the name of the beloved functions as a kind of supersymbolic utterance, fetishized by the lover for its ability to call up a sense of her presence.

This poem, again like Percy's discussed above, concludes with a threat that exposes the violence behind its postures of suffering. Killing the beloved off in his imagination, the *Zepheria* poet threatens to withhold his own words: "Dead, may her graves stone be her Epitaph." The movement in each poem from masochistic suffering to sadistic threat instances the shifting modalities of fantasy. A masochistic sexuality of meekness, complaint, and affliction is prolonged through imagined scenes of "willow shades" and a shipwrecked "barke." For the duration of these lines, the reflexive focus remains on the suffering poet. Only at the conclusion of the utterance, when the message is ostensibly delivered ("no more," "this sayd"), does the beloved take center stage, as savage aggression is expressed. These reversals, resembling the fantasies Freud analyzes in "A Child Is Being Beaten," evidence the primacy of masochism yielding, within the terms of cultural expression, to the normalization of heterosexual aggression.

The concluding poems of *Coelia* and *Zepheria* reveal a complex but unresolved awareness of the misfit between symbolic language and the suffering of lovesickness. Each poem appeals to bodily communication as more authentic than language, but each indicates an understanding of the limitations imposed by rejection of symbolic language. The intensity of these utterances includes the aggression toward the lady that displaces more obvious postures of masochistic suffering. In the midst of the poet's analysis of linguistic crisis, a heightened emotionality emerges, escaping or even resisting symbolization. Where the symbolic order, the determinant of meaning and significance, collides with the order of lived existence, a residue of impossibility is exposed, what fails to be contained by either the ruling symbols or by ordinary lived experience. For instance, Petrarchanism fashions the beloved as a beautiful but cruel goddess, while lived experience may suggest that she is rather more familiar and ordinary. Where these two planes fail to merge and the distance between them is revealed, the poet, unexpectedly, finds his jouissance, in the dizzying possibilities of multidimensional communication, including the expression of violence. Moreover, here the reader is offered jouissance, in the gap between levels of reality exposed by the crises of Petrarchan poetry.

Unlike Foxe's martyrologies, which sought to shock complacent readers into a shared commitment to Protestant ideology, the Petrarchan poets envision sympathetic readers. Or at least, a distinction is made between the levels of understanding possible to those who are themselves lovesick and those who escape the plight. Samuel Daniel writes of the readerly destination of his efforts in sonnet 3 of *Delia:*

> *If so it hap this of-spring of my care,*
> *These fatall Antheames, sad and mornefull Songes:*
> *Come to their view, who like afflicted are;*

> *Let them yet sigh their owne, and mone my wrongs.*
> *But untouch'd harts, with unaffected eye,*
> *Approch not to behold so great distresse:*
> *Cleer-sighted you, soone note what is awry,*
> *Whilst blinded ones mine errours never gesse.*
> *You blinded soules whom youth and errours lead,*
> *You outcast Eglets, dazled with your sunne:*
> *Ah you, and none but you my sorrowes read,*
> *You best can judge the wrongs that she hath dunne.*
> *That she hath doone, the motive of my paine;*
> *Who whilst I love, doth kill me with disdaine.*[24]

Daniel turns on its head love's tendency to erode reason, asserting that "blinded," "dazled," lovesick readers may overlook his authorial "errours" but will correctly "read" his "sorrowes" and "judge" the beloved's offensive slights. If lovesickness compromised judgment, apparently it did so selectively, producing something more akin to obsession than to lunacy.

Lovesickness was obviously symptomatic, producing an array of physical and emotional complaints. Burton sees this is as one of its eroding characteristics: "there is no end of Loves Symptomes, 'tis a bottomlesse pit."[25] Burton's remark recalls Lacan's sense of the neurotic symptom as an eruption or bubbling up of the Real into a world of symbols; its alien provenance explains why a symptom typically cannot be read or understood. A symptom persists not because of its symbolic capacity (or lack thereof) but because it provides an established "way for the subject to organize his enjoyment."[26] In a related idea, Kristeva in *Black Sun* reads melancholia as productive for artists who are able to convert their suffering into creative acts, whereas ordinary melancholiacs display only symptoms.[27] We could perhaps understand Petrarchan poetry analogously to be the expressive form taken by more creative victims of lovesickness. Yet the self-defeating mechanism built into the Petrarchan structure complicates this interpretation, for the Petrarchan poet does not merely confess and convey pain or describe and praise a remote beloved. Instead, the Petrarchanist wins (poetry) by losing (the beloved). The situation is intensely masochistic, but not, or not only, in the simple sense of involving self-punishment. The pleasure for both poet and reader consists precisely in the beloved's denial, her cruelty, and the impossibility of satisfaction, as these simultaneously are suffered and provide occasions for poetic utterance. As Daniel writes in *Delia*, "O had she not beene faire, and thus unkinde, / My Muse had slept, and none had knowne my minde." Her cruelty moves his Muse. Consequently, what seems to be a poor bargain in terms of emotional economies, since the lover pays and pays with little or no reward from the beloved, comes into focus when we recognize the masochistic link between pain and pleasure. Rejection, far from being an impediment, works productively here; denial inspires a flood of feeling and the occasion for further poetry and analysis; it enables proliferating discourse. In this way, we can see how Petrarchan poets' continual fantasizing about the anguish of unrequited love corresponds to the Lacanian notion of jouissance, defined by Bruce Fink as "what the subject orchestrates for him or herself in fantasy."[28]

Jouissance is an overwhelming experience of shattering pleasure/pain that cuts through the orders of Symbolic, Imaginary, and Real, although Lacan associates it particularly with the Real. For the Petrarchanists, the fantasy, the jouissance, is about the lovesick pleasure of pain, not only as a thematic situation but precisely as a challenge to poetic utterance. When Lacan observes that "to speak of love is in itself a jouissance," he does not refer to an orgasmic pleasure but to an unsettling of the self, as the collision of language and love in Petrarchan poetry allows us to see (*Seminar XX*, 83).

With its sadomasochistic conjunction of pleasure and pain, lovesickness undoes the constructed self, dissolving symbolic certainty and creating a challenge for linguistic utterance. Shakespeare's astonishing sonnet 147 expresses this crisis. The first line announces it as a poem of lovesickness:

> *My love is as a fever, longing still*
> *For that which longer nurseth the disease,*
> *Feeding on that which doth preserve the ill,*
> *Th' uncertain sickly appetite to please.*
> *My reason, the physician to my love,*
> *Angry that his prescriptions are not kept,*
> *Hath left me, and I desp'rate now approve*
> *Desire is death, which physic did except.*
> *Past cure I am, now reason is past care,*
> *And frantic mad with evermore unrest,*

> *My thoughts and my discourse as madmen's are,*
> *At random from the truth vainly expressed;*
> > *For I have sworn thee fair, and thought thee bright,*
> > *Who art as black as hell, as dark as night.*[29]

Intensely diagnostic in its energies, the poem is ultimately less concerned with physical, moral, or emotional effects of the "disease" than with its debilitating effect on "discourse." The quatrains recount how the speaker has been abandoned by reason and now is left "frantic mad." The couplet offers what seems both the illustration of this madness and its cause: "I have sworn thee fair, and thought thee bright, / Who art as black as hell, as dark as night." Realizing his radical misprision—taking dark for light—the speaker is left without an epistemological foundation; his senses and his judgment have been thrown into doubt, so that his relation to truth is skewed, "at random." Speech in the midst of this crisis is purportedly impossible, and the ending ostensibly casts the poem into jeopardy. Yet the continuous present of the opening line—"My love is as a fever, longing still"—works against and effectively overrides the couplet's recounted act of variance from the truth ("I have sworn . . . and thought"). As a result, the poem speaks directly out of the occasion of linguistic crisis, at once analyzing and performing it.

Syntactically, the erosion of linguistic certainty is enacted in the recurrence of prepositional phrases and relative pronouns: "is as," "that which," "that which," "as . . . are," "art as . . . as . . . as . . . as." These formulas suggest a straining after clarity, as meaning seems to slide away from the certain pole of truth. Countering this effect, precisely centered in the sonnet, stands the firm equation "Desire is death." Such a lodestone of a statement is bound to attract attention to itself, and often it has been related to the statement against lust of sonnet 129. But as Jonathan Dollimore points out, sonnet 147 speaks of love, not lust, so the experience here seems even more encompassing. Dollimore reads the poem as recounting "a love wrecked by the desire it would contain"; he hears an ambiguity in "desire is death" between a demonstrative statement about desire and an evoked wish for death. Dollimore's thematic focus on death leads him to privilege it as a static state and to underestimate the poem's anguished deviance from quiesence. Similarly, Dollimore defines Freud's concept of the death drive as "an instinctual reaching towards that state in which there is the complete absence of excitation, a state of zero tension characteristic of the inorganic or the inanimate,"[30] but moves quickly in discussion to overlook the aspect of "reaching" that makes the death drive an active, hydraulic force for Freud, not simply a passive state. If "desire is death," then, by the logic of equation—emphasized here by the contrast with other claims that are couched as comparatives—death is also desire: and thus burning, eroding, anything but a static escape. "My love is as a fever, longing still" is not a poem with a death wish, but one about seemingly incurable lovesickness.

The connection Dollimore draws between Shakespeare's sonnet and the death drive exemplifies a critical tendency to seek interpretive closure for Petrarchan poems. The Renaissance sonnet sequences offer hints of continuous narrative, and customarily readers have appealed to some sort of story to hold the poems in relation. That all the sonnet sequences except Spenser's *Amoretti* end unhappily tells us something about the dynamic of Petrarchan love: the unlikelihood of its successful outcome and the poet's tolerance of failure. The cycle into despair also tells us something about the formal pattern of the poems within each sequence. As Margreta de Grazia acutely notes, "The form repeats itself because the desire it articulates, be it erotic, political, artistic, can never be satisfied." I would push this even further: the resistance to closure that characterizes the sonnet sequences, the way poems consist of various approaches to expressing the same ideas over and over again, shows them to be driven by a desire for their own perpetuation. Arguing along similar lines, Heather Dubrow appeals to the Freudian pattern of *Fort/Da* to explain how sonnets are poised between winning and losing. In her analysis, the *Fort/Da* pattern applies only in the narrative terms of a search for mastery—that is, according to Freud's initial theory about the child's pattern of throwing away and retrieving a toy. Similarly, Dubrow's appeal to Lacan's complication of the theory stays within those terms; Lacan, she writes, sees the drive for mastery as "doomed to failure."[31] As I discussed above in chapter 1, psychoanalytic discussions of the dynamic of repetition and reenactment open complex resonances that go beyond the question of success or failure. Freud himself proceeded to question his own initial reading of the *Fort/Da*. After observing that the child repeats the first part of the pattern (pitching the toy) more than the second (retrieving it), Freud concludes that a pleasure of sorts must be gained from the apparently painful action of losing a valued object, and he suggests the existence of "primary masochism" (*BPP*, 38, 54–55). Lacan's attention to the matter of symbolic conversion further complicates a mechanistic reading of the scenario.

Were Petrarchan poets really interested in mastery, we would expect themes of dominance, structures of increasing distance, or secure formal closure to prevail. Instead, the English Petrarchanists indulge in the poetic equivalent of casting away their toy, over and over again. We might compare the logic Marshall Grossman identifies in Andrew Marvell's "The Mower's Song." Appealing to Freud's analysis of the *Fort/Da* scene, Grossman notes that for the poet's speaker "desire . . . has replaced Juliana with Damon's imagination of her, mastered her absence by bringing her into the timeless present of the lyric, and so, ironically, Damon seizes his own subjectivity by imagining her image of him."[32] In Grossman's account, the poem achieves closure when the speaker objectifies himself in Juliana's eyes, actually imagining his own death. Certainly, there is a masochistic element here, but it works in the service of poetic closure, as Grossman notes. By contrast, the sequential aspect of the sonnets necessitates and provokes a proliferating desire. Even at the level of the single poem, the formal structure may consist of simply recounting the various forms the repeated action of rejection or betrayal might take. One example is sonnet 29 from William Smith's *Chloris*:

> Some in their harts their Mistres colours bears,
> Some hath hir gloves, some other hath hir garters,
> Some in a bracelet weares hir golden hears,
> And some with kisses seale their loving charters.
> But I which never favour reaped yet,
> Nor had one pleasant looke from hir faire brow,
> Content my selfe in silent shade to sit
> In hope at length my cares to overplow.
> Meanewhile mine eies shall feede on hir faire face,
> My sighs shall tell to hir my sad designes,
> My painefull pen shall ever sue for grace
> To helpe my hart, which languishing now pines.
>   And I will triumph still amidst my woe
>   Till mercy shall my sorrowes overflowe.[33]

The imagined "triumph" here takes place "amidst my woe," scarcely separate from it, and the final appeal to the lady's "mercy" envisions it as a kind of tidal wave capable of "overflow[ing]" his "sorrowes"—presumably washing him away with them. Thus, even success in love (winning her mercy) takes the form of masochistic self-erasure.

Daniel, though a stronger poet, similarly offers a poem built of lists that culminates in a fantasy of extinguishing the self.

> *Those amber locks, are those same nets my deere,*
> *Wherewith my libertie thou didst surprize:*
> *Love was the flame, that fired me so neere,*
> *The darte transpearsing, were those Christall eyes.*
>   *Strong is the net, and fervent is the flame;*
> *Deepe is the wounde, my sighes do well report:*
> *Yet doe I love, adore, and praise the same,*
> *That holdes, that burnes, that wounds me in this sort.*
>   *And list not seeke to breake, to quench, to heale,*
> *The bonde, the flame, the wound that festreth so;*
> *By knife, by lyquor, or by salve to deale:*
> *So much I please to perish in my wo.*
>   *Yet least long travailes be above my strength,*
>   *Good Delia lose, quench, heale me now at length.*[34]

The reiterated triplets (lines 7, 8, 9, 10, 11, 14) bespeak a poetic equation out of balance, its words in excess of the syntax, as though the emotion overwhelms the symbolic structure. The final request is oddly contradictory: to be "lose[d]" from the lady's nets would provide a liberty that her "heal[ing]" of his wound would deny; likewise, to be "heal[ed]" implies a wholeness and autonomy that being "quench[ed]"—satisfied but also destroyed—would eradicate. This ambivalence is also built into the phrase "now at length" which suggests both "finally, at long last" and "continuously, from now on."

The scene of perpetuated torment takes on particular vividness in sonnet 50 from Michael Drayton's *Idea*:

> *As in some Countries, farre remote from hence,*
> *The wretched Creature, destined to die,*

Having the Judgement due to his Offence,
By Surgeons beg'd, their Art on him to trie,
Which on the Living worke without remorse,
First make incision on each mast'ring Veine,
Then stanch the bleeding, then trans-pierce the Coarse,
And with their Balmes recure the Wounds againe;
Then Poyson, and with Physike him restore:
Not that they feare the hope-lesse Man to kill,
But their Experience to increase the more:
Ev'n so my Mistres workes upon my Ill;
    By curing me, and killing me each How'r,
    Onely to shew her Beauties Sov'raigne Pow'r.[35]

The extension of suffering effected here—the condemned "Creature" brought agonizingly close to death only to be pulled back to endure further agony—is so extreme that it challenges the purported analogy between experimental practices in "Countries . . . remote" and the cruel tricks of the "Mistres." Indeed, the energy of the imaginative act lies in the first eleven lines of the poem, unfolding the slow torments of "bleeding," "transpierc[ing]," and poisoning, with the comparison to the beloved's power serving only as a kind of justificatory epigram. The physical suspension that characterizes masochistic narratives here carries over into a metaphysical suspension, with the condemned hovering perforce between life and death (*Coldness*, 33).

The sadomasochism in the English Petrarchan sonnet sequences involves posturing and violent fantasies, but most of all it is a matter of the manipulation of poetic form and theme to achieve heightened emotional effect. Emotion is foregrounded over narrative, as seen in this example, from the *Zepheria* sequence:

[O] then Desire, father of jouisance,
[Th]e life of love, the death of dastard feare,
[T]he kindest Nurse to true perseverance,
[M]ine heart enherited with thy loves revere.
    Beautie peculiar parent of conceite,
[P]rosperous Midwife to a travelling Muse,
The sweete of life Nepenthe eyes receite,

Thee into me distild oh sweete infuse.
  Love then the spirit of a generous sprite,
An infant ever drawing Natures brest,
The summe of life that Chaos did unnight
Dismist mine heart from me with thee to rest.
  And now incites me cry double or quit,
  Give back my heart, or take his body to it.[36]

Here the first eight lines consist of little more than exclamation, while the final six lines, repeating Petrarch's trope of heart-theft, recount a reciprocity of bodies, body parts, and subjective identities. Poetry replicates and prolongs the undoing of the ego or self, delivering jouissance through forms of wounding, penetrating, and dissolving and through images of bodies in states of undoing. In the 1590s, the meaning of jouissance (now archaic in English) was in process of changing from "possession and use of something affording advantage" (OED 1) to the more general "pleasure, delight, merriment, mirth, festivity" (OED 2). Referring to "jouisance" as the child of "Desire," Smith employs the earlier sense of the word as a pleasure in possession, closely anticipating the Lacanian definition of desire as lack.

Had an epidemic of cruel ladies or mismatched couples occurred in the years in which Petrarchan poetry was written, we might account for poets' languishing, piteous postures in historical terms, as simply realistic. However, this sort of cultural-historical explanation cannot be granted causal weight, for the sonneteers quite evidently pursue their own romantic torment, seeking poetic occasions to reiterate their suffering, in order to lament and ponder upon it. They pursue love in order to feel lovesick, rather than suffering lovesickness as an unhappy result of misbegotten love. Petrarchanism thus presents the structural puzzle of masochism, or what Freud called its "economic problem" (*EPM*). We might state this generally as "why would the pleasure-loving subject pursue its own pain?" In structural terms, the question is one of the relation between experiencing absence or loss (the departing mother of the *Fort/Da* scenario) and the subject's symbolic repetition of the painful event (the child's tossing the toy away). In the ordinary terms of representation, the symbolic rendering of a lost object negates its loss. For instance, in Christian theology the cross so fully stands for the absent Christ that his loss can cease to be painfully difficult, for he is symbolically or spiritually present. In its happier manifestations, Petrarchan poetry likewise endorses language as a symbolic substitute for full presence; sonnets 87–89 of the *Amoretti* offer a notable example.[37] A more eroding sense of the relation between signifier and signified is registered by Sidney, for whom the beloved's cruelty means that her "presence, absence, absence presence is."[38] Characteristically, Petrarchan poems reiterate loss and refuse the consolation of symbolic presence. In this they accord with Lacan's reading of the *Fort/Da* schema, which shows (as I discussed above in chap. 1) linguistic conversion of loss to function as a form of negation, reversing the valences. "Don't forget," Lacan writes, "when he [the child in Freud's anecdote] says *Fort*, it is because the object is here, and when he says *Da* the object is absent" (*Seminar I*, 173).

In Petrarch's *Rime Sparse*, language serves a substitutive, symbolic purpose. Enterline convincingly shows the fetishistic logic by which "Petrarch substitutes words for sexual relations," arguing that the process reaches the point where "linguistic form usurps bodily form." Representing Laura in poetry, Petrarch confines her to his own use, shapes her to his own purpose. Further, through the blazon, he fragments her body, and his fetishizing rhetoric of bodily parts functions to "affirm absence by their presence," as Nancy Vickers argues. However, such substitution is inherently unstable, not only because the poet attempts to cover over his own fear of dismemberment (specifically, of castration), but because the linguistic means used as a replacement introduces its own forms of lack. Enterline ultimately detects in Petrarch's poetry not only a thematic use of dismemberment, whereby linguistic presence compensates for actual absence, but an eroding recognition of loss associated with language itself. The speaking subject is "utterly implicated" in the signifier's constitutive absence, its distance from what it signifies.[39]

For the English Petrarchanists, a troubled awareness of linguistic instability becomes so profound that the *absence* of the beloved is fetishized. Rather than substituting words for presence, these poets perform a more complex but less satisfying maneuver. They rivet themselves to the very language of absence and pain, creating fantasies of destruction while destroying fantasies of happiness. Their poetic process involves both negation and disavowal, in effect combining the two types of negation Deleuze would isolate in sadism and masochism. For Deleuze, there is a "fundamental distinction" between sadistic negation (destruction and cruelty) and masochistic disavowal (suspending reality in fantasy) (*Coldness*, 35). But in the Petrarchan sonnets, negation pressures the way the beloved is present because doubly absent (because she is cruelly rejecting and because she is linguistically rendered). Likewise, the poet declares himself through his double rejection (by the beloved and through masochistic self-obliteration). Their habit of disavowal allows these poets, in Sidneyan fashion, to affirm nothing and therefore never lie, although their fantasies of sadistic destructiveness and masochistic frenzy lie open for our analysis.

We can see these odd linguistic reversals, with their contained violence, occurring in sonnet 63 of Barnaby Barnes's *Parthenophil and Parthenophe*, a translation of a poem by Ronsard and a work notorious for its anatomical imagination:

> Jove for Europaes love tooke shape of Bull,
>   And for Calisto playde Dianaes parte
>   And in a golden shower, he filled full
>   The lappe of Danae with coelestiall arte,
> Would I were chang'd but to my mistresse gloves,
>   That those white lovely fingers I might hide,
>   That I might kisse those hands, which mine hart loves
>   Or else that cheane of pearle, her neckes vaine pride,
> Made proude with her neckes vaines, that I might folde
>   About that lovely necke, and her pappes tickle,
>   Or her to compasse like a belt of golde,
> Or that sweet wine, which downe her throate doth trickle,
>   To kisse her lippes, and lye next at her hart,
>   Runne through her vaynes, and passe by pleasures part.[40]

Barnes expresses his love by imagining himself literally dissolved into the beloved. His attention to her physical parts complicates the misogynistic scattering that Vickers identifies as the informing energy of the blazon. While Barnes's rhetoric follows the practice of parceling the beloved into pieces (concluding with a pornographic focus on "pleasures part"), the poem's imaginative structure also posits the speaker's own disintegration. The plurality and fluidity of identities imagined for the lover indicate how desire itself, as process, takes precedence over adoration of the beloved. Love figures as self-erasure, a wish to perpetually renew desire, even though that means continual transformation of the self. Barnes ambivalently asserts himself through an identification with Jove in his deific acts of erotic transformation; by evoking a rapist with mutable physical form, the poem conveys sadomasochistic sentiments. Barnes's self-erasure goes even further, as he proceeds to imagine himself as his beloved's accoutrement and then as wine that she ingests and digests. Technically an act of imagined penetration, Barnes's digestive journey from another angle accomplishes mutuality, although by an odd route.

Dubrow observes how Petrarchan poets enact "fluid" gender boundaries, so that "often one cannot talk with confidence about a powerful male poet and subservient mistress, or vice versa, because those two figures so frequently appear to merge, to dissolve in each other's subjectivity, even though they never achieve sexual union."[41] "Jove for Europaes love" illustrates this logic of dissolution, actually literalizing Dubrow's discursive metaphors. Barnes's poem not only merges the figures of poet and mistress but also challenges the terms of subjective identity. The speaker proclaims himself undone, liquefied, and swallowed, but for all that he manages to humiliate and penetrate the beloved. Language works here at cross-purpose to conveyed effect or meaning: "When he says *Da* the object is absent."

Because Lacan refers repeatedly in *Seminar XX* to troubadours and discusses courtly love in *Seminar VII* and because Žižek has further developed these references in "Courtly Love, or, Woman as Thing," it is important to note the relation between these earlier forms and the English Petrarchan poetry under discussion here. The thirteenth-century troubadours sang of exalted, idealized women; Petrarch was influenced by this tradition and in turn inspired the rash of sonnet sequences written in England in the 1580s and 1590s.[42] Treating the mythos of courtly love, Lacan and Žižek consider it a relatively closed structure. For instance, Lacan writes: "What is courtly love? It is a highly refined way of making up for (*suppléer à*) the absence of the sexual relationship, by feigning that we are the ones who erect an obstacle thereto" (*Seminar XX*, 69). While the English Renaissance Petrarchanists draw on this mythos, within their poetry it is submitted to question, scrutiny, and problematization, as Dubrow has suggested with her observation of the interpenetration of anti-Petrarchanism with Petrarchan forms. As a symbolic form, courtly love—roughly equivalent to the idealizing part of Petrarchanism—

attempts to encompass and cover over the experiential level that Lacan calls the Imaginary. So, for instance, in Barnes's poem the eroticizing admiration of the beloved barely conceals a fantasy of rape. Manipulating his fantasy through imagery of dismemberment and dissolution, the speaker indulges his aggressive desire within the terms of Petrarchan admiration. At the same time, the poem illustrates the ego to be, as Lacan calls it, an imaginary construction, whose ideological character is subject to cultural alteration. The imperfect fit between the speaking subject ("I") and the desires expressed in the poem suggests how illusory the ego really is. Although we detect the troubling emergence of heteroaggression, presumably traceable to the cultural diminishment of the feminine object, "Jove for Europaes Love" also documents a distinct unease with the autonomy of the speaking self.

The forms of courtly love also attempt to efface altogether the existence of anything outside symbolism's scope. Yet as we have seen, repeatedly in the poetry of English Petrarchanists the gaps between an idealizing symbol and mundane ordinary experience are disclosed, and often there is a disclosure of a level beyond either of these—a realm of vivid excitement, which linguistic terms strain to accommodate. Seemingly perverse rhetorical techniques evidence Petrarchanism's reference to something that actively resists language. Barnes's sonnet 31, for instance, is a paradigmatic instance of these poets' notorious fondness for oxymorons.

> *I burne yet am I cold, I am a could yet burne*
> > *In pleasing discontent, in discontentment pleased*
> > *Diseas'd I am in health, and health-full am diseased*
> > *In turning backe proceede, proceeding I returne*
> *In mourning I rejoyce, and in rejoycing murne*
> > *In preasing I steppe backe, in stepping backe I preased*
> > *In gaining still I loose, and in my losses gaine*
> > *Grounded I waver still, and wavering still am grounded;*
> *Unwounded yet not sound, and being sound am wounded:*
> > *Slayne yet am I a live, and yet alive am slayne:*
> > *Hounded mine hart restes still, still resting is it hounded:*
> *In paine I feele no greef, yet voide of greefe in payne*
> > *Unmov'd I vexe my selfe, unvext yet am I moved*
> > *Belov'd she loves me not, yet is she my beloved.*[43]

Wearisome in its repetition of the rhetorical motif, Barnes's poem is hardly a triumph of form or sensation. However, when read as structurally indicative rather than merely an obsessive exercise, the sonnet attempts to articulate an experience that language cannot name but can only point to, something hidden in the knots of logical contradiction. Lacan relevantly suggests that "the real can only be inscribed on the basis of an impasse of formalization" (*Seminar XX*, 93). When symbolic forms or formal structures fail, as with the excesses of Petrarchanism, an unintended result may be the exposure of the Real. Sympathetic readers, such as those for whom Daniel wishes, could thus experience the swooning pleasure of lovesick jouissance. Critical readers also stand to gain because, even though the Real, in Lacan's schema, does not correspond to reality, its exposure signals the limitation of the symbolic and thus allows an understanding of the several nonsymmetrical registers of human existence.[44]

In chapter 3, I will turn to moments in Foxe's *Acts and Monuments* that rupture Christianity's symbolic fabric, showing how Foxe's readers are delivered provocative challenges, such as imagining their own death at the stake, in order to prompt their devotion. The space of textuality introduces a slippage from an overtly heroicizing discourse, leaving the way open to contemplation of, for instance, the physical pain of death and the spiritual horror of failing in the martyr's role. The thrill or jouissance associated with reading the "Book of Martyrs" derives from this exposure of the Real, the parts of recounted martyrdom that Christian ideology does not adequately contain. By the same logic, when the ideology of courtly or romantic love figures seamlessly in a love lyric, the poem will inspire formal admiration and deliver a civilized sort of pleasure; the more shattering, disturbing experience of jouissance occurs when the symbolic order somehow falters. The English Petrarchanists, with their challenges to the idealized forms of love, devastate at those moments when the mythic or ideological surface cracks and terrifying or thrilling possibilities are exposed. Elements of significant violence are likely to surface, as are wishes to obliterate the self; these impulses, ordinarily kept in check within the ideology of romance, break out in the midst of linguistic and subjective crisis.

Obviously, such crises in the romance form are functions of gender, and in naming the masochism in the sonnets I am suggesting that they problematize established gender identities. The standard Petrarchan trope of the cruel beloved and the long-suffering lover clearly corresponds to the paradigm of masochism instanced in the work of Leopold von Sacher-Masoch.[45] Readers have debated the nature and meaning of Sacher-Masoch's fictions in ways that are useful to our understanding of Petrarchan poetry. Deleuze, in particular, has written compellingly of the distinction between masochism (especially as evidenced in Sacher-Masoch) and sadism (as evidenced in the work of the Marquis de Sade). For Deleuze, masochism involves rejection of the oedipal father and corresponding magnification of the phallic mother; he calls masochism "a story that relates how the superego was destroyed and by whom, and what was the sequel to this destruction." Sadism, by contrast, documents "how the ego . . . is beaten and expelled; how the unrestrained superego assumes an exclusive role" (*Coldness*, 130, 131). This paradigm has gained considerable acceptance; it helps to make sense of two baffling psychological phenomena, and it makes a certain amount of sense in relation to the core texts by Sacher-Masoch and the Marquis de Sade. But Deleuze's scheme fails to accord with the tradition of Petrarchanism, where the mutuality of images of power and submission was evidently necessary to produce in readers a pleasurable shattering of subjective reality. The sonneteers' lack of linguistic fixity and their bizarre manipulation of patriarchal order illustrate a rejection of established symbolic codes and go beyond a merely thematic masochism. On the other hand, the sadistic rape fantasies, misogynistic blazons, and obliteration of the lady's voice clearly exhibit a punishing superego unrestrained by an organizing ego. The shaping fantasies of Petrarchan poetry involve postures of mastery and submission in various and changing configurations. In sum, while masochism is the underlying psychic phenomenon, in gaining expression it encompasses and makes use of sadism.

Deleuze's effort to segregate masochism from sadism "politically sentimentalizes masochism as a resistance to power."[46] His paradigm may appeal to the liberal scholarly community because it implies that submissive behavior can subvert an established order. But disavowing the draw of sadism carries the danger of simply overlooking the ideologies that an "unrestrained superego" tends to embrace. For instance, the resolution of masochistic suffering into heteroaggression, such as occurs in the poems by Percy and the *Zepheria* poet analyzed above, reveal the fallback position of gendered interaction. Barnes pathologically anatomizes his lady to locate "pleasures part"; Shakespeare declares his lover "as black as hell, as dark as night." While the symbolic order of Petrarchan romance posited the lover as beautiful, remote, chaste, and untouchable, the gendered ideology of early modern life suggested that women were dirty, penetrable, and immoral.[47] The fact that resonances of this latter Imaginary break out at certain moments does not alter—indeed, it would seem to underline—the sense of abjection provoked in male readers by a strategic inversion that places men beneath women.

Although the gender of their authors and their presumed appeal to male readers could lead one to suspect otherwise, the Petrarchan sonnets aim to instill a shattering pleasure that seems not to accord with orgasmic release or what Lacan terms "phallic jouissance." Lacan writes also of an "other" jouissance, which he sometimes associates with religious ecstasy, most famously in his remark about Bernini's statue of Saint Teresa: "You need but go to Rome and see the statue by Bernini to immediately understand that she's coming. There's no doubt about it. What is she getting off on?" (*Seminar XX*, 76). Lacan's notorious remark has been taken as a forced or anachronistic substitution of the terms of sexual pleasure for those of mystical ecstasy,[48] but in context it suggests an overwhelming experience of conjoined pleasure and pain, which is bodily but not specifically or exclusively sexual.[49] This affiliation between mystical religious jouissance and romantic or sexual love in fact reproduces the terms of Burton's *Anatomy*, in which religious melancholy is treated as "a distinct Species of Love Melancholy."[50] Burton's perception that the psychic, emotional, and physical experiences of lovesickness and religious despair were similar indicates an early modern sense of the congruency between erotic and religious jouissance. Perhaps the dominant trope of the beloved as "goddess" draws on this conjunction. Further, the link testifies to the absence of gender fixity in these experiences, since religious ecstasy is associated in a Christian culture with a male deity, whereas sufferers of lovesickness might be men or women attached to objects of either sex, although the dominant situation in Petrarchanism involves a male lover and a female beloved. Lacan associates "other" or surplus jouissance with those in the feminine speaking position, meaning not women as empirically defined but those whose relation to the dominant symbolic order is skewed, as women's typically is in patriarchy.[51] As we have noted, male Petrarchan poets, in their recurrent masochism, situate themselves in oblique relation to the master's discourse of the patriarchal order. They convey in their poetry an unsettling experience at once pleasurable and painful, involving loss or shattering of selfhood, a jouissance that overwhelmed language yet seemed to call for expression.

A discussion of jouissance circles around what current criticism terms *the body,* and indeed it is worth asking how the physical selves of the poet, the beloved, and the reader figure into Petrarchanism. My argument suggests that the body remains the traumatic Real outside the terms of a troubled symbolic exchange, in which the idealizing love conceived in the symbolic realm fails to match up with the imperfections encountered in the Imaginary order. At once a site of jouissance and an aspect of existence impossible to understand, the body provokes defensive gestures of violence. Feminism alerts us to the sexual politics of this arrangement: deemed the cultural holders of physicality, women are idealized, silenced, and symbolically fragmented.[52] In a strikingly aggressive poem, Drayton imagines himself the "Tormentor" who will "crucifie" his beloved:

> Now Love, if thou wilt prove a Conqueror,
>> Subdue thys Tyrant ever martyring mee,
>> And but appoint me for her Tormentor,
>> Then for a Monarch will I honour thee.
> My hart shall be the prison for my fayre,
>> Ile fetter her in chaines of purest love,
>> My sighes shall stop the passage of the ayre:
>> This punishment the pittilesse may move.
> With teares out of the Channels of mine eyes,
>> She'st quench her thirst as duly as they fall:
>> Kinde words unkindest meate I can devise,
>> My sweet, my faire, my good, my best of all.
> Ile binde her then with my torne-tressed haire,
>> And racke her with a thousand holy wishes,
>> Then on a place prepared for her there,
>> Ile execute her with a thousand kisses.
> Thus will I crucifie my cruell shee,
> Thus Ile plague her which so hath plagued mee.[53]

The savagery with which Drayton imagines torturing his beloved renders the poem distinctly sadomasochistic. Since her rejection is understood as cruelty, the beloved is granted no opportunity for choice or agency. The poem projects the infantile vision of the abandoned child who persists in throwing his plaything away.

Nevertheless, because of the masochistic pleasure taken in pain, the violence provoked in a poem such as Drayton's is not reliably bound by gender. Envisioning their own jouissance in terms of wounds and pain, poets extend the same to their beloved in perversely attempted mutuality. William Smith makes memorable use of the trope of wounding his beloved:

> *Tell me my deere what mooves thy ruthlesse minde*
> *To be so cruell, seeing thou art so faire?*
> *Did Nature frame thy beautie so unkinde?*
> *Or dost thou scorne to pitie my despaire?*
> *O no it was not natures ornament,*
> *But winged loves unpartiall cruell wound,*
> *Which in my hart is ever permanent,*
> *Untill my Chloris make me whole and sound.*
> *O glorious love-god thinke on my harts griefe,*
> *Let not thy vassaile pine through deepe disdaine,*
> *By wounding Chloris I shall finde reliefe,*
> *If thou impart to hir some of my paine.*
> > *She doth thy temples and thy shrines abject,*
> > *They with Amintas flowers by me are deckt.*[54]

Where love is experienced as pain, wounding the beloved figures as the logical means toward mutuality. No wonder there was little tenderness or nurturant attention in the affections of Petrarchanists; for the beloved to share the poet's emotion, she would need to suffer like him. One is reminded of Lacan's remark about the cruelty of loving one's neighbor as oneself (*Seminar VII*, 194). The Petrarchanists instance the possibly greater cruelty of seeking a shared experience of romantic love under a social regime that understood love to entail pain and grief. By giving language to an experience of love as violence, Petrarchan poetry helped establish the currency of a concept that extends into our time.

Despite feminism's exposure of the political grounding and implication of attitudes toward love, especially heterosexual erotic love, Petrarchan poetry remains by traditional standards an ornamental discourse elaborating the private lives of individuals. Not so John Foxe's *Acts and Monuments:* few texts were so influential on the political debates of the day, shaping the attitudes of individual readers and consolidating the English Protestant church by supplying a set of shared stories of persecution and suffering. How, though, did Foxe's text effect the link between individual readers and the corporate body of Protestantism? In the next chapter, I show how Foxe used the allure of shattering the self to gather in and indoctrinate believers.

CHAPTER THREE

Foxe and the Jouissance
of Martyrology

An art that appeals to a mimetic fascination with the violence it represents
frequently denies that appeal by monumentalizing the scene of violence.
—Leo Bersani and Ulysse Dutoit, *Caravaggio's Secrets*

JOHN FOXE OPENS HIS NARRATIVE ACCOUNT of English martyrdom for
the year 1552 by transporting his audience, rather in the style of Shakespeare's
Henry V, to the European continent: "Commyng now to the yeare next
folowyng, 1552, we will somwhat steppe aside and borow a little leave,
coastyng the Seas into Portyngale amongest the Popishe Marchauntes there"
(1570, 1541; CT, 6:274).[1] Foxe's purpose is to recount "the history, no lesse
lamentable then notable of William Gardiner an English man," martyred
"for the testimony of God's truth" (1570, 1541; CT, 6:274). Like many of his
fellow martyrs in the *Acts and Monuments,* Gardiner provokes the suffering he
endures: attending mass in the presence of the king and his court, Gardiner
seizes the sacrament from the cardinal's hands and grinds it beneath his feet.
Refusing to repent for his action, Gardiner is subjected to a series of ordeals.
One form of torment involves forcing a linen ball "unto the bottome of his
stomacke," then pulling it up by means of an attached string and "pluckyng
it to and fro through the meate pipe" (1570, 1543; CT, 6:280). This yo-yo-like
action is repeated when Gardiner, both his hands now cut off, is taken to the
place of execution and placed on a pulley: "Then was ther a great pile of

Fig. 1. "The order and maner of the cruell handlyng of William
Gardiner, an Englishe Marchaunt, tormented and burned in Portugall
in the cause of God and of hys truth." From *The First Volume of the
Ecclesiasticall history*. . . . (London: John Day, 1570), p. 1544.
By permission of the Folger Shakespeare Library.

woode set on fire underneath him, into the which hee was by little and little let downe, not with the whole body, but so that his feete onely felt the fire. Then was he hoysted up, and so let downe agayne into the fyre, and thus oftentymes pulled uppe and downe" (1570, 1544; CT, 6:280).

Gardiner remains faithful, refusing the exhortations to repent that are made "when hys feete were consumed." Eventually, "the rope beyng burnt a sonder," he falls into the flames and "the body of the sayd Gardiner [is] consumed" (1570, 1544; CT, 6:280–81). Foxe reports that God took vengeance against Gardiner's tormentors, and "yet for all that," his story will not seem to die, for "there are some (as I have heard divers reporte) out of whose myndes the remembraunce of this constant Martyr can never be pulled" (1570, 1545; CT, 6:281). Converting the yo-yo action of Gardiner's tormentors into a trope for mental retention and release, Foxe extends Gardiner's suffering to readers, who will have "remembrance" agitatingly placed and "pulled" from their minds. Beyond lending formal patterning and coherence to his narrative, Foxe's rhetorical extension of torment invites or enables readers' involvement with the suffering martyr. The gagging ball and the pulley, ostensibly deployed to force Gardiner's repentance, prolong his torment and frustrate a wish for the closure death would provide. In his presentation of this episode, Foxe rhetorically mimes the persecutors' actions, so that readers drawn into this compact play martyrs to Foxe as tormentor. This reading economy, I suggest, should alert us to the peculiar dynamic behind the astonishing popularity and impact of the *Acts and Monuments*.

A landmark text of Reformation England, the *Acts and Monuments* has defied interpreters' attempts at generic classification. Strong arguments have been advanced for its inclusion within the fields of ecclesiastical history, nationalist politics, apocalyptic, and hagiography.[2] Recently, it has been asserted that the *Acts and Monuments* can best be thought of as many works rather than a single coherent one: the four editions of the book published during Foxe's lifetime (in 1563, 1570, 1576, and 1583) represent not only an accumulating mass of material but variations of emphasis and presentation.[3] For instance, Tom Betteridge suggests a distinction between the prophetic (1563), apocalyptic (1570), and monumental (1583) versions.[4] Enormously influential from the time of its first English publication in 1563 through the nineteenth century, the *Acts and Monuments* was sanctioned by members of the Anglican hierarchy and placed in many English churches beginning in 1571.[5] Although it remained too large and in the sixteenth century too expensive for many in-dividuals to purchase, it was "generally available," and its vivid stories "en-tered into the public imagination."[6] That a work originally begun by an ex-iled Anglican would eventually be adopted by other resistance movements indicates that Foxe's text had the capacity not only to spawn ongoing reform but also to appeal to general readers.[7] It was from the beginning a quintes-sentially popular text, widely read, noted, and remembered by all sorts of readers. Furthermore, the illustrations in the numerous reprintings furnished the visual imaginations of sixteenth- and early-seventeenth-century minds.[8]

In spite of its acknowledged influence and popularity, the question of readerly pleasure in relation to the *Acts and Monuments* has rarely been ad-dressed.[9] Even though Foxe's relentless cataloguing of the torments suffered by martyrs strikes most modern readers as excessive, even obsessive, the effect is ordinarily ascribed to his Protestant zeal, a move that blocks inquiry into the extent to which Foxe explicitly appeals to his audience by way of violent interactions. To some, I expect that pleasure seems entirely the wrong topic to pursue in relation to Foxe, an appropriation of theological writing for secular or even frivolous purpose. Yet, as George Eliot suggested with the familiar example of young Maggy Tulliver (inspired by Defoe's *History of the Devil* and an illustrated image of Jael destroying Sisera) indulging the "luxury of vengeance" against her fetish, readerly pleasure follows varied and sometimes violent paths. Eirwen Nicholson's observation that the *Acts and Monuments* carries the reputation of a "video-nasty horror packaged in the brown-paper wrapper of cautionary history and Protestant national destiny" nicely articulates the traditional licensing of the violence in Foxe's text.[10] Further, Nicholson's crude cloaking metaphor suggests that the problem might be traced to the difficulty of discovering the appropriate language to explain a deadly serious work that appealed to readers by offering them a kind of narrative pleasure. As a result, an important dimension of this text's significance and influence has been elided.

By inquiring into the emotional attraction Foxe's text held for its early audiences, I mean to direct attention past its institutional moorings to probe its imaginative appeal for individual readers.[11] As a text presented to encour-age Protestants to remain mindful of the sacrifices others had made in the defense of their faith, the *Acts and Monuments* participated in the development of the individual as reader and the reader as individual. While the pleasures it offered were thus in part those affiliated with institutions and their power—the satisfactions of knowledge, of inclusion within a religious community, of national pride—each of these would be heightened, and perhaps secured initially, by the readerly excitement of imaginative involvement with suffering martyrs and their persecutors. That the Marian martyrs, though condemned under ecclesiastical jurisdiction, were executed by civil authorities reminds us of the congruency between the martyrs' dramas and those of other sorts of condemned criminals.[12] Public executions were designed as spectacles of humiliation and hatred, mobilizing witnesses to enforce a community's morality. Foxe proceeds by renaming as martyrs those condemned as heretics under Marian rule, thereby redirecting the passionate condemnation of those executed toward those who prosecuted them. In other words, the thrill of watching or imaginatively participating in a scene of tortured death was reassigned from affiliation with the tormentors (sadistic pleasure) to sympathetic identification with the victim (masochistic pleasure), with hatred of the Papists supplying further opportunity for sadism.

Not only did the emphases of the *Acts and Monuments* shift over the course of its publication history, but also individual readers inevitably responded in different ways as a result of variations in education, experience, and taste. In their historical particularity and individuality, the responses of readers are unavailable. However, probing the way Foxe typically positions and presents his accounts of martyrs over the course of his proliferating text (a double folio by 1570, with more additions following in subsequent editions) allows us to gauge the sort of appeal he expected to make. Through both structure and style, Foxe encourages readers' participation in the drama of martyrdom. His teleological structure, stretching from the primitive church to the Marian martyrs of the mid sixteenth century, illustrates a line of holy "acts" extending to the present day for its original readers. Readerly participation could mean, on the one hand, imaginative involvement in the reading process (aided by Foxe's vividly evocative details) or, on the other, preparation for an active role in defending the faith, although as even Foxe admits, few among his readers were likely to be called upon to offer their lives in defense of the faith. He counsels readers "if we can not willingly put of this lyfe, yet let us not bee slow to amend and correct this same: and though we can not dye with them in lyke martyrdome, yet let us mortify the worldly and prophane affections of the flesh which strive against the spirit" (1570, 1542; CT, 6:276).

However readers participate, the *Acts and Monuments* uses martyrology to create a sense of separateness and particularity among them, given that any decision about faith must be made on an individual basis. Yet paradoxically, in seeking to arouse his readers' passions, to excite and horrify them with vivid accounts of torture, Foxe was encouraging a contemplation that could shatter readers' defensive structures and undermine a sense of personal autonomy. In this sense, the *Acts and Monuments* urges readers' identification with suffering martyrs as a means to break down established subjective identity. Foxe's ultimate goal was to recuperate that shattered subjectivity as the basis for individual dedication to the Protestant cause. In the language of conversion, he sought to destroy the "old man" so that a new one could be born. In the language of psychoanalysis, Foxe offered readers a jouissance that cut through and unsettled the terms of identity.

In this chapter I argue that the *Acts and Monuments* can be understood as itself a monument to a particular time in the history of subjectivity, a moment when developments in technology, literacy, and religious politics made it possible for a massive textual detailing of physical suffering to occupy the imaginative screen of English readers. I suggest a scandalous pleasure offered by the "Book of Martyrs," a pleasure in reading about violent acts of torture and domination that should not be overlooked because of its manifestation within a work whose goals were both lofty and polemical. Indeed, its polemicism may be determinative rather than incidental to its appeal, given the link between transgression and jouissance. Ultimately, I will suggest a crucial distinction between those more ordinary pleasures that affirm the self, solidifying its nature and boundaries, and the more radical modes of pleasure, which Lacan calls jouissance, that effectively dissolve the constructed ego or sense of self.

SINCE MY INQUIRY IS CONCERNED with the peculiar pleasure of this text,[13] it will be useful to begin by identifying two general forms of pleasure that Foxe's text could offer its readers. One of these would be rendered formally, in ways that are connected to the historical context in which the *Acts and Monuments* appeared: in a hierarchical society structured according to relations of domination and subordination, textual images of the interplay of power relations could grant a subversive pleasure, allowing the embrace of subordination as an emotionally rich or even potentially powerful position. Foxe organizes his presentation of events to stress the way martyrs outsmart and triumph over their prosecutors, at least from the perspective of sympathetic Protestant readers. Moreover, the topos of martrydom presupposes a higher realm of spiritual authenticity, in which suffering for the cause of truth will be redeemed and glorified; thus, it displaces the dominant figures of this world by trumping their authority. The text could also offer pleasure through what we can understand as psychological means: Foxe assumes that readers will share in the sufferings of martyrs, through sympathetic imagination, and he provokes this imaginative link with vivid details, dramatic scene painting, and memorable dialogue. Foxe explicitly theorizes the responsibility of readers to honor the martyrs through appropriate means—to engage so thoroughly with the martyrs' textual "monuments" that their "acts" of suffering might be perpetuated, either in the temporal world or in the identifying consciousness of readers. By aligning formal, psychological, and rhetorical approaches, I mean to direct attention to the readerly act of response and the way it is shaped, ordered, and theorized within *Acts and Monuments*.

Unlike more strictly informative propagandistic texts, *Acts and Monuments* aims to incite or inspire its readers by encouraging them to share the experience of the martyrs. Although the *Acts and Monuments* could never be called pornographic in the familiar sense of the term, we miss something crucial about the work if we pass too quickly over the provocational agenda it shares with pornography, the way it explicitly serves as a call to Christian and specifically Protestant action. In its appeal to the reader's existence, the words of the *Acts and Monuments* seek actually to embody meaning, not simply to convey it. Words and bodies interact in complex, multifaceted ways in the *Acts and Monuments*. While Foxe's martyrs demonstrate their transcendence of the flesh by enduring its torturous destruction, theirs is no dualistic logic of body and soul. If the body were completely devalued, as martyrs and mystics sometimes claim, its loss could not occasion martyrdom. Under a rule of asceticism, authorities would not seek to burn supposed heretics, and accused Protestants would not assent to their fate by way of proving their devotion.[14] When Bishop Cranmer famously thrusts his own hand into the flames to illustrate his repudiation of an earlier act of recantation, he uses his body as his persecutors do, to endure the flames as punishment for misdeeds (1570, 2067; CT, 8:90). By feeding his hand to the fire, however, Cranmer subverts their authority, splitting himself into both active, condemning subject and passive, martyred object. Just as the prosecutors show their paradoxical valuation of the martyrs' bodies by condemning them to the stake rather than allowing them to expire less spectacularly in prison, so Cranmer secures a metonymic significance for the hand that signed the recantation, when his mind or entire self might be understood to bear responsibility for the action.

Foxe's attention to the repeated parceling of the martyrs' bodies—the way arms drop off into the fire, as when Richard Bayfield, after burning for a half-hour "for lacke of a spedy fire," rubs his left arm, which then "fell from his body" (1570, 1164–65; CT, 4:688), or an unburnt, stockinged foot is recovered in the charred remains of John Noyes (1570, 2218; CT, 8:426), or relics are gathered from the ashes of John Hullier, whose "bones stood upright" after his flesh was consumed (1570, 2197; CT, 8:380)—all this underlines the poignancy and horror of the martyrs' suffering, indicating the value of the fleshly self they have sacrificed. Some martyrs repeat some version of Matthew 10.28, such as John Noyes's claim not to fear "them that can kill the body" but "him that can kill both body and soul, and cast it into everlasting fire" (1570, 2218; CT, 8:425), a heroic and distinctly nondualistic formula illustrating their phenomenology of the composite self.[15] Similarly, Laurence Saunders claims to taste the communion of saints in a bodily fashion (1570, 1666; CT, 6:616–17, 623) during his imprisonment.

The significance of physical suffering in the *Acts and Monuments* has recently been discussed by Janel Mueller, who suggests a metaphysical link between the logic of Protestant martyrdom and Reformation debates about transubstantiation. Pursuing the question of what burning meant for those who suffered it, Mueller proposes that it served as an implicit replacement for the real presence of Christ during the Mass: "Displacing the crucial site of human access to divinity from the Mass to the stake, the Marian protestant ontology of presence centered itself in the physical body and agency of the believer. It invoked no miracle, only the workings of natural processes of dissolution and transmutation. Yet as it burned for failing to believe in the miracle of transubstantiation, the martyr's body experienced just such a miracle."[16] Impressively sensitive to historical context, Mueller's argument suggests the ideal understanding of burning that enabled martyrs to go to the stake willingly. Nevertheless, in Foxe's account it often seems that human ineptitude or unfavorable circumstances (green wood, insufficient faggots, adverse wind) prevent the quick incineration a victim might be expected to prefer and Mueller envisions when she writes of "natural processes of dissolution and transmutation."

Considerable slippage occurs in the *Acts and Monuments* from the supposed miracle of "natural processes" to Foxe's horrifying stories of botched burnings. The keen attention Foxe pays to the particular events of each burning undermines the miraculous understanding with which the martyrs themselves might have approached the stake, turning readers' imaginations instead to grim physical situations such as that of William Flower, who was forced to lie down in the fire because of an inadequate supply of wood and whose lips continued to move after his "neather part was consumed" (1570, 1749; CT, 7:76). The *Acts and Monuments*, after all, seeks to incorporate its readers into the "body" of the militant church, and thus it is situated on a dialectical tension between individuals' material and subjective concerns and the encompassing identity of the church. Mueller's argument provides a provocative answer to the historical and theological question "Why fire?" but many readers would also ponder "Why (not) me?" The entire teleological force of the *Acts and Monuments* drives toward this second question, as Foxe moves from the ancient church to events within recent memory, from remote locations to the English countryside, and accordingly from abstract theological formulations to events with a bearing on the individul, physical selves of readers.

Yet Foxe problematizes individuality. Paradoxically, despite his insistence on the particular details of the various Marian martyrdoms, each incident seems to end in the same fiery way. Martyrs invariably die at the stake, usually meeting this fate meekly and often raising their arms or offering a devout exclamation at a late moment in the burning process.[17] Foxe works to maintain and support the martyrs' individuality through his detailed textual record of their separate stories, each account announced by a new title. For instance, probably the most famous narrative in the *Acts and Monuments*, that of the deaths of Bishops Latimer and Ridley, turns on the contrasting portraits of the two and on the difference between Latimer's mercifully rapid end and Ridley's agonizingly prolonged one ("let the fyre come unto me, I cannot burne") (1570, 1939; CT, 7:551). Although they all die, it seems to matter that Christopher Wade arranged the faggots around himself, that John Denley sang a psalm as he burned, that George Roper extended his arms "lyke a roode" until they were burned off (1583 ed., 1679; 1570 ed., 1867, 1960; CT, 7:320, 334, 604). If Foxe, in producing these narratives, works to guarantee his subjects' individuality in the way they secure the glorious new name of "martyr," he also records and even seeks to emphasize the way their fleshly fate erases personal identity. He writes of the jumbling together of bodies, as when thirteen martyrs are burned together in one fire at Stratford Le Bow (1570, 2096; CT, 8:154) or when, after the heads of three martyrs tied to the same stake had "fallen together in a plumpe or cluster," "sodenly [Julius] Palmer as a man waked out of a sleepe, moved hys tounge and Jawes and was hard to pronounce JESU" (1570, 2123; CT, 8:218). Foxe offers the peculiar observation that Rose Allin and the nine others burned with her together numbered 406 years of age (1570, 2202; CT, 8:392–93). Beyond simple narrative interest, these details testify to the way martyrdom's course threatens to eclipse individuality, to enact a reduction of human identity to mere flesh, and then to destroy even that.

By recording the martyrs' bodily dissolution in graphic terms, Foxe attests to the technical success of their persecutors. He does so strategically. Training readers' minds to the details of physical destruction is a powerful method of provoking questions about personal autonomy and identity. When he encourages admiration for individual martyrs and readerly sympathy with them, Foxe offers textual pleasure of a fairly straightforward sort, pleasure that affirms the self by solidifying its nature and boundaries. When, however, he challenges readers to take up the cause and identity of martyrdom, he provokes the radical, unsettling textual interaction of jouissance, for a reader who truly identified with a martyr would feel herself undone, the structuring terms of identity shattered. Foxe presumably worked for this effect in order to encourage shaken readers to dedicate themselves to a sustaining structure of religious faith. His aim, in other words, was to recuperate for the church the loss of selfhood provoked in readers by their contemplation of martyrological horrors.[18]

Foxe highlights the martyrs' acts of devotion and submission during their burnings, such as lifting the hands up "to heaven" (although I suspect this action may have been primarily a physiological response),[19] and he emphasizes the late utterance of God's name as a sign of sanctity. Mueller cites the prolonged consciousness of many of the martyrs as evidence for her claim that "braving torture works to catalyze strong individual identities in the *Acts and Monuments,*" in contradistinction to Elaine Scarry's theory that torture unmakes the self.[20] Foxe's rhetoricity may be more important than his content, however. Clearly, a victim's state of mind or spiritual disposition would be determinative of his or her ability to withstand pain, and circulating stories of martyrs' deaths evidently provided a model for those who were sent to the stake, so many of the martyrs no doubt did meet their horrid fate meekly. Still, I question the validity of reading these accounts as historical evidence that the martyrs "experienced [death] as willingly as if it were the satisfaction of a species of desire."[21] My point is not to reopen the debate about Foxe's value as a historian, although recent attention to the theatricality of martyrdom promises to add a needed richness of dimensionality to understandings of Foxe.[22] Rather, I suggest the relevancy of reading his lurid narratives as the textual opportunity for *readers* to contemplate submission to death as "a species of desire." The potential masochism here is on the part of readers, not the martyrs themselves, whose enforced subordination denied the imaginative space for masochism to occur. It is this sort of imaginative space—the space of textuality—that later would distinguish the Marquis de Sade's fantasies of torture and dismemberment from the execution chamber.

The force of textuality is overtly championed in the *Acts and Monuments.* Central to Foxe's Protestant cause was the promotion of individual literacy, and he does his part to advertise the power of the word, presenting his work written "in the popular toung" in accordance with "the necessitie of the ignorant flocke" (1570, "To the Queenes Majestie"; CT, 1:viii). The book is offered as a "monument" honoring and standing in for the martyrs who have died while upholding the gospel. The martyrs are bound to God, through their words as well as their deeds, including the crucial act of dying at the stake; the valuation accorded their words is evident in Foxe's treatment of their writings and the record of their speech.

Less obvious is the way Foxe understood his own authorial task as the counterpart of the martyrs' actions; in the preface to Ridley's *Friendly Farewel,* a precursor text to the *Acts and Monuments* published in 1559, Foxe proposed that in "double ways are we bound to the Lord, who not only by the Word and death of the saints confirmeth the testimony of his truth but also besides their death leaveth such monuments behind them which no less confound the adversary as confirm the godly."[23] Foxe was confident that the "godly" might "confirm" themselves through further reading of textual monuments such as the one he offered. After 1576, the "Book of Martyrs" closed with an injunction to the "gentle reader" to "so employ thy self to read, that by readyng thou mayst lerne haply to know that may profite thy soule, may teach thee experience, may arme thee with pacience, and instruct thee in all spirituall knowledge more and more, to the perpetuall comfort, and salvation in Christ Jesu our Lord to whom be glory in secula seculorum" (1576, 2008; CT, 8:754). Foxe strongly advocated the value of reading a godly text such as his own rather than other "prophane" works offering "delite" in "the variable eventes of worldly affaires, the stratagemes of valiant captaines, the terror of foughten fields, the sacking of Cities, the hurly burlies of Realmes and people" (1570, "To the true Christian Reader"; CT, 1:xxv). He implicitly acknowledges that readers might choose to read profane works rather than godly ones, and he works to secure readers by mixing pleasure with the "experience and wisedome" his monument provides (1570, "To the Queenes Majestie"; CT, 1:viii).

In the radical collapsing of word and deed, whereby the martyrs speak and the author acts, the *Acts and Monuments* seems intent on encouraging readers to read as much as, perhaps even more than, it seeks to inspire them toward acts of godliness and sacrifice. Reading itself is claimed as a godly act, just as writing can be: Foxe refers to his readers when he enjoins, "seying we have found so famous Martyrs in this our age, let us not fayle then in publishing and setting forth their doinges." Thus, in "double ways" Foxe and his audience justify and even sanctify their textual involvement, so that the martyrs live on through their embodied words: "And though we repute not their ashes, chaynes, and swerdes in the stede of reliques: yet let us yelde thus much unto theyr commemoration, to glorify the Lord in his Saintes, and imitate their death (as much as we may) with like constancy, or theyr lyves at the least with like innocency" (1570, "To the true Christian Reader"; CT, 1:xxvii). In Foxe's theology of the word, textuality subverts the force of physical presence.

For readers, an unremarked result of this folding back of presence into textuality is a displacement of affect, a wrenching of the emotional response ordinarily associated with felt experience. Rather than collapsing a reader's imaginative experience into that of textual figures, according to a paradigm of readerly sympathy and involvement, the *Acts and Monuments* calls up a different form of response in readers than what is reportedly felt by figures within the narrative. Foxe purports to be a solicitous author, concerned not only with his readers' spiritual welfare but with their imaginative involvement with the scenes he describes. Foxe himself seems to become so involved with the scene at hand that occasionally he must rhetorically shake himself to escape, as when, after his lengthy narrative of the deaths of Latimer and Ridley, he interposes, "Wel, dead they are" (1570, 1939; CT, 7:551). Foxe's choice of vividly excruciating details seems gauged to inspire readers' involvement. One of the most horrible narratives recounts the prolonged effort to burn John Hooper. Not only does the narrative involve details of chaining the victim to the stake and recital of the conditions necessitating the kindling of three separate fires ("and all this while his neither partes did burne"), but it concludes with a description of his black and shrunken gums, his swollen tongue, and the way "he knocked hys brest with hys handes untill one of his armes fell of, and then knocked still with the other, what tyme the fat, water, and bloud dropped out at his fingers endes, untill by renewyng of the fire, his strength was gone, and his hand did cleave fast in knockyng, to the yron upon his brest" (1570, 1684; CT, 6:658).

While ordinarily one would judge that such a narrative aims to impress with the suffering the victim endured, Foxe concludes his account by claiming Hooper's contentment in his death. "Even as a Lambe, patiently he abode the extremity therof, neither movyng forwardes, backwardes, or to any side: but hauvyng his nether partes burned, and hys bowels fallen out, he dyed as quietly as a child in his bed" (1570, 1684; CT, 6:659). Readers are led to imagine Hooper's agony and then to differentiate their own responses from the martyr's heroically humble one. Through a narrative bifurcation, Foxe calls up his readers' horrifed, suffering sympathy but indicates that the martyr, protected by what Caroline Bynum calls the "anesthesia of glory," felt no pain or triumphed over it through faith.[24]

For Foxe's martyrs, faith provides what Lacan would call the *point de capiton*, which halts the potential slide of meaning in human existence. Faith orders their existence, it enables their submission to the word of God (the symbolic order), and it makes their physical ordeals both endurable and meaningful. Secure within their belief, the martyrs have integrated the dimensions of their existence; this enables them to bear torturous death and to express confidence in their speeches from the stake. In Lacanian terms, the Imaginary and the Symbolic converge for the martyrs, so that the Real (the suffering body) is effaced. Foxe's martyrs, as I have indicated, are not mas-ochistic because, within their system of meaning, death at the stake is the path to glory. With their existence governed by the symbolic order associ-ated with their faith, burning at the stake may not even be painful.[25] When it comes to Foxe's readers, however, the situation is more complex. Foxe per-haps intended to reach (or to produce) readers located so fully within the structure of religious faith that they would share the martyrs' own set of articulated meanings. But more skeptical, less sanctified readers would neces-sarily participate in the martyrs' torment differently. To read without com-plete doctrinal assurance means existing outside the knot of meaning that se-cures the martyrs themselves to their fate as godly. Positioned as consumers of Foxe's text, such readers are wondering or admiring observers of the mar-tyrs' deaths, unable to collapse the ideological, historical, and textual dis-tance that separates them from full participation in martyrdom. Indeed, be-cause textuality opens a space that inevitably involves slippage, we need not posit agnostic or skeptical readers but only active, thinking ones, who would find in Foxe's narratives the seeds or provocations of intellectual debate (did he really maintain his faith through his ordeal? did she not suffer horribly?).

Moreover, through his focus on the physical suffering of the martyrs, Foxe appears to force readers into a confrontation with what Lacan terms the Real—those aspects of existence that escape symbolic articulation alto-gether. This focus seems a purposeful part of Foxe's design: readers, con-fronted by the horrors of the Real (the possibility of dying in torment without the supporting comfort of religious belief) would experience an overwhelming sense of shattering jouissance. Foxe provokes this sort of emotional shattering to motivate readers toward the simpler, more comfort-able, and abiding pleasure of Protestant belief. A confrontation of this sort can scarcely be supposed pleasurable, but judging from Foxe's enormous influence, it certainly seems to have been compelling.

The jouissance I am identifying in readers' experience would be discon-certing and unsettling rather than pleasurable or erotic per se. Although Lacan's ideas evolve more than is usually acknowledged, jouissance consis-tently functions as a specialized term within his usage, naming something more than and other than pleasure; it refers to an experience "*beyond* the plea-sure principle" (*Four Concepts*, 281 [translator's note]) because it "implies pre-cisely the acceptance of death" (*Seminar VII*, 189). The practice of translating the French term as "bliss," with a suggestion of "orgasm," has led to a domesticating misconception of Lacanian jouissance among many Anglophone readers. Moreover, as I discussed in chapter 2, Lacan designates an "other" or feminine jouissance, which he associates with mystical experience in which the self is dissolved into a mode of bodily—but not specifically sexual—ecstasy (*Seminar XX*, 60).

Lacanian jouissance articulates and furthers Freud's formulation of the death instinct in *Beyond the Pleasure Principle* and bears a resemblance to the concept of primary masochism that Freud finally admits to in that work. The link between jouissance and the death instinct is most evident in Lacan's concept of the Thing *(das Ding)*, which names an "emptiness at the center of the real," a kind of vacuole or "black hole" condensing the properties of everything existing outside of the signified (*Seminar VII*, 121). The Thing connotes a limit experience; in Bruce Fink's words, *"the subject comes into being as a defense against it, against the primal experience of pleasure/pain associated with it."*[26] As I have suggested, the *Acts and Monuments* provoked an overwhelming jouissance; it moved readers to glimpse the Thing, in an effort to catapult them into religious acceptance, because devotion could provide a necessary defense against the horrific spectacle of individual disintegration. Foxe, in other words, sought to shatter readers by bringing them up against the Real in extreme form and did so by way of motivating their embrace of the protective identity of Christian faith. Faith could protect against confrontation with the Thing; for Lacan, religion "consists of avoiding this emptiness" in the Real, by attaching meaning to it (*Seminar VII*, 130).

In short, my inquiry rests on a distinction between pleasure and jouissance.[27] In *Seminar XX*, Lacan associates jouissance with the Real and pleasure with the covering over of the Real.[28] For the martyrs themselves, burning evidently produces jouissance—a pleasure beyond happiness, an absolute of the unbearable, access to and acceptance of death, dissolution of meaning into a real that is beyond signification. We might suppose Foxe's purpose to be the extension of the individual martyrs' jouissance to the community of faithful readers, encouraging their incorporation within a shared absolute meaning. But when it came to communicating jouissance, the *Acts and Monuments* could succeed only to the extent that readers were able to participate imaginatively in (what we would assume to be) the martyrs' torments. And perhaps no reader could fully do so: to the reader imagining a martyr's death, its horror would in a sense turn inside out, becoming the road to glory for the martyr him/herself and the occasion for the *reader's* traumatic contemplation. Foxe insists so strongly on his martyrs' secure placement within a belief system capable of sanctifying their sacrifice that a reader might well suppose them actually to escape confrontation with the Thing, even though it comprises the body in its states of extremity, such as burning. Readers, on the other hand, who might be caught in ambivalence, aware of the gaps within signifying systems or constructions of faith or distanced in their perspective, would necessarily negotiate the possibilities of both horror and glory in the experience of burning at the stake. Because their experience remained the least secured, readers would have the fullest sense of overwhelming terror, glimpsed glory, shattering pain/pleasure.

I emphasize that the issue here is one of textual dynamics, not religious or ontological validity. I am contrasting the portraits of martyrs as constructed by Foxe with the readers whom he rhetorically positions. Jonathan Culler famously used the premise of reading "as a woman" to demonstrate the absence of secure self-identity in the reading process.[29] Along the same lines, I would suggest that reading "as a martyr" involves an impossible positionality, a necessary oscillation between sharing a martyr's profundity of faith (which at the limit would negate the horror of death at the stake) and sharing a martyr's horrific experience (not a literal option in most cases, but even contemplating the flames could be expected to threaten a reader's resolve and dedication). The reading dynamic itself would work against secure positioning through full identification with a martyr (or other person) and thus contribute to jouissance.

The tropes of reading as a woman or as a martyr carry suggestions of disempowerment, but I am not arguing that the reading audience passively received Foxe's efforts. For if Foxe sought to unsettle his readers from the security of settled identity, to provoke them with a difficult, demanding text, to shatter them into an embrace of Protestantism, the net effect was the creation of motivated individuals. Moreover, the split or gap occurring in readerly consciousness through the effort to read as a martyr could be subversively empowering, much as the embrace of lovesick jouissance served paradoxically to elevate Petrarchan poets by placing them beneath the deified beloved.

Huston Diehl has recently argued that Foxe creates narrative dramas as part of the process through which he "constructs his own readers as witnesses." In Diehl's view, illustrations in the *Acts and Monuments* "forge [readers'] identifications with the eyewitnesses" and thus enable Foxe to emphasize the responsibility accruing to spectators of martyrdom.[30] Indeed, Foxe's narratives indicate the complexity with which historical spectators responded to these events: to enable the flames (by piling up faggots or by supplying a necklace of powder) could be an act of mercy, to turn away from the condemned in horror an act of complicity with torturers. Reversals and complications resulted from the split identities of the martyrs, who understood themselves to be spiritually bound for heaven as their bodies were spectacularly destroyed on earth.[31] Perhaps the most useful model for thinking about Foxe's construction of his readers as witnesses to martyrdom is the theater, where viewers could and did take up shifting positions of sympathy and judgment.

Nevertheless, there are significant, relevant differences between reading about violence and witnessing it or its theatrical image. Viewing violence, one might take any number of emotional positions—resisting, sympathizing, criticizing, admiring, or identifying with the victim or the persecutors and potentially shifting between these responses. As I have suggested, the complex difficulty of reading "as a martyr" also causes shifting and split positionality. Still, violent texts tend primarily to expose the position of the victim. The entry into language of the inchoate material of violence brings a degree of logical order that reveals the victim's experience, even when there is no expression of overt sympathy or respect. For instance, Georges Bataille observes how Sade's "language takes us out of the field of violence . . . [and] into something else, something necessarily its opposite: into a reflecting and rationalised will to violence."[32] Furthermore, a degree of imaginative sympathy is necessary for verbal exploration of a victim's suffering. Slavoj Žižek articulates this point when he claims that even Sade himself, as a writer, does not qualify as "sadistic" because his exposure of cruelty renders its logic inoperable. Such structural sympathy effects a displacement whereby the "position of enunciation" is necessarily that of the victim.[33]

Lacan goes on to observe that, in Sade's fictions, the victim seems indestructible, showing no trace of the abuse she or he endures. Instead the victim "separates out a double of himself . . . inaccessible to destruction . . . [enabling] the play of pain." By splitting the victim, Sade explores what

Lacan calls the "second death," the fantasy of continued "suffering beyond death" that animates the idea of hell (*Seminar VII*, 261, 295). This doubling of the victim effects a kind of thickening or swelling out of fantasy to form the space of textuality, allowing the fantasy to be put into language. For Žižek, the "place 'between the two deaths' . . . is the site of *das Ding*. . . . This place is opened by symbolization/historicization: the process of historicization implies an empty place, a non-historical kernel around which the symbolic network is articulated."[34] We can compare how the victim is similarly split in Foxe's martyr narratives, divided under the aegis of neoplatonized Christianity into destructible flesh and transcendent body-and-soul. With this theological division, martyrs are saved from masochism through the insistence that they are not "really" destroyed but transferred to another dimension. An observer of a martyr's burning would only actually *see* destruction of the flesh; the further dimension of a transcendent soul is accomplished through "symbolization"—hence the importance of the martyr's own words of faith and assurance, as collected and reiterated by Foxe. So, too, the promise of the martyrs' redemption turns on projection of a further temporal existence and hence is built on an implied "historicization."

Reading back from our era, the *Acts and Monuments* seems proleptically sadistic in its focus on suffering bodies, the excitement of cruelty, and relationships of domination and subordination. But this is not to say that the *Acts and Monuments* offered its early readers erotic pleasure; indeed, following Foucault one would have to say that what it offers is specifically *not sexual* because chronologically prior to the development of a discourse of sexuality.[35] Yet Foxe's text offers a form of sadism *avant la lettre*—a pleasure derived from the three interlocking dialectics of (de)valuing the flesh, promoting/erasing individuality, and strategically collapsing the domains of word and deed. Lacan writes in *The Ethics of Psychoanalysis* of what he calls the paradox of jouissance: "What is the goal *jouissance* seeks if it has to find support in transgression to reach it?" (*Seminar VII*, 195). Following this point, Lacan proposes that Sade articulates a fundamental ethical problem: "To love one's neighbor may be the cruelest of choices." For Lacan, this amounts to an "antimorality," a recognition that "my neighbor possesses all the evil Freud speaks about, but it is no different from the evil I retreat from in myself. To love him, to love him as myself, is necessarily to move toward some cruelty" (*Seminar VII*, 194, 198). Given the evident similarities between Sade's and

Foxe's work, we might begin to see the problems attaching to a religion of love that disavows the human capacity for cruelty.

The power of the *Acts and Monuments* to fuel Protestantism depended, of course, on the purported distinction between the martyrs and their persecutors. Yet many have commented on the irony that the text of Foxe's reform effort was later used against the church in whose support he wrote. Perhaps we can glimpse in Lacan's analysis of "the *jouissance* of destruction" a further link with the paradox of founding a religion of love on acts of suffering (*Seminar VII*, 197). The Reformation was, in ways Sade can demystify, built on the appeal of transgression: the martyrs' defiance of institutional authority produced their spirited acceptance of the stake, and Foxe incorporated readers into the Protestant church by fueling both their opposition to Roman tradition and their willingness to embrace suffering. Considering Sade's penchant for sullying the stuff of religion[36] and Leopold von Sacher-Masoch's claim to have been excited by reading the tales of suffering saints,[37] one suspects that the specific psychology of sadomasochism emerged from the ruins of politicoreligious means for achieving submission or shattering of the self. The discourses and practices of sexuality gradually usurped these and other purposes previously tied to the institutional authority of church and state.

The inclusiveness of Foxe's world and his textual aims meant that *Acts and Monuments* could serve for pleasure, polemic, history, and ecclesiastical record all at once. Because of the changing position of the writing subject in relation to both authority and desire, a severing and specialization of the textual world and the effects it produced had taken place by the time of Sade. In Foxe's case, wide acceptance of the Protestant ideological structure meant that, in context, neither he nor his martyrs were sadistic or masochistic; their actions were in line with established meanings. But readers, with the intrinsic freedom to be less securely positioned within the governing ideology and with the unavoidable double consciousness that the reading experience entails, could respond more variously and transgressively, in ways we can identify as sadistic or masochistic. Their pleasure would be located, as with reading Sade, in the textual space that allows a shattering of established boundaries. Readerly pleasure of this sort is a matter of the textual articulation of physical extremity, as distinguished from a response to suffering in the phenomenal world, although it would be left for later eras to rediscover the necessarily reciprocal relations between violence and violent texts.

In conclusion, I look briefly at a text written between the times of Foxe and Sade, which illustrates the relationship between textuality and an emerging literature of sadomasochism. Thomas Nashe's *The Unfortunate Traveller* closes with a spirited account of the burning of the Jew Zadoch, in revenge for his offenses against two women—violent sexual offenses themselves described with relish in the text. The death of Zadoch recapitulates the deaths at the stake of Foxe's martyrs but casts them into a harsher light:

> To the execution place was he brought, where first and formost he was stript, then on a sharp yron stake fastened in the ground he had his fundament pitcht, which stake ran up along into the bodie like a spit; under his arme-holes two of like sort; a great bon-fire they made round about him, wherewith his flesh roasted, not burnd: and ever as with the heate his skinne blistred, the fire was drawen aside, and they basted him with a mixture of Aqua fortis, allum water, and Mercury sublimatum, which smarted to the very soul of him, and searcht him to the marrowe. . . . To his privie members they tied streaming fire-workes: The skinne from the crest of the shoulder, as also from his elbowes, his nuckle bones, his knees, his anckles, they pluckt and gnawed off with sparkling pincers . . . his nailes they halfe raised up, and then under-propt them with sharpe prickes, like a Tailers shop window halfe open on a holy daie: every one of his fingers they rent up to the wrist. . . . In conclusion, they had a small oyle fire, such as men blow light bubbles of glasse with, and beginning at his feete, they let him lingringly burne up lim by lim, till his heart was consumed, and then he died. Triumph, women, this was the end of the shipping Jew, contrived by a woman, in revenge of two women, her selfe and her maide.[38]

In this purported parody of martyrs' deaths,[39] we encounter a complication of textual positioning: while Nashe's narrative seems to be a fantasy—and hence more kin to Sade than to Foxe—the hatred expressed is so vividly felt as to seem "real."[40] Indeed, there is none of the self-conscious textuality one finds in Sade, no doubling of the victim to enable the continuation of fantasy, and as a result the authorial self seems actually to *be* sadistic. Nashe's text is peculiarly able to reveal Sade's relative tameness. By the same token, it is what Nashe shares with Foxe that renders this account sadistic—the ideological confidence about right and wrong, the secure belief about what the burning means, the necessity to provide vivid details of the torment, and the evident desire to move readers into identification with the suffering portrayed, so that Nashe "imagines for the reader what the torments felt like to Zadoch"[41] (they "smarted to the very soul of him"). That Nashe's descriptive details extend so fully beyond anything Foxe wrote illustrates how textuality puts sadomasochism into play: it is not the fact of the martyrs' deaths that Foxe uses to impress readers but the conveyance through language of their experience. As Jonathan Crewe notes, *The Unfortunate Traveller* "suggest[s] the possibility of an aesthetic appreciation of violence."[42]

Foxe's early readers were positioned historically between the time of living witnesses to the Marian martyrdoms and that of theatrical spectacles of fictional suffering, such as *Titus Andronicus* and later *The Broken Heart*, which would enable the jouissance of future generations. With theater and sophisticated parodic treatment such as Nashe's, jouissance separates off from religious conviction or the excitement provoked by spiritual controversy. As the world became more stratified, so that politics and religion occupied increasingly separate spheres, it also developed more space for and need for violent aesthetic pleasures. The public theaters, as Stephen Greenblatt has argued, adopted forms and adapted purposes of religious ritual, providing a secular site for communal involvement with emotionally wrenching spectacles. As I will show in chapter 4, the Shakespearean theater not only secularized but sexualized the image of martyrdom through the character of Lavinia in *Titus Andronicus*.

CHAPTER FOUR

The Pornographic Economy
of Titus Andronicus

[P]erhaps we may say in terms recalling the prophecy made by the Three
Witches to Banquo: "Not clearly sexual, not in itself sadistic, but yet
the stuff from which both will later come."
—Freud, "A Child Is Being Beaten"

AFTER SEVERAL CENTURIES OF CRITICAL CONDESCENSION, *Titus Andronicus*
has been reassessed in the last fifty years, mostly on the evidence of several successful theatrical productions. The two most notable were strikingly different
in style—Peter Brook's in 1955 was highly ritualized, with crimson streamers
suggesting blood, and Deborah Warner's in 1987 was intimately realistic—yet
both provoked extremely emotional responses from audiences. A theater
official reported laconically of the Brook production, "At least three people
pass out nightly. Twenty fainted at one performance. Ten swooned on Friday."[1] Warner's production had a similar casualty rate; I saw four people faint
during a Saturday matinee. Theatrical productions are frequently instructive
for revealing the formal cohesion of a play or demonstrating its appropriateness to a particular historical or cultural context. But the extreme audience response to *Titus* tells us something else as well, something about spectacle,
about identification, about what viewers can and cannot bear to witness.

Certainly, the violence in *Titus* is horrific, and, as D. J. Palmer observes,
"the horrific of its very nature is that from which the mind shrinks, that

which repels the senses, feelings and understandings."[2] It is easy to assume, with Palmer, that certain actions are inherently repellant—too easy, in fact, since *Titus* features most of the acts likely to appear on such a list (cannibalism, dismemberment, sexual violence), yet its early popularity has been well documented as well as recently repeated. So while it is an interesting sociological point that the Elizabethans had, like us, a penchant for gory entertainments, the correspondence of tastes is merely tautological when it comes to explaining the problematic appeal of this play's violence. Moreover, to subordinate the intensity of theatrical effect to the play's narrative or thematic lessons may produce a structure of meaning but does so without fully acknowledging the theatrical dynamic.[3] To see the play as demonstrating the destructive cycles of revenge, for instance, or offering the recuperative comfort of fantasy, or training its audience in acceptable responses to unimaginable grief—each of these approaches leaves the most basic question unanswered: why would an audience, any audience, enjoy *Titus's* reiteration of violence against the human body? "Enjoy" may seem an odd verb to use here, since most viewers today will claim to appreciate the play *in spite of* its violence or alternatively to reject it *because of* the effects Palmer calls horrific. Yet enjoyment or pleasure of some form is the goal of any paying theatrical audience, as Shakespeare was well aware. The brilliance of *Titus Andronicus* lies in the way it allows viewers to be scandalized and morally outraged by events portrayed on stage but also and at the same time to identify with characters who suffer and commit acts of horrific violence.

This accomplishment depends upon a shifting dynamic of sympathetic identification, Shakespeare's exploitation of drama's capacity to fracture its audience in several ways. Individual viewers respond differently to the unfolding events on stage; individual characters make changing, competing claims on viewers' sympathies. The effect is to break down established viewer subjectivity, to undermine supposedly firm positions from which to watch and make sense of the play. Diagnosing this situation in the abstract is, however, a far simpler matter than intervening at any particular point to expose the meanings pressuring a response. Because of the play's unsettling features, locating points of pleasurable interaction is extremely difficult, for *Titus Andronicus* effectively *negates* the viewing subject. The disappearing position of the viewer of *Titus Andronicus* can be traced to two factors, one having to do with codes of bodily integrity and the other an effect of gender.

In a recent overview of critical explorations of bodies or "the body," Keir Elam notes how such work often misses its mark. The Lacanian paradigm I have used in preceding chapters helps to explain why: the body as Real remains foreclosed from the symbolic language of academic criticism. For the semiotician Elam, performance offers a way beyond this impasse, since it "permits us to read Shakespeare's bodies both in their non-idealized or em-bodied corporeality and in their signifying power."[4] However, bodies on stage do not exist as stable objects read by disengaged viewers. The phenomenology of theater structures an interaction through which viewers are aware of their own physical existence in the presence of other highly marked bodies on the stage. Therefore, to understand bodies we need to "read" the engagements and responses of viewers as they process the signifying corporeality on stage. The spectatorial crises recurring in productions of *Titus Andronicus* register the impact of images of bodily disintegration. The handless, headless, tongueless bodies represented on stage offer a mirror stage gone tragically amuck. In place of the "statue" or "orthopaedic" image of bodily totality that Lacan's paradigmatic infant admired, what stares back to viewers of this play is the "fragmented body" of the disintegrating individual (*Écrits*, 2, 4). The many anxious jokes about mutilation, both within the playtext and in the criticism it inspires, testify to the horror these images provoke. Here, the truth one reads in performance involves a challenge to fundamental ideas of bodily presence and totality. Fascination with mutilated forms is leveraged by the terrifying threat to one's own bodily form and the subjectivity mapped onto it.

With the brutalized figure of Lavinia, in particular, *Titus Andronicus* explicitly confronts viewers with the disappearance of subjectivity into a gulf of silence. The male characters in the play construct sympathetic responses to her, claiming her story and then, uncannily, her mutilation, as their own. Lavinia occasions the political argument with which the play begins, she inspires the rapists, she motivates the revenge plot, and she incites the horror of viewers. But none of these acts affirms her subjective agency. In each case it is a matter of others reading in her the cause of their own passion. With the compulsively repeated act of placing Lavinia at the site of others' emotion, the play feeds on her femininity. As a result, her nascent subjectivity is undermined, turned to other purpose by the exigencies of plot and the requirements of passion. Liberal feminist criticism would recognize and speak for the silenced woman, but because Lavinia has already been so thoroughly spoken for, her position exposes a structural limit on feminist solidarity, a point at which the sympathetic effort to share another's pain slides into appropriation. It is neither the play's suggestion, nor my assumption, of Lavinia's individuality that makes her proof against political rescue; rather, it is the structural challenge her plight presents to those who would see and respond.

To bring these central issues of dismemberment and gender into focus, I will explore the ongoing stage presence of the mutilated and raped Lavinia, beginning with the crucial passage in which she is slowly recognized by her uncle Marcus. Despite the wealth of critical commentary on this scene, especially in recent years, its full material horror—the way Lavinia is presented on stage as a mutilated sex object—remains unacknowledged. The prevailing paradigm sees Lavinia as a woman whose brutal rape motivates the Andronican revenge plot. But at the moment of her first appearance, Marcus's address disconcertingly offers his niece as a sexual image for spectators' contemplation. If we pay attention to the theatrical dynamic, it is clear that dismemberment does not figure here simply formally (as a strategic response by her attackers to illicit sexuality) or symbolically (as a sign that Rome itself has been attacked or as an image of castration). Instead, mutilation is granted its own fetishistic attraction. When Aaron describes her as "trimmed" (5.1.93),[5] the word distressingly compounds two available meanings of "to cut off the excrescences of" and "to make comely, adorn, dress up" by way of suggesting a third, overarching meaning: "To put into proper condition for some purpose or use" (OED 11, 7, 2). By "lop[ping]" (2.3.17) her limbs, the attackers have rendered Lavinia useful, appropriate, and thus in their eyes perversely attractive. Montaigne reports on an early modern taste for physically incomplete women: "they say in Italy as a common proverb that he does not know Venus in her perfect sweetness who has not lain with a cripple."[6]

Furthering this connection, we might recall how images of martyrs in the early modern period frequently conjoined mutilation with eroticism. Given the availability in our own culture of pornographic images of battered women and of amputees whose stumps or prostheses are used as sexual fetishes, it is worth wondering why the fetishizing of Lavinia's maimed body has not been generally acknowledged. Bardolatry and critical prudery aside, there are moments at which critics are unable to comprehend the way the early modern theater titillated with violence. When the mix strikes us as too perverse or too threatening, we are inclined to block out the sexual resonances and to focus on other terms of significance. Indeed, even with current critical discourses emphasizing power and sexuality, critics have had a particular investment in *not* seeing Lavinia's postrape appearance as perversely pornographic. Pondering viewers' fascinated resistance to the spectacle of Lavinia's mutilated body in terms provided by the discourses of pornography and sadomasochism can expose the horror attaching to the play. They show *Titus Andronicus* to instance a kind of Shakespearean "hardcore" that conjoins the available imagery of martyrdom with that of early modern pornography. With this play, Shakespeare accomplishes a two-part innovation in the entertainment industry—first, by transferring images of martyrs from the page to the stage where they could be bodied forth and, second, by explicitly sexualizing Lavinia's martyrdom through the rape narrative.

In labeling *Titus Andronicus* a form of pornography, my point is not to express disapprobation of the play, nor do I mean to suggest that Lavinia's appearance is sexually explicit in the familiar sense of that phrase. Rather, I am using the term *pornographic* to describe material that uses sexuality to activate a voyeuristic response. The striking congruency between the fields of pornography and theater can be helpful in understanding the dynamics of dramatic form and in particular the difficulties for some viewers of confronting the action of *Titus Andronicus*. We might begin with the rather obvious point that pornography, like theater, foregrounds the physicality of the human body yet calls into question the status of the "real." In Kaja Silverman's terms, "pornography leans . . . upon real bodies";[7] with her ambiguous verb formulation, Silverman captures the action of pornography as a discourse dependent on real bodies but also pressuring them. In a parallel way, the bodies of actors provide the ground in which dramatic texts are realized, but those bodies are shaped and presented by texts. The dependency of the performative body on dramatic and cultural texts is what compromises the ability of performance to expose bodies in the way Elam suggests.

Three characteristics of *Titus Andronicus* suggest why it can appropriately be included within the discourse of pornography. First, pornography specifically, even formally, thematizes looking; its regime is intensely and often self-consciously scopic. Classic voyeuristic images position an illicit, peeping viewer at a window or keyhole; trick perspective pictures designed to be viewed through a lens have been a popular form of pornography since at least the seventeenth century;[8] and pornographic photography uses the confrontational look of the subject to more directly "interrogat[e] the very act of viewing, making the viewer self-conscious."[9] Shakespeare evidently understood this motif well: In *Cymbeline*, for instance, when Iachimo creeps from the trunk in Imogen's bedchamber to gaze first at the decorative scenes from erotic myths and then at the exposed breast of the sleeping Imogen, he enacts the viewing position of spectators in the theater. *Titus Andronicus* contains reiterated instructions for characters to "look on" the mutilated Lavinia (3.1.111; see also 3.1.60–66, 4.1.10–15, 30–65), instructions that are inevitably and purposefully extended to theatrical spectators. Moreover, the effort to read her body, to "understand her signs" (3.1.144), thematizes looking as an epistemological act.

Second, pornography has traditionally been understood as material designed to arouse a sexual response. In this sense it troubles the boundaries between textual and phenomenal worlds. Kenneth Clark, for instance, distinguished the relative containment of art from the imperatives of pornography, and James Joyce contrasted "aesthetic emotion" that was "static" from the "improper arts" he understood to be "kinetic."[10] The classic liberal view of this matter is exemplified by Roland Barthes's praise for the erotic photograph that avoids showing the sexual organs and thereby "takes the spectator outside its frame, and it is there that I animate this photograph and that it animates me."[11] Another view has been popularized by Catharine MacKinnon, who agrees that pornography extends, or trespasses, into real life but disagrees about the desirability of its doing so. Rather than objecting simply to the individual reader's or viewer's response to a piece of pornography as a formal object, MacKinnon is concerned with how pornographic images are produced as well as how they are used, and with long-term as well as immediate responses. MacKinnon's argument emphasizes the "transitiveness" of representations, in the words of Frances Ferguson, by "acknowledg[ing] the recommendation implicit in any representation as both an object for evaluation and also a representation of an evaluation."[12] In this sense, MacKinnon's argument coincides with Silverman's, for both grant to pornographic discourse the power to shape bodily existence in the real world. MacKinnon's polemicism has often distracted from her lucid recognition of pornography's power to shape events. In fact, the position she has so vigorously argued—that pornography is not "only words" but has real power to harm—uncannily reproduces Shakespeare's extension of the rhetoric of dismemberment by representing it in *Titus Andronicus* as lurid fact.[13] Surely, the most striking linguistic feature of the play is its use of perversely literalized metaphors—"handle not the theme, to talk of hands, / Lest we remember still that we have none" (3.2.29–30), "set a head on headless Rome" (1.1.189)—through which Shakespeare calls attention to the collapse or reversion of language into violent action.

Because of its troubling of the phenomenological border between the real and the representational, *Titus Andronicus* bears comparison to hard-core pornography.[14] In a strictly formal sense, the comparison does not stand, since hardcore designates filmed actions that (supposedly) cannot be faked, and a stage performance of *Titus Andronicus* is filled with necessarily representational action performed by actors (including a male actor playing Lavinia, in the early modern theater) who do not suffer actual bodily harm. Yet no matter what the style of presentation, the dimensional difference between pictorial depiction of mutilation and live enactment of it is startling. As Thomas Heywood explained in his *Apology for Actors* (1612), "A Description is only a shadow received by the eare but not perceived by the eye: so lively portrature is meerely a forme seene by the eye, but can neither shew action, passion, motion, or any other gesture, to moove the spirits of the beholder to admiration: but to see a souldier shap'd like a souldier, walke, speake, act like a souldier: to see a Hector all besmered in blood, trampling upon the bulkes of kinges. . . . To see as I have seene, Hercules in his owne shape hunting the Boare, knocking downe the Bull, taming the Hart, fighting with Hydra, murdering Gerion, slaughtering Diomed, wounding the Stimpholides, killing the Centaurs, pashing the Lion, squeezing the Dragon, dragging Cerberus in Chaynes, and lastly, on his high Pyramides writing Nilultra, Oh, these were sights to make an Alexander." Heywood recognizes that the formal differences between drama and other representational modes carry with them differences in the phenomenology of response: "so bewitching a thing is lively and well spirited action, that it hath power to new mold the harts of the spectators and fashion them to the shape of any noble and notable attempt."[15]

By depicting on stage in *Titus Andronicus* events ordinarily relegated to fiction or the private hells of a few unfortunate individuals, Shakespeare ups the theatrical ante. Readers often assume that *Titus* was intended as parody, for reasons including the sheer technical difficulties of staging so many "lopped" limbs (2.3.17). With its insistence that viewers witness Titus losing a hand, Chiron and Demetrius having their throats cut, the heads of Quintus and Martius being bartered, and the ongoing spectacle of the mutilated Lavinia, the play pushes toward graphic confrontation. In *Titus Andronicus*, it is insufficient just to die; explicit, and often prolonged, physical suffering is required. Bringing events of this sort onto the public stage, Shakespeare challenges viewers to think about issues of bodily autonomy and wholeness, about the bounds of personhood. Fragmentation not only is a metaphor for social, political, or moral undoing but also is made literal, graphic, hard-core.

For these reasons, it is interesting that the long history of spirited opposition to *Titus Andronicus*—as not truly Shakespearean, not worthy of admission to the canon—constitutes a kind of implicit censorship comparable to that mounted against pornography. For it is not simply the play's content that has offended: instead, its determined exposure of the vanishing line between the real and the representational causes profound discomfiture. The plight of critics who find their language infected by the play's characteristic tropes of bodily mutilation illustrates how *Titus Andronicus* deconstructs an opposition between words and action, drawing critics into its grasp. One response to such linguistic stickiness is to seek recourse in the supposedly pure standards of literary excellence. The move recalls MacKinnon's paradoxical effort to stave off the performative power of hate speech by enacting legislation—more words—to control a distressing linguistic function.

In her analysis of MacKinnon's opposition to pornography, Judith Butler detects an impulse to halt the free play of discourse. Calling attention to the contextual embeddedness of every utterance, including MacKinnon's denunciation, Butler asks: from what position is the argument against pornography (or hate speech generally) uttered? and what work does it do? When Mac-Kinnon urges recourse to an increased governmental role in regulating pornography, she grants the state a position of sovereignty and objectivity that Butler disputes.[16] MacKinnon's "idealization of the speech act as sovereign action (whether positive or negative) appears linked with the idealization of sovereign state power or, rather, with the imagined and forceful voice of that power" (Butler, *Excitable Speech*, 82). In Butler's view, not only does Mac-Kinnon presume overmuch agency in the speaking subject (by deemphasizing the derived nature of any speech), but she repeats the error on a grander scale by supposing that the state might intervene from a neutral position to grant agency to those who would otherwise be deprived of it.

Butler's sense of the inappropriateness and futility of using words to fence out performative utterances bears strongly on *Titus Andronicus*. So, too, does her attention to the complex position of the audience or addressee of hate speech or pornography. In response to MacKinnon's argument that pornography "proclaims and effects the subordinated status of women," Butler objects that she moves too quickly to place women in the position of victim, falsely equating woman as depicted in pornography with woman as viewer (73). In general, MacKinnon discounts the role of fantasy, which effectively fractures and complicates the viewing subject, in order to sustain her moral argument. For Butler, MacKinnon's energies are misdirected because she would enact prohibition against a "domain of the phantasmatic [that] is precisely *suspended* action, neither fully affirmed nor fully denied, and most often structured in some form of ambivalent pleasure ('yes' and 'no' at once)" (95). The point is not that fantasy and pleasure should license objectionable behavior but that the ends of discourse demand to be analyzed, as well as its context, history, and addressee. For these reasons, Butler calls for "a feminist reading of pornography that resists the literalization of this imaginary scene" (69).

Butler's insistence on the significance of fantasy points toward the third characteristic that *Titus Andronicus,* and theater in general, shares with pornography: both are designed and intended to produce pleasure in viewers. Although considerable attention has been paid to the eroticism of the early modern theater, the strong traditional sense that a formal or aesthetic pleasure defined the experience still blocks an understanding of how Shakespeare and some of his contemporaries depended on sexual titillation to arouse viewer involvement.[17] This theater regularly employed the imagery of sexual violence—sometimes, as in *Titus,* in the context of a plot encoding a moral argument against such violence. Bruce R. Smith points out that "to speak of 'sex' on the one hand and 'violence' on the other presumes that those two terms designate distinct categories of experience. In early modern English such a distinction was even less certain than it is now."[18] My argument in this chapter begins with consideration of early modern pornography and its congruency with the imagery of martyrdom. Then, because erotic and pornographic imagery inherently calls up questions about viewer response, my inquiry proceeds through consideration of the politics of representation and into the psychology of identification. Ultimately, the question of what it means to label the play "pornographic" returns us to consideration of the troubled relation of *Titus Andronicus* to the Shakespearean canon.

TECHNICALLY SPEAKING, any reference to pornography in the early modern period is anachronistic, since neither the term nor a distinct category of written or visual representation existed before the nineteenth century. Although most cultures have produced some form of sexually explicit images or texts, "pornography" proper comes into existence as a category of thinking, an effort at regulation; in Walter Kendrick's terms, pornography is "not a thing but a concept." Nevertheless, as Lynn Hunt points out in *The Invention of Pornography*, something like pornography had a long prior history as "an adjunct to something else." In early modern Europe, images of the kind our culture typically considers pornographic were often put to political purpose, "using the shock of sex to criticize religious and political authorities."[19]

Certainly the most famous example of early modern erotica or proto-pornography is the series of engravings by Giulio Romano called *I Modi*, published in 1524 and suppressed by papal order. Learning of the arrest of the engraver, Pietro Aretino composed a series of sonnets to accompany the graphic illustrations of sexual postures. After his daring act of resistance, Aretino's name came to be associated with not only this particular set of poems and engravings but also the numerous imitations that sprang up. References to "Aretino's postures" are made in many English works of the early seventeenth century. Henry Peacham, for instance, complains "what hurt hath that beastly booke of *Aretines* done abroad in the world." Peacham's remarks are especially interesting because he is himself linked with *Titus Andronicus* through the famous sketch of the play's characters ascribed to him. He associates Aretino with a whole tradition of Continental pornography: "what lewde art is there showne in many printes and peeces that are daily brought over out of Italy, Flanders, and other places, which are oftner enquired after in the shops then any other, little use else is there of most of the wax pictures of Curtizans in Rome and Venice being drawne naked, and sold up and downe as *Libidinis Fomenta*, surely I cannot but commend art in them, as many times there is excellent good, but verily doe hate their wicked makers and abhominable ends."[20]

With his vilification of the pornographers' "abhominable ends," Peacham expresses the classic, defining case against such images: they provoke too active a response. Peacham goes on to discuss idolatrous imagery he regards as "blasphemous, and utterly unlawfull, and whatsoever the Romane Catholickes thinke of it . . . no waies allowable by the word of God." Peacham's set of associations provides a sense of how the pornographic tradition had a familiar political resonance in early modern England. For English Protestants, there was only a short step from Italian erotica to Roman Catholic idolatry; in each case, the flesh was the focus of all too much attention. As David O. Frantz puts it, "On the one hand the English admired and imitated much in the way of Italian learning, general culture, and especially literature. On the other hand, the English abhorred and feared Italy as a land of Catholicism, lewd living, and lewd writing."[21]

Peacham's elision of Italian erotica with Roman Catholic idolatry is understandable in terms of style as well as geographical provenance. To Protestants of the late sixteenth and early seventeenth centuries, one of the most dangerous aspects of Catholicism was its promotion of luxuriously fleshly images. That such images could inspire sensual as well as spiritual responses is illustrated by Vasari's anecdote of the Saint Sebastian produced by Fra Bartolomeo "with very good flesh colouring, of sweet aspect and great personal beauty." The painting's "comely and lascivious realism" supposedly elicited sinful responses: "the friars found by the confessional that women had sinned in looking at it."[22] The temporary solution to the problem—moving the painting from the church into the chapter house, where only men could see it—may suggest that male viewers took delight in the provocative image themselves.[23] Martyrdom scenes, in particular, unabashedly conflated sensuality with suffering. Images of Saint Sebastian, for instance, were typically quite erotic; in the view of historian Peter Webb, Guido Reni's Saint Sebastian in the Capitoline Museum in Rome "could almost be posing for a male pin-up photograph." Paintings such as Nuvolone's *Saint Ursula* (Karlsruhe Gallery), showing "the saint in an ecstatic fit with an arrow penetrating her body between the breasts," or Sebastiano del Piombo's *Saint Agatha* (Pitti Palace, Florence), showing "two men attacking her breasts with tongs,"[24] or Lelio Orsi's *Martyrdom of Saint Catherine* (1555–63), showing the

Fig. 2. **Three martyrs.** From Antonio Gallonio Romano, *Trattato de Gli Instrumenti di mortirio* (Rome, 1591), p. 69. By permission of the Folger Shakespeare Library.

wide-eyed saint about to suffer death by the wheel, exemplify this characteristic blending of eroticism, violence, and spirituality.

Such imagery was not limited to the high art of Italian Renaissance paintings; it had its counterpart in readily available materials. While the popularity in England of Foxe's *Acts and Monuments* testified to the appeal of violent
imagery and narrative, its woodcut illustrations, though terrifying, were
hardly sensual. However, the *Acts and Monuments* had a sensational counterpart on the continent, the *Trattato de Gli Instrumenti di mortirio* of Antonio
Gallonio. Appearing originally in Rome in 1591, Gallonio's book represents a
wide variety of instruments of torture and systematically illustrates their
modes of application. Included in this textbook of tortures are several meth-
ods reminiscent of *Titus Andronicus:* burying alive (as Aaron is at the end of
the play); roasting of bodies or body parts in frying pans, pots, and caldrons;
lopping off of hands; and cutting out the tongue. The illustrations are not
sexually explicit, but the gracefully fleshed bodies and sensual suffering depicted in Gallonio's book conform with a classical style. Gallonio's martyrs
appear to be fragmentary statues, suggesting a broken or interrupted trans-
mission of the classical past to the Renaissance world. Gallonio includes images of women's breasts being amputated, a form of torment not illustrated
in sixteenth-century editions of Foxe's *Book of Martyrs* but included in later
editions. As the appropriation of this image suggests, one of the ways the
English devised to counteract the effects of Italian and/or Catholic art was
to turn it to Protestant purposes. Shakespeare played a version of this role
late in his career when he made Giulio Romano, the engraver of *I Modi,* the
supposed sculptor of Hermione's statue in *The Winter's Tale.* The producer of
Italian erotica was thus domesticated, his images of courtesans' bodies
redesignated as the memorial image of a wife and mother.

At the time of *Titus Andronicus,* Shakespeare seems more concerned to reiterate than to appropriate Italian sources. Long considered more "Roman"
than Shakespeare's three Plutarchan plays, even though it lacks an identifiable
Roman source, *Titus Andronicus* was said by T. J. B. Spencer to "includ[e] *all*
the political institutions that Rome ever had. The author seemed anxious,
not to get it all right, but to get it all in."[25] Obviously, Shakespeare distinguished between the ancient Rome in which the play is set and the early modern Rome in which voluptuous images abounded, yet the zealous attention to
Romanness that characterizes the play seems to have brought a sliding of

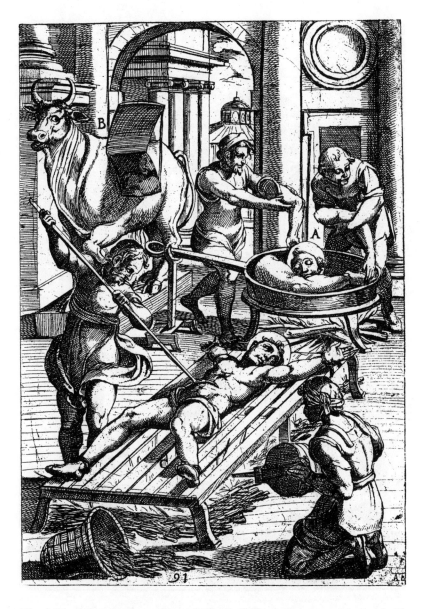

Fig. 3. Roasting martyrs. From Antonio Gallonio Romano, *Trattato de Gli Instrumenti di mortirio* (Rome, 1591), p. 91. By permission of the Folger Shakespeare Library.

Fig. 4. **Martyrs dismembered and severed.** From Antonio Gallonio
Romano, *Trattato de Gli Instrumenti di mortirio* (Rome, 1591), p. 123.
By permission of the Folger Shakespeare Library.

associations, similar to that glimpsed in Peacham's remarks. Contemporary connotations of Rome as the site of lewd religion and lewd art were projected backward onto the Rome of *Titus Andronicus*.[26] Among the indications of the play's Reformation context,[27] we should note especially the repeated references to Lavinia as a "martyr": "Speak gentle sister: who hath martyred thee?" (3.1.82), "I can interpret all her martyred signs" (3.2.36).

In documenting the availability of materials conflating eroticism and suffering within the context of sixteenth-century religious disputes, I have thus far been concerned primarily with the images as a factor in the political world. But martyr images did not function simply, or primarily, as propaganda; they were intended to serve as devotional aids. As I indicated in chapter 3, Foxe explicitly invites, encourages, and discusses his readers' involvement with his book. Inviting imaginary participation in the suffering of martyrs or saints, such images, both visual and verbal, encouraged viewers to identify with those experiencing ecstatic pain. The martyrs' torments were presented to occasion an unsettling of the established self, a religious jouissance. Eventually, as I have suggested, martyrdom would provoke another sort of shattering pleasure: Leopold von Sacher-Masoch recalls "devouring the legends of the Saints" as a child and being "plunged into a state of feverish exictement on reading about the torments suffered by the martyrs."[28] The "martyrd" Lavinia instances a significant step toward the later, explicitly sexualized form of masochism, since her violation is offered as potentially exciting to viewers. In presenting a feminine sexual object as beautiful, suffering, and available, the play's structural dynamic accords with standard pornographic codes.

However, since Lavinia's image is not isolated but presented within a narrative plot, the questions of response and viewer identification must be considered. Much as I would like to think that few viewers in any era actively identify with Chiron and Demetrius in their attack on Lavinia, her subsequent presentation achieves its effect by merging sexual provocation with evidence of cruelty. Presumably, the majority of viewers identify chiefly with Marcus and Titus; for them, sadistic aspects of Lavinia's rape and mutilation are briefly activated but foreclosed by being put to the service of a humanistic plot. Lavinia's objectified stance presents a particularly interesting point of identification, one that proceeds from a feminine viewing position, although those who occupy this position are not necessarily women. With

Lavinia, the play solicits a masochistic response. As we will see, however, analyzing a masochistic viewing position proves difficult, not only because the play disavows its sadomasochistic potential by encasing violence within a revenge plot but also and more generally because of the paradoxical nature of spectatorial identification itself.

As critics have begun to demonstrate, Lacanian models of desire and identification productively reveal the blind spots and displacements that feature so regularly in Shakespeare's plays. Of course, Freud himself saw subjectivity and desire as mimetic and unstable, nowhere more explicitly than in his writings on masochism, and yet he never entirely abandoned his sense of the innately desiring subject. Pondering Freud's 1919 essay "A Child Is Being Beaten," Mikkel Borch-Jacobsen locates a "blind spot" concealing the identification at the very core of Freud's concept of subjectivity. Freud maintains that the violent beating-fantasy stated objectively in the phrase used as the essay's title actually culminates a set of earlier fantasies. The first phase is sadistic—"my father is beating the child"; the second phase inverts this into masochism—"I am being beaten by my father." The essay treats the patient's fantasies as a form of internal theater: it analyzes three related scenes of fantasy, devoting much attention to the movement between phases; it scrutinizes the patient's identifications; and, unusually for Freud, it uses a quotation from the patient as the essay title. In addition to providing a way to locate various critical orientations, the model Freud develops here demonstrates how the shifting logic of fantasy documents subjective orientations toward the human body. The model turns, however, on a "blind spot": Although, Freud states, the second (masochistic) phase is "the most important and the most momentous of all," yet "it is never remembered, it has never succeeded in becoming conscious. It is a construction of analysis" (*Child*, 185). The hidden masochistic fantasy—imagining oneself as victim—is the lynchpin activating pleasure in spectacles of violence. But because the fantasy remains hidden from consciousness, delight or gratification in violence remains difficult to theorize, except in the blunt terms of opposing it.

Freud's early comments on Hamlet and Oedipus make clear that his sense of the theatrical dynamic is founded on a perceived connection between the presented characters and the observing audience.[29] As further developed in Freud's later work, the concept of identification takes on a bodily component, and the theatrical model becomes the basis for understanding subjective identity per se. That is, not only an analytic paradigm for a subjective position but an actual lived sense of *who one is* as a desiring subject is attained through processes of identification.[30] Identification can be so complete as to mask its own action, so that the subject may remain blind to its ever having occurred. Partly as a consequence of identification's self-canceling mechanism, the subject forgoes any direct understanding of his or her own body. This is what Lacan theorizes as the occlusion of the Real within the lived framework of the Imaginary and the Symbolic.

The problem of identification forms the crux of Borch-Jacobsen's argument that Freud's model of subject formation contains unacknowledged divisions. Borch-Jacobsen emphasizes the essential theatricality of the entire psychoanalytic enterprise; he examines the "representative theatricality" of Freud's model of the unconscious, maintaining that "unconscious thought is always conceived as visual thought" (*Freudian Subject*, 26, 244n). The riddle or "blind spot" that Borch-Jacobsen locates in Freud's model is the priority of mimesis. Rather than following upon and fulfilling desire, identification makes desire possible: "Mimesis informs desire, directs it, and, more broadly speaking, incites it" (*Freudian Subject*, 23, 27). Where Freud seems committed to an original desiring subject whose wishes are met through identification— as, most notably, in the identification that resolves the oedipal conflict and inaugurates emotional and sexual maturity—Borch-Jacobsen follows Lacan in locating a hidden early mimesis inaugurating the first desires.

The importance of specularity in this model becomes clear in his extended reading of "A Child Is Being Beaten." Borch-Jacobsen locates a "transitivist indistinction of self and other" that precedes "any differentiation of roles" (*Freudian Subject*, 38). This point of mimesis remains hidden from the subject, who cannot remember or verbalize it because it has not been observed. Why can't the subject see himself or herself playing the part of the other in the crucial second phase of the fantasy? Because "when the subject goes up onto the stage, enters the scene, *he no longer represents it to himself.*" The point of identification is the point of splitting, where the subject becomes the other and so simultaneously gains through mimesis what is lost through cleavage. The transitivist phase, says Borch-Jacobsen,

constitutes the blind spot of the fantasy, for it is the spot or standpoint from which the subject sees ... *the point of otherness* (since the other whose place is occupied by the subject is *not* apprehended as other). This point is invisible to the subject; it is not perceived. The subject cannot see himself miming another at the moment he is miming, just as he cannot say that he is playacting precisely while he is acting. In order to do that—in order to see the invisible, or say the unsayable—he would have to reflect himself . . . he would have to arrive at the vantage point of the lucid spectator (philosopher, analyst, director). (*Freudian Subject*, 39)

Given the eroded foundations of this model of subject formation, one has to wonder whether it is ever really possible to arrive at the objective "vantage point of the lucid spectator" or whether the best that could be hoped for would be a further mimesis—taking on the *role* of philosopher, analyst, director. For Borch-Jacobsen, the subject's identifications inevitably elude him or her. Since there seems no alternative model available within his theory, Freud has constructed a trap into which he himself falls. Unable to "see" the priority of mimesis in his own developmental model, he fails in particular to acknowledge the male child's early identification with his mother, as feminist psychoanalytic theorists have pointed out.[31]

Borch-Jacobsen's model of identification has a further important implication, one that takes my argument from simply locating Freud's blind spots and returns it to the more relevant questions of seeing, knowing, and talking about the body. A theory that gives priority to identification displaces the possibility of bodily knowledge leading to a body-ego. Indeed, a subject who originally identifies with an other would gain a sense of the *other's* body, rather than the subject's own. It becomes necessary at the very least to see knowledge of one's own body to be secondary and dependent, as in the Lacanian concept of the specular ego. Psychoanalysis thus suggests how approaches to the body are inherently flawed, to the extent that the subject sees through the eyes of an other, without seeing that this is its vantage point. This, in part, is what Slavoj Žižek, adopting a Shakespearean phrase, calls "looking awry."[32]

Moreover, as Lacan emphasizes, desire is organized through identification: "The subject originally locates and recognizes desire through the intermediary, not only of his own image, but of the body of his fellow being. It's exactly at that moment that the human being's consciousness, in the form of consciousness of self, distinguishes itself. . . . It is in so far as his desire has gone over to the other side that he assimilates himself to the body of the other and recognises himself as body" (*Seminar I,* 147). This sense of the necessary triangulation of desire provides the groundwork for understanding the theatricality of sadomasochism as an erotic economy. But a new problem opens up with a recognition of how identification displaces both desire and self-awareness, a hermeneutic one, since critics can scarcely claim to be immune from the effects they analyze. The slippery slopes of identification imperil the legitimacy of analytic claims of all sorts, and those explicitly concerned with variations of viewer response may be most jeopardized.

The problem of objective judgment of plays that demand personal response is one Stanley Cavell has masterfully addressed. Foregrounding the question of limitations on knowledge, Cavell reads Shakespeare's plays as interpretations of the skeptical dilemma: "how to live at all in a groundless world," or, more prosaically, "whether I know with certainty of the existence of the external world and of myself and others in it."[33] His readings return over and over again to the imagined theatrical scene of the plays. "It is the work of this theater to present itself as an instance of the ceremonies and institutions toward which our relation is in doubt, exists in doubt, is unknowable from the outside," and, conversely, "Our task is exactly to determine our relation to the events specifically before us" (Cavell, *Disowning Knowledge,* 29). Cavell acknowledges instances of specific partialities, as in his consideration of how and with what effects skepticism is a masculine affair (15–17, 34–35). Yet his writing is marked by a tension between his commitment to confronting the "specifications and doubts" of his own relation to the theater's events and his wish to speak more widely of the achievement of the plays. Every act of criticism must construct a position from which to speak, and Cavell takes on a double challenge in writing from a performance standpoint (where the temptation to record or at least to rely on anecdotal theatrical experiences is large) *and* making the question of specificity, or partiality, of response his very theme. When he generalizes about response—which typically occurs, in the essay on *King Lear* especially, when he is accounting for critics' failure to *see* certain meanings (81)—Cavell constructs a position that conjoins moral imperative with psychological involvement.

For instance, asking why readers or viewers or critics fail to notice that Gloucester has not mentioned Dover before Regan "thrust[s] him out" to "smell His way to Dover" (3.7.92–93), Cavell grants no quarter to confusion or inattention: "We 'do not notice' Regan's confusion of identity because we share it, and in failing to understand Gloucester's blanked condition (or rather, in insisting upon understanding it from our point of view) we are doing what the characters in the play are seen to do: We avoid him. And so we are implicated in the failures we are witnessing; we share the responsibility for tragedy" (54). The argument here is about the power of Shakespeare's theater to confront its audience in their inadequacies, to place spectators or readers in the position of epistemological untenability. The theater forces viewers, that is, into blind spots: how can viewers do otherwise than understand "from our point of view"? Yet, Cavell asserts, by rendering any particular viewpoint "partial," Shakespeare's theater displays the limitations of its viewers. The argument is largely congruent with Borch-Jacobsen's about Freud. Viewers fail to notice the guilt they share: here, as in "A Child Is Being Beaten," identification produces the blind spot. Just as Freud calls the second phase of fantasy, the occluded masochistic phase, the "most momentous," so Cavell believes that Shakespearean drama is constructed to point to the viewer's particular partiality.

Can we see our way around such spots, construct a periscope that will extend our perceptions? Cavell has himself been criticized for "fall[ing] short of profiting from feminist reconsiderations of male psychoanalytical baggage." Timothy Murray sees Cavell's "impressive achievement" in *Disowning Knowledge* of revealing "the extensive role of skepticism in empowering early modern culture and political philosophy" as intimately bound up with a problem "typical of skepticism itself": a refusal "to acknowledge a representation of the female outside of the parameters of male loss."[34] The blind spots in some of Cavell's readings may be exacerbated by his tendency to analyze *imagined* performances; responding to a theater within his own mind, Cavell creates models that may not be truly subject to the skeptical dilemma because they are not truly other.

Despite these concerns, *Disowning Knowledge* presents an appealing model of a skeptical stance. Cavell's limitations are intrinsically bound up with his larger understanding of how the plays work. What could more aptly demonstrate, for instance, how *The Winter's Tale* presents "the skeptic as a fanatic" than Cavell's own overdetermined identification with Mamillius? (206).[35] He couples his disturbing insight that what we fail to see is precisely what is most important with another, more reassuring thought: that Shakespeare's theater "giv[es] us a place within which our hiddenness and silence and separation are accounted for" so that we are allowed "a chance to stop" theatricalizing, stop hiding behind customary defenses. In response to worries that philosophy is jeopardized by the seductive powers of theater, Cavell simply admits that "we are always already seduced" (104, 37). Caught in the web as we are, there is no chance of achieving perfect or perfectly objective knowledge, and accepting that limitation becomes the precondition for a meaningful encounter with a play. Cavell thus privileges the dramatic fiction, granting it license to confront viewers in their/our peculiar inadequacies. As I have implied, Cavell presupposes an ethical drama, one whose confrontations will make viewers both more honest and more aware of the needs of others. *Titus Andronicus* has sometimes been understood as this sort of drama, its excesses put into the service of moral lessons: appreciating how cycles of revenge perpetuate themselves; learning to confront suffering; perhaps even, in the Andronican response to Lavinia, learning to speak from the position of the other. Certainly, the grieving tenderness with which the Andronici respond to Lavinia encourages viewers to share this response.

Nevertheless, it is important to reflect how few experiences in life are so open to skepticism as rape. That the event is beyond question in *Titus Andronicus*, all doubt stilled by the extra evidentiary acts of mutilation, demonstrates the hyperbolic aspect of this rape. Since the violence itself is not (cannot be) shown on stage, the mutilated Lavinia serves as its emblem, as well as its victim. She confronts viewers in this emblematic sense, assaulting their/our sensibilities with the too-apparent evidence of what has happened to her, the act encoded on her body. Like a pornographic image that destroys eroticism by showing too much, Lavinia's postrape display is excessive. So thoroughly is she undone by this overexposure that for many viewers Lavinia fails to acquire a sense of subjective identity altogether; for them, she remains merely a sketch, a cartoon, an unfortunate image.[36] Evidently this is the case for Marcus: one of the distinct horrors of his long speech of discovery is his inability to fit her blasted appearance into a framework that will enable an appropriate response. Narrative ordering must occur for Lavinia's plight to become the occasion for sympathy. Without a narrative framework, the figure of a mutilated woman in extreme circumstances functions ambiguously, as if oscillating between the possibilities of sensual appeal, ecstatic self-abnegation, shamed self-effacement, and imploring neediness.

Once the narrative of rape is deployed, Marcus and other characters, as well as viewers and critics, can construct coherent responses to Lavinia. I suggest, however, that the humanist narrative of rape serves as what Cavell might call a "customary defense" against the raw spectacle of the theatrical moment. Further, the shifting dynamic of responses to this scene indicates the intrinsic instability of the narrative frame.

Bringing Lavinia from object to subject status has been a project of liberal feminist criticism. Traditional humanist criticism assimilated Lavinia's plight to Titus's tragedy; Albert Tricomi, for example, remarked that "Lavinia's violated chastity . . . was to Titus the worst violation of all."[37] The patriarchal standard was also upheld by early psychoanalytic criticism emphasizing oedipal or castration themes.[38] David Willbern's important essay "Rape and Revenge in *Titus Andronicus*" suggested that the play's aggression stems from "a more primary source than castration anxiety": it emerges from "a fear of the catastrophically perceived preoedipal mother, who threatens total dismemberment and destruction (the devouring mother)." His attention to preoedipal dynamics allowed Willbern to diagnose "the murderous hostility toward women which informs the play,"[39] although Lavinia seems more a symbol than a represented person in Willbern's account. More recently, feminist critics have seen Lavinia's plight as emblematic of women's troubled relation to the symbolic order.[40]

All of these approaches position themselves as objective, disinterested accounts of the play's action; they resist involvement with the play as fantasy. In this sense, criticism corresponds to the third phase of Freud's model of fantasy, the phase that "neutralizes the subject (who is doing the beating?) as well as the object (what child is being beaten?) in the impersonal 'a child is being beaten.'" The neutrality of this position, Žižek notes, allows the advent of "compassion and guilt."[41] Freud's claim that this third phase presupposes the other two (sadistic and masochistic) forms of fantasy and Cavell's injunction that Shakespeare's plays are specifically designed to locate our blind spots as viewers together suggest the importance of also exploring alternative modes of relation that may be compacted within the morally ordered one. Even if neutrality is attainable, it may mask other forms of connection activated by the play. Since many feminist interventions are willing to challenge the claims of objectivity, we might expect to find criticism from this perspective to be more "interested," but this is only partially the case.

Bringing the character from objectification into full(er) subject status has meant (re)constructing a sense of Lavinia's desires and motivations, discovering traces of an inner dimension in a character previously understood as merely an Ovidian reference point. Much has been gained in this project, but something important has been overlooked as well, for focusing on Lavinia as subject has meant denying how the play itself presents her and insisting that an audience view her as a sexual object. So one might move from Marion Wynne-Davies's comment that "*Titus* is about . . . the point at which woman as subject is confronted with a destructive depersonalization" to consider how problematically woman (Lavinia at least) achieves subject status in the play—if she does so at all.[42] Sara Eaton, combining Laura Mulvey's analysis of the gaze with Elaine Scarry's formulations of the dialectic of physical torture, offers a crucial insight: "Tortured women on the stage are substantiated and acquire presence . . . because the male characters and the audience see them hurt. . . . Representations of women must be fetishized by viewers if self-consciousness . . . in the spectator is to result."[43] Eaton isolates the fetishizing dynamic of Lavinia's presentation in *Titus Andronicus* and suggests how it might be expected to appeal to some viewers. According to Mulvey's model, viewers' pleasure is either voyeuristic or identificatory; she explicitly labels the scopophilic position sadistic.[44] As Silverman has shown, masochism can motivate the alternative, identificatory mode of pleasure.[45] In the case of *Titus Andronicus*, readers or viewers who are positioned as feminine identify masochistically with Lavinia.

In the Introduction to the Arden 3 edition of *Titus Andronicus*, Jonathan Bate quotes Anna Calder-Marshall, who played Lavinia in the BBC television production of the play. She recollects: "'Someone said to me, "It's just like a video nasty, isn't it?" and it is very, very frightening.' 'But,' she went on, 'somehow, we've found—or I think we have—that the characters through their suffering get closer. Titus has committed the most appalling deeds and it isn't until he's maimed and his daughter's maimed that he learns anything about love.'" Bate goes on to say that understanding *Titus Andronicus* means "perceiv[ing] its proximity to *King Lear*" and "apprehend[ing] the difference between a slasher movie and a tragedy."[46] But that difference is undermined by Calder-Marshall's sense of the play's frightening proximity to a "video nasty" and her uncertainty about whether a humanistic lesson is actually achieved.

Considering the haunting similarities "between a slasher movie and a tragedy" would mean activating Cavell's question: What does it mean to *see* the
mutilated Lavinia? Why does the play specifically and repeatedly demand that
the audience look at her? Is it possible to overcome the pornographic objectification of the raped woman? Most readers or theater viewers would not understand an appearance such as Lavinia's with "her hands cut off and her
tongue cut out, and ravished" (2.3.1sd), as even remotely erotic. Yet such are
the terms used by Lavinia's uncle Marcus in confronting her. His references to
her arms as "sweet ornaments / Whose circling shadows kings have sought to
sleep in" (2.3.18–19), to the "crimson river of warm blood . . . between thy
rosed lips, / Coming and going with thy honey breath" (2.3.22, 24–25), to her
"pretty fingers" and her "lily hands [that could] / Tremble like aspen leaves
upon a lute / And make the silken strings delight to kiss them" (2.3.42, 44–
46)—this rhetoric, especially in combination with Marcus's overall tone of
aghast speculation, marks Lavinia, even in this moment of distress, as an erotic
object. Marcus even uses a term—"encountered" in line 32—that was standard vocabulary "for the accosting of a prostitute."[47] The point has been reiterated that the speech is poetic in a specifically Ovidian way and that its logic
should not be confused with conventions of realistic drama. But granting
Marcus's characteristically remote and aesthetic mode of response does not
limit the speech from marking an erotic appeal in the woman as object of rape
and mutilation. Whereas morally scrupulous members of the audience might
be expected to differentiate their own responses from those of the thuglike
Chiron and Demetrius, Marcus's own moral authority ironically legitimizes a
sense of Lavinia's sexual desirability even when, or especially when, she has
been mutilated.

The amount of critical ink devoted to discussing this speech suggests just
how uneasy it makes commentators. As Bate suggests, "For all that it is an attempt at empathy, might Marcus' perversely Petrarchan display of the raped
Lavinia be a kind of second rape upon her?"[48] At that uncomfortable overlap
between slasher film and tragedy, Marcus offers his violated niece as a sexual
image for the audience's contemplation. His lengthy apostrophe arrests the
temporal movement of the plot as he trains all eyes on her. The effect is that
of a photograph or a freeze frame in cinema, the sort of suspended image that
Gilles Deleuze associates with the rituals of masochism (*Coldness*, 33). Moreover, the play specifically frames Lavinia's mutilated entrance between build-

ing expectations of illicit sexual expression and Marcus's eroticizing address.[49] It presents her not only as a wounded and pitiable person but, in structural terms, as a sexual object.[50]

Within the play's action, Lavinia's dismemberment is eventually understood, by means of its Ovidian parallel, as a secondary result of the rape. The Philomel story has taught her attackers that cutting out a victim's tongue is not enough, so they have severed her hands as well to forestall discovery of their identity. This narrative order has shaped critical responses: in terms of chronology as well as significance, Lavinia is seen as first raped and then mutilated. But because the rape is not shown, viewers, including Marcus, will ordinarily realize first that she has been mutilated and then surmise that she has been violated. Retaining the experiential chronology reveals further resonances of the play's misogynistic violence. Focusing on her dismemberment reminds us that the lost parts—her hands, her tongue—are those through which a woman might express herself and also those through which she could be active as a sexual being. Moreover, her bleeding mouth figures in Marcus's apostrophe as a displaced image for the vagina,[51] suggesting his implicit understanding that her attackers have rendered her mouth as well as the stumps of her arms into passive receptacles, as if they have attempted to make her, like a sex toy, all vagina. This is indeed a moment of hard-core realization.

Stephanie Jed has influentially demonstrated how rape served as a central trope of Western humanism, and *Titus Andronicus* provides a clear example of the trope at work: "The physical violation of [a woman's] body [is] transformed into an injury to the honor of her male survivors."[52] In our culture rape has traditionally been defined as a property crime, and this logic obviously produces the view of Lavinia's suffering as an offense against Titus. Some have argued that rape is more appropriately seen as a crime of power than as an instance of sexuality.[53] Most of those who understand Lavinia's dismemberment symbolically endorse one or both of these views; the character's fate thus becomes emblematic of a largely male disenfranchisement, a contribution to the furthering of the tragic hero's suffering. Bate believes that "our culture is more conscious of rape and its peculiar vileness than many previous cultures have been" and that modern productions, notably Warner's, with Sonia Ritter as Lavinia, have been strong "because rape matters to them as late twentieth-century women more than it could possibly

Fig. 5. Removal of breasts, teeth, and tongue. From Antonio Gallonio
Romano, *Trattato de Gli Instrumenti di mortirio* (Rome, 1591), p. 125.
By permission of the Folger Shakespeare Library.

have done to Shakespeare writing for Marcus and to the boy who first played Lavinia."[54] Of course, constructing and advancing a moral argument against rape are fairly straightforward tasks, since it has no public supporters: that is how rape fits into the humanist project. More difficult to comprehend is the way *Titus Andronicus* traffics in images of violent sexuality, offering them for viewer consumption even while condemning them as outrageous and morally loathsome. As Marcus is struggling to make sense of the moment and the humanistic plot is activated around Lavinia, making her the cause célèbre of the play's revenge plot, the moment showcases in the actor's/character's body a conjunction of violence and sexuality that makes its own perverse appeal to the audience.

This is why, I think, Marcus's address to Lavinia marks a crisis point for many viewers: it hovers over a blind spot, a near-impossible realization. To approach Lavinia as a fully realized character, as a represented person, makes it impossible to accommodate the pornographic aspect of her presentation. To consider the image unrealistic, staged, and merely distasteful is to reduce the moment's tug of reference. This blind spot marks the intersection of two currents of representation: on the one hand, the brutally objectifying presentation of Lavinia as recipient of sexual violence; on the other, the nascent development of Lavinia as a character. The first mode involves sadism, which the play authorizes, allowing it to be foreclosed and disavowed through identification with the revenging Andronici. The second mode involves a masochistic identification with Lavinia, which the play invites but does not fully authorize. We can compare Linda Williams's analysis of the "impossible" pleasure of a woman viewer who identifies masochistically with the victim in a snuff film. Williams is not concerned to label such a pleasure "politically incorrect" but literally impossible, for in her view "there can be no pleasure . . . without some power."[55] The masochistic position is dangled before viewers but suppressed by the overwhelming costs of identifying with the brutalized Lavinia.

As I have suggested, spectatorial relation to theatrical violence may be split not only among individual viewing positions but also within individual viewers. The play's presentational dynamics will complicate these relations. Marcus's inability to determine what he is seeing, what has happened to Lavinia, when he finds her after the rape exaggerates the possibilities for splitting of response. Alan Dessen describes how spectators at Warner's production of *Titus* were required to "observe Marcus, step-by-step, use his logic and Lavinia's reaction to work out what has happened, so that the spectators both see Lavinia directly *and* see her through his eyes and images." Bate writes that Marcus "has to make himself *look* steadily at the mutilated woman, just as we, the offstage audience, have to look at her."[56] But the difficulty of knowing *how* to look at her—of seeing adequately, in Cavell's sense—is largely a function of the queasy construction of the viewer's gaze.

Late in act 1, viewers observe Chiron and Demetrius "braving" (1.1.524sd) for one another and then for Aaron. Ultimately, they seek to prove their boastful claims, and the attack on Lavinia is performed to demonstrate to one another that they have "no cowardice" (1.1.632) and to show the lustier, more violent Aaron that they are indeed "brave boys" (1.1.629). As spectators in the theater, viewers form the third party for whose gaze the rape and mutilation are carried out. Chiron and Demetrius do not act out of "blind lust"; they attack in order to show off. The viewer's horror registers compliance with the episode's structure, following the dynamic of pornography; Žižek explains: "In pornography, the spectator is forced a priori to occupy a perverse position. Instead of being on the side of the viewed object, the gaze falls into ourselves, the spectators." Pornography typically acknowledges its viewer and consciously displays its object. Together with the paralyzed Marcus, the typical viewer's onstage double, spectators who look on Lavinia in 2.3 see too much: the excessive, sadistic confirmation of Chiron and Demetrius's daring and lust. And it is not Lavinia (or the actor playing her) who is degraded by this encounter. Žižek continues: "Contrary to the commonplace according to which, in pornography, the other . . . is degraded to an object of our voyeuristic pleasure . . . it is the spectator himself who effectively occupies the position of the object. The real subjects are the actors . . . trying to rouse us sexually, while we, the spectators, are reduced to a paralyzed object-gaze."[57]

When Marcus says that "such a sight will blind a father's eye" (2.3.53), he indicates the perverse power of the mutilated Lavinia: it will not be the horror of what Titus will gaze upon, but his dawning recognition of his own inability to respond adequately that might blind him. Rendered impotent by the rape of his daughter, Titus is further differentiated from her attackers. Similarly, Willbern's reading points to the pornographic dynamic of this line while implicitly connecting it with castration anxiety: "The imagined blindness is both a defense against having to look at such a horrible symbolic image, and also a punishment *for* seeing it. Lavinia has become a kind of Medusa."[58] In the event, Lucius testifies to the power of the image and his own reduction by it: "Ay me, this object kills me" (3.1.65).

Titus, significantly, goes on to mime Lavinia's loss by sacrificing one of his own hands. Motivated by family loyalty and honor, Titus, Marcus, and Lucius all profess eagerness to send a hand as ransom for Quintus and Martius. When Titus deceives the others and has Aaron cut off his hand, he enters into a deeper identification with Lavinia, sharing her inability to "passionate . . . grief" (3.2.6) and declaring himself, through his masochistic self-sacrifice, the most loyal of the Andronici. His movement from an originally proprietary relationship with Lavinia to one in which he participates in (one of) her specific loss(es) signals shifting identifications of the sort characteristic of fantasy. Titus's excesses, after all, have led to Lavinia's plight; by masochistically sharing in her mutilation, he disavows his own guilt without forsaking the position of power that leads him to kill his daughter in act 5. Similarly shifting identifications are also operative in the theater.[59] As Smith points out, the playhouse is distinctive in that "it denies the spectator a fixed point of view. In watching a play, as in living a life, the Subject Position is in fact the intersection of many different subject positions." Smith notes further that the viewing position of women spectators was particularly ambiguous in relation to the early modern theater's "economy of violent objects and subjective pleasures." I would extend this point to say that men or women might occupy a feminine, masochistic position, although social codes result in women's more frequent placement there. Certainly, the theater's "fluid boundary between victim and victimizer" that Smith compares to "the psychological dynamics of sadomasochism" unsettles established gender positions.[60] Nevertheless, the model so strikingly played out in *Titus Andronicus* is the traditional one of woman as victim whose suffering is taken up and used by men to their particular purposes.

Earlier I located the objective stance of compassionate but purportedly disinterested criticism in the third, "neutral" phase of fantasy, as its logic is articulated by Freud. The first, sadistic phase of the fantasy ("my father is beating the child") corresponds with the pornographic aspect of Lavinia's presentation. It entails a viewer's structural coincidence with the brutal Chiron and Demetrius and hence a forced identification of some sort with them. Spectators are required by the structure of *Titus Andronicus* to confront and gaze upon the mutilated Lavinia, to observe her with a pornographer's eye. Alternatively, one may view her with a humanist's neutral compassion; the play's action, in fact, works to modulate the pornographic posture into one of "compassion and guilt." But no space is readily available from which to view Lavinia empathetically or to identify with her. Structural impediments block identification with a character presented as a brutalized sexual object: in Lacanian terms, the constructed gaze is in discord with the empathizing viewer's eye. Those who persist in an inclination to identify with the tormented character are required to construct a masochistic fantasy. Such a fantasy, Freud writes, "is never remembered, it has never succeeded in becoming conscious" (*Child*, 185); it is the impossible point of trauma, the patient's "I am being beaten by my father," or here, "I am raped and dismembered." This type of fantasy renders the identification an abject one that is intolerable for many viewers, in keeping with Freud's view that masochism necessarily escapes consciousness. But, of course, masochism *does* enter into consciousness and has taken its place in the world of textuality; the insistence to the contrary constitutes Freud's defensive strategy. *Titus Andronicus* illustrates how Shakespeare participated in the development of sadomasochistic fantasies as part of the Renaissance theatrical experience.

Butler's critique of MacKinnon's stance against pornography corresponds to my own view of the apparent sins of *Titus Andronicus*. I have urged in this chapter a confrontation with the play's pornographic economies not to censor them but to expose the layering of sadomasochistic fantasy at work. Much as Butler worries that localizing the cause of violent behavior can work to "silence a discussion of the broader institutional conditions" underlying that violence (Butler, *Excitable Speech*, 22), so the omission of *Titus Andronicus* from the high canon of Shakespearean literature has enabled critical blindness to the deep appeal of sadomasochistic fantasy as a force in early modern (and later) English texts. Despite its popularity in the early modern period, *Titus* has been deemed uncharacteristic of Shakespeare's work. However, "what we mean by 'normative' necessarily alters once we recognize that the very field of speech is structured and framed through norms that precede the possibility of description" (140). What we mean by "Shakespearean" has been structured by Enlightenment norms of subjectivity and aesthetic function.

But as *Titus Andronicus* shows, Shakespeare draws on traditions of martyrology in bringing living images of torment and prolonged suffering onto the public stage, audaciously vivifying the images presented in two-dimensional form in illustrations of religious torment. He secularizes and, in the case of Lavinia, sexualizes motifs of bodily fragmentation familiar from images of saints and martyrs. *Titus Andronicus* has long been considered a false start in Shakespeare's career of tragedy writing, since it features a sensationalistic physical dynamic that contrasts with the more philosophical movement of the later tragedies. Yet we see here the first efforts toward psychologizing the suffering self: challenging his viewers to empathize with the mad and psychically fragmented Titus, Shakespeare induces a type of temporary shattering of viewers. In the case of Lavinia, the conflict between modes of presentation—objectifying and empathetic, sadistic and masochistic—complicates identification in disturbing ways. Nevertheless, we can attribute the play's power, for good or ill, to its activation of energies that some audience members find overwhelming. If earlier images of martyrdom provoked a jouissance that could be recuperated into religious identity, *Titus Andronicus* takes a decisive step toward the sort of sexualized shattering that we know as sadomasochistic.

Titus Andronicus presents the paradox of extreme imagery of physical violence existing outside an available framework of emotional response. The play deploys physical violence in disturbingly revelatory ways, troubling the familiar claims of audiences and critics to oppose violence, challenging the humanist aesthetic that sees suffering and pleasure as inherently unrelated. No wonder, then, that *Titus Andronicus* was for so long rejected as ridiculous and un-Shakespearean: it exposes the limits of cherished precepts of humanist aesthetics. The play's presentational economies elicit sadistic and masochistic responses that are disassociated from the established sense of Shakespearean drama today but that Shakespeare was evidently not loath to activate. Or I should say to capitalize on, for not least among the pornographic functions of his theater was the economic motive for creating a pleasurably erotic dynamic.

If its access to discourses of martyrdom activated the pornographic potential of early modern theater, the understanding of emotions as physical empowered this movement onto the stage. In my final chapter, I return to the discourses of the passions and humoral theory, showing how the Caroline playwright John Ford drew on familiar bodily economies to occasion emotional shattering of viewers.

) (

$\mathcal{F}$orm, $\mathcal{C}$haracters, $\mathcal{V}$iewers, and $\mathcal{F}$ord's The Broken Heart

IN THEIR ATTEMPT TO ESTABLISH A LINK between the body and social theory, M. L. Lyon and J. M. Barbalet grant emotion a vital, active role. Emotion, they write, "activates distinct dispositions, postures and movements which are not only attitudinal but also physical. . . . Emotion is precisely the experience of embodied sociality."[1] Lyon and Barbalet's sense of emotion as marking the bodily intersection of an individual, psychological existence and a shaping social order corresponds in interesting ways to the concept of dramatic catharsis. Aristotle's idea of the purgative function of tragedy has usually been understood to mean that individual viewers are purged of excessive emotion through their social experience of attending a play. Some maintain that Aristotle meant to grant a social utility to theater, as a means to siphon off the unruly emotions of the masses. Others stress the individualistic possibilities of the idea, extending to the ethical realm the educative possibilities of catharsis. A minority view understands the idea in formal terms, seeing the catharsis as occurring within the structure of the play. As Stephen Orgel notes, the conversation about catharsis has taken on a life of its own, so that Aristotle's intentions may now be deemed less important than the evolving influence of the idea,[2] and what it has provided is a familiar site for understanding emotion as "embodied sociality."

Thus, while high-minded theorists have taken Aristotle's term *catharsis* to mean "cleansed" or "purified" (resonances that support the moral emphasis and suppress the physical one) or have lamented it as an unfortunate metaphor,[3] there exists a particular relevance to Renaissance drama of a theory that sees emotion as bodily, as something that might be purged. Whatever the Greek may have meant, his conflation of the emotive and the physical makes good sense in relation to the early modern era, when the governing concept of the humoral body made emotions a function of physiology. Although available moral codes counseled the importance of asserting the superior will to subdue the passions, the experience of attending the theater was not only or even primarily an affair of the mind and spirit. It was instead a shared group experience in which emotions were pricked and inflamed—an effect to which the hand-wringing antitheatricalists testify when they offer their ironical endorsements of Aristotelian theory.[4] Given the visibility and importance of emotional responses to this drama, theories that concentrate on strictly cognitive dimensions of the viewers' experience (whether intellectual, moral, political, or aesthetic) remain inadequate.[5] As we have seen, within the historical context of humoralism, Renaissance drama was simultaneously a matter of emotions and bodies, since the balance of bodily fluids within the individual was understood to largely determine his or her emotional state. What we think of as private or internal experience was mediated by a set of social norms that structured individuality along rather different lines than those to which we are accustomed. Gail Kern Paster has brilliantly demonstrated how the tumultuous internal experience of the humoral body is inscribed in the drama of Shakespeare and his contemporaries.[6] In this chapter I am building on her insights about the physical and emotional lives of early modern subjects in order to revisit the concepts of dramatic form and viewer response associated with the debate about catharsis. The problematically negative implications of purgation will be brought to bear on the problem of locating either pleasure or aesthetic value in the reception of John Ford's *The Broken Heart* (c. 1629).

Unlike *Titus Andronicus* or the numerous spectacularly violent seventeenth-century tragedies, *The Broken Heart* eschews extravagance in favor of forms of violence that are not merely restrained but actually accomplish destruction and death *through* restraint. Extreme forms of control and self-torment—starvation, bleeding to death, dying of a broken heart—demonstrate divided selves. But, crucially for my inquiry, the division does not conform with the division between body and soul that a dualistic interpretive tradition has taught us to expect. When Penthea speaks of a "divorce betwixt my body and my heart" (2.3.57),[7] she riddlingly problematizes the significance of "heart," making it at once physical and emblematic.[8] The effect is a far more subtle version of Giovanni's appearance at the end of *'Tis Pity She's a Whore* with Annabella's heart on his dagger's point, where the literal presentation of the heart (given further emphasis in the early modern theater, where an animal's heart would be on the dagger) complicates the Cardinal's more typically metaphoric reference to how Giovanni's deed "broke thy old father's heart" (5.6.63). Since Penthea's heart is not removed from her body, the divorce she refers to can only be an internal division, but psychomachia is itself literalized by her self-starvation. Oscillating meanings of "heart" continue throughout the play (e.g., 3.5.85–86, 4.2.129) and contribute to a complex exploration of the terms of subjective identity.

One critical tradition has understood the play to validate honor and virtuous resolve through its extreme demonstrations of the destructive power of passion.[9] But given the complicated relationships between the terms and boundaries of body and soul repeatedly demonstrated in the play, we can more accurately see it as an inquiry into the location of the self, an exploration into what Lyon and Barbalet call the "tension between having and being a body."[10] Precisely because of *The Broken Heart*'s failure to achieve an entirely convincing moral resolution of these issues, an alternative critical tradition has labeled it "decadent,"[11] at best limited by the "absence of purpose" T. S. Eliot complained about and at worst associated with perversity and a "frank enjoyment of sin."[12] As Rowland Wymer notes, in such arguments the term *decadence* can "conveniently combin[e] moral and aesthetic implications."[13] Along with Wymer and several other critics, I see *The Broken Heart* as more intent on arousing emotions than on delivering didactic lessons.[14] But I think this recognition introduces several further sets of questions: about the associational meanings of the play's terms for the body and emotions; about the sort of pleasure afforded by theatrical representations of suffering through starvation, bleeding, restraint, and heartbreak; and about the connection between its characteristic themes and *The Broken Heart*'s peculiar reluctance or difficulty in ending.[15]

Simply put, I argue that *The Broken Heart* offers its viewers, in ways that can be understood both formally and phenomenologically, experiences of heartbreak. Although for us a mostly dead metaphor, a broken heart had for seventeenth-century audiences a rich set of associational resonances, many of them emblematic but others, derived from religious imagery and humoral physiology, spanning the bodily and the emotional dimensions. However sweetly savored by Petrarchan poets, heartbreak is not generally deemed a pleasant experience, and since *The Broken Heart* offers so unsatisfying a moral distance from it, we need to address the further difficult question of how such an experience might be construed as theatrical entertainment or pleasure. I posit that the play offers a complex manipulation of proffered pleasure and pain and is structured to intensify viewer emotion through the alteration of images of restraint and those of release or shattering. Although formal patterning of control and release characterizes all drama, *The Broken Heart* offers an extreme example, which is a late moment in the Renaissance tradition of textual self-shattering.

PERHAPS BECAUSE OF ITS STATIC, restrained quality—Marion Lomax says its action takes place in "slow motion against a muted background of tension"—*The Broken Heart* has generally been approached through the lens of formalism or ethical criticism, as though, in lacking excitement, its effects on viewers must be limited to intellectual and moral rather than emotional zones. As Harriet Hawkins has observed, that *The Broken Heart's* moral lessons can be interpreted in diametrically opposite ways indicates the appropriateness of another approach to understanding Ford's play. For her, the play's meanings concern "emotional and biological needs" as much as "moral and rational" ones, and she quotes Saint Augustine in support of the view that "people go to tragedies because they 'wish to be made to feel sad,' and the 'feeling of sorrow is what they enjoy.'"[16] I follow Hawkins in locating tragedy's meanings in the responses of viewers, but where her references to Augustine, Erasmus, and Sylvia Plath suggest a universalist understanding of tragic effect, I want to explore specific historical contexts within which *The Broken Heart* took its significance.

Commentators have noticed that the play essentially consists of several significant tableaux, linked by a rather improbable plot and somewhat inconsistent characters.[17] Not surprisingly, the most memorable scenes are those dramatizing the deaths of the four central characters: Penthea revealed as starved (4.4); Ithocles caught in a mechanical device and stabbed by Orgilus (4.4); Orgilus opening his veins and bleeding to death (5.2); Calantha contin-

uing to dance as she receives word of one death after another and then suc-
cumbing to "silent griefs which cut the heartstrings" (5.3.75). Although the
critical charges of decadence imply the presence of perversion, the forms of
suffering that are displayed are all relatively familiar corporeal experiences, or
would have been for the play's original audiences. Few people among the
playgoing set were threatened by imminent starvation, but the sensation of
hunger would not have been unknown and, among the growing numbers
of rural poor, starvation did occur, especially in years of poor harvest. Phlebotomy, or bloodletting, was recommended as therapy for an astonishing variety of ailments and formed part of the health regimen practiced by many
people. Although it is difficult to generalize about an experience such as
forced physical restraint, one could simply note that bodily punishments
were common in the early modern period, for children and others deemed
disobedient, and that the practice of swaddling infants meant that everyone
had begun life in a posture of restraint. As for heartbreak, its feasibility was
documented, and thereby encouraged, by the discourses of religion, erotic
love, and humoral psychology. The representation of each of these experiences engages a corporeal dynamic. Unlike plays of the period that accomplish violence through such common dramatic means as stabbing, decapita-
tion, or poisoning (much less more exotic suffering such as being sodomized
with a burning poker or having one's tongue cut or bitten out), *The Broken
Heart* affects viewers not through extravagant displays but by arousing the
memory of familiar, or at least readily conceivable, forms of uncomfortable
experiences. In the intimate indoor space of the Blackfriars theater, where the
play was originally staged by the King's Men, viewers' physical proximity to
the stage would heighten evoked sensations of discomfort.

By means of this sort of appeal, what phenomenologists would consider
the perceiving body of a viewer would be engaged; in Maurice Merleau-
Ponty's terms, "the body is our general medium for having a world." As
Merleau-Ponty acknowledges, the body is an ambiguous site of subjectivity,
since people do not exactly coincide with their bodies but cannot exist independently of them. A person may simultaneously experience her or his body
as subject and as object—for instance, when one (subject) hand deliberately
touches another (object) part of the body. In the phenomenology Merleau-
Ponty outlined, one can't simply opt for a simplified relationship to the
body or the physical world, nor can one subjugate bodily impulses and in-

stincts, as the Stoics would counsel. Instead, bodily experience is constitutive of knowledge; "it is through my body that I understand other people, just as it is through my body that I perceive 'things.'"[18] In applying this theory to drama, it would be a mistake to collapse the distinction between (viewing) subject and (performing or mimed) object; the viewer does not become, except through sympathetic imagination, the figure(s) represented on stage. Yet phenomenology offers a powerful tool for understanding the physical dynamic of drama, its ability to engage the bodies as well as the minds and hearts of viewers—or, as was the case with early modern viewers, how matters of the mind and heart were at once matters of the body. Certainly, a metaphysical split between mind and body was known in the early seventeenth century, although the division we call Cartesian may not have been as sudden or as definitive as some modern commentators suppose.[19] Emotion, however, was simultaneously an affair of the humoral body and of the thinking mind, so that through emotion the body served as what Merleau-Ponty calls "expressive space."[20]

To move from consideration of the drama as staged to the viewers' emotional responses, we need to examine the discursive contexts within which emotion would have been structured. I will primarily be concerned here with early modern understandings of the humoral body and the physiology of emotion. Starvation and bloodletting are the two specific experiences that I will examine; the generality of restraint demands that I give it less attention. Heartbreak is the encompassing physical-physiological experience of the play; Penthea's starvation and Orgilus's bleeding to death are each specialized instances of the general theme, emphasized by the climactic nature of Calantha's death in the final scene and, of course, by the title. In successive waves, the play exposes its viewers to the deaths of Penthea, Orgilus, and Ithocles; each grants a further involving instance of the sort of death by dissolution in which the play specializes, so that viewers are prepared to imagine, virtually on their own, the sensation of Calantha's "heartstrings" bursting. But I also examine briefly the emblematic religious associations of broken hearts and other body images, since Ford's seventeenth-century audience would have known the politics of religious influence as a dynamic factor in their "experience of embodied sociality." Although today we situate discussions of subjectivity and personhood in the domains of psychology and philosophy, in the early modern period these were primarily issues for theological debate.²¹ Moreover, theological debates were themselves physical in reference, encouraging certain attitudes toward the body as well as particular physical behaviors. Use of bodily imagery in seventeenth-century religious poetry illustrates, as does *The Broken Heart*, Merleau-Ponty's phenomenological view of the human body as "transform[ing] ideas into things. . . . The body can symbolize existence because it brings it into being and actualizes it."²² In my argument, humoralism provides the nouns, the established context for understanding the bodies that are involved, while religious literature provides the verbs, the language of breaking and submitting that activates what occurs in theater.

David Hillman observes that "religion has always positioned the body's inner realm as the ultimate site of faith." The Psalms, for instance, draw on images of the human body in compelling tropes that are not strictly metaphorical. The Psalmist who writes "I am poured out like water, and all my bones are out of joint: my heart is like wax; it is melted in the midst of my bowels" (Ps. 22.14, KJV) captures the visceral sensations of overwhelming grief and loss. While inevitably culture-bound to some extent, the trope transcends historical moorings; the description of the feeling of internal dissolution one experiences in moments of great emotional pain remains as vivid today as it was several thousand years ago. In the early modern period, religious bodily imagery came into special prominence, as "Christ's wounds, blood, heart, and bowels become a near-obsessive topic of sermons, poems, and visual representations."²³ The influence of Jesuit meditation practices that sought to dramatize the events of Christ's life, especially his suffering, in painstaking detail lent specificity and vividness to English devotional poetry. The method of "affective meditation" involved a visual "composition of place" followed by "application of the senses."²⁴ Contemplative focus on the body of Christ appealed to Anglican as well as Catholic poets, in spite of the general Anglican concerns about Roman overemphasis on the sensual aspects of religious practice. The Anglican priest George Herbert, for instance, wrote both a devotional poem on Christ's crucifixion ("The Sacrifice") and many poems of spiritual self-examination using tropes of the body.

Ford, however, may have had his own reasons for emphasizing bodily images: evidence amassed by Lisa Hopkins links Ford with a coterie of aristocrats holding Catholic sympathies.²⁵ Although, as Hopkins notes, there is no direct proof that Ford was himself a practicing Catholic, the linkage helps to account for the significance he grants to the language of the body. Reiterating in his work "terms traditionally associated with Jesuit devotional discourse"—blood, heart, tears, sweat—Ford tends to invest these bodily terms with the spiritual dimensionality they hold for Roman theology and art. As Hopkins observes, with Protestantism becoming increasingly "an intellectual religion" in early-seventeenth-century England, Catholicism "aimed to recapture a sense of mystical spirituality which was very strongly rooted in the experiences of the body."[26] In Hopkins' view, Ford's attention to the parts of the body fails in a primary aim of mystical spirituality: she understands his characteristic attention to hearts and blood to instance rather than forestall a haunting sense of fragmentation, a point to which I shall return.

Herbert, with whom Ford was associated through his ties to the Pembroke/Sidney circle,[27] uses the heart as a recurrent image, often as an emblem of the spiritual self. In Herbert's *The Temple*, the heart might be "peevish," "thankfull," "greedie," "enquiring," or "wither'd"; it can contain "closets" or "holes," be "hammer[ed]" by sin, or be "broken . . . so long That eve'ry part Hath got a tongue."[28] The active, discerning roles Herbert gives to the heart were common in seventeenth-century usage, as Scott Manning Stevens notes: "Because the heart, enlightened by the Holy Spirit, could *perceive*, it was more than the receptor of the passions. The heart could on some level compete with the brain as a locus of perception through its ability to perceive things unseen."[29] For Herbert, a broken heart, while painful, is less lamentable than a hard or stony heart. The Christian's goal is attaining the yielding heart of contrition, and in Herbert's imagery, shattering the heart can lead to softening it: "For with love Stonie hearts will bleed" ("Discipline"). Herbert also puts the heartbreak trope to metapoetic use in "Deniall," creating a formal structure that mimes the narrative: "then was my heart broken, as was my verse."

Herbert's effort to suggest an analogy between poetic structure and the structure of belief indicates the deep significance of bodily autonomy or shattering within his spiritual system. The way the heart functions for him not *like* but *as* religious faith corresponds to Merleau-Ponty's sense that the body literalizes belief, or "transforms ideas into things." Similarly, Elaine Scarry observes that, in Old Testament texts, belief is literally a matter of physical surrender and not merely figured in its terms: "The withholding of the body—the stiffening of the neck, the turning of the shoulder, the closing of the ears, the hardening of the heart, the making of the face like stone—necessitates God's forceful shattering of the reluctant human surface and repossession of the interior. . . . The fragility of the human interior and the absolute surrender of that interior . . . *is itself belief*—the endowing of the most concrete and intimate parts of oneself with an objectified referent."[30] Herbert's usage provided Ford with a close contemporary model of bodily imagery put to this sort of strong usage, whereby the structure of belief might actually be felt by and in the body, not expressed in its terms metaphorically. That Herbert himself builds on the analogy between religious belief and aesthetic form (in "Deniall") gives us warrant to extend this visceral model of involvement to theater and compare it to dramatic empathy. For Herbert, as for biblical writers, the broken heart indicated submission to a higher, divine force; Ford is concerned with secular meanings of the broken heart, but he also is concerned with the dynamic force of release or submission. An analogy exists, I am suggesting, between the pleasure of release from the prideful demands of self into subjection to divine power and the theatrical pleasure of submitting to an imaginative fiction. In each case, boundaries of the self or ego are (at least temporarily) lifted, the self purged.

Leo Bersani, we recall, has developed a theory of art as maintaining a masochistic tension that is libidinally invested by readers or viewers because it corresponds to the paradoxical configuration of subjective identity. Bersani draws from Jean Laplanche a notion of the subject as formed through and in response to a wish for its own dissolution. According to Bersani's "esthetics of masochism," readers take pleasure in the sense of release or "shattering" afforded by immersion in violent art.[31] Considering the relevance of this approach to *The Broken Heart*, one notices how the play instances prolonged forms of suffering—starving, bleeding, heart breaking—and how each experience brings about calamitous death in which consciousness slowly slips away. The person who starves or bleeds to death feels a gradual ebbing of strength and awareness, a literal dissolution of self. A reader or viewer participating imaginatively in the death of Penthea or Orgilus would thus experience the masochistic prolongation of a shattering of the character's self. And seventeenth-century audiences would be especially well equipped to participate in this way, not only because of the familiarity of religious tropes of battering the heart or shattering the body but also because of contemporary psychological and physiological theories and the practices they encouraged.

In the late sixteenth and early seventeenth centuries, advances in the field of anatomy were altering the understanding of the heart's role in physical functioning. According to traditional physiology, the heart functioned to distribute heat through the body, with the lungs providing cool air to moderate temperature, and arteries and veins were thought to comprise two separate vascular systems. Since its specific workings were undifferentiated, "the heart could still be regarded as a kind of diverticulum arising from the vena cava as it passed on its way carrying venous blood from the liver to the head."[32] The path to the discovery of circulation began with a controversy about venesection in the first half of the sixteenth century, which led to the recognition of venous valves and, more abstractly, to the recognition of Galen's fallibility in anatomical description.[33] Building on a century of evolving knowledge and offering a demonstrative argument, William Harvey's *De motu cordis* (1628) offered proof for the circulation of the blood through the body, granting the heart new anatomical importance as the center of this complex system.

Perhaps not entirely coincidental to growing understanding of the heart's role in circulation was a firmer sense of the heart as the center of the emotions.[34] Aristotelians had always considered the heart the central organ and seat of vital pneuma,[35] but established Galenic theory located different emotions variously in the liver, kidneys (or reins), brain, and womb, as well as the heart. Consequently, Timothy Bright in the 1580s found it necessary to argue for the heart's "prerogative above the liver" as the distributor of "the spirit of life" through the body and for its priority above the humors in receiving sensory data first. By 1618, Helkiah Crooke declares the heart's importance but "not as Aristotle called it principall, who placed in it all the actions of life and sense"; Crooke argues for the brain's priority in matters of sense and cognition. The heart, in his view, serves as "the fountaine of the Vitall Faculty and spirit, the place and nourishment of naturall heat" and, by naming the heart "the seate of the Irascible or angry parts of the soule," he secures what we would consider an emotional component in the "naturall heat."[36] The anatomist's view was in keeping with the opinions expressed by humoral theorists; when Thomas Wright declared the heart to be "the very seate of all Passions," he referred not to vital spirit but to the individual passions or emotions. Wright cites experience as the best evidence for this claim. Sounding much like the psalmist quoted above, he asks "who loveth extreamely, and feeleth not that passion to dissolve his hearte? who rejoyceth, and proveth not his heart dilated? who is moyled with heavinesse, or plunged with payne, and perceiveth not his heart to bee coarcted? whom inflameth ire, and hath not heart-burning?" Wright explains emotional response on the model of a castle maintaining its defenses: when the brain is met with sense impressions, it sends a message "by certayne secret channels to the heart, where they pitch at the doore, signifying what an object was presented, convenient or disconvenient for it." Roused into action, the heart prepares either to pursue or repel the object, and for assistance "draweth other humours to helpe him," although humours are also independently sent by "the same soule that informeth the heart residing in other partes."[37] Through this account, Wright is able to reconcile the heart's centrality with the fluidity and variability of humoral theory.

The relevance of humoral theory to *The Broken Heart* was established many years ago when S. Blaine Ewing described the play's characters in terms of Burtonian melancholy, as so many case studies in the various effects of misbegotten desire.[38] The discourse on melancholy had, of course, long provided material for dramatic characters; what sets Ford apart is his attention to the physiology of the disorder. He details melancholic symptoms of refusal to eat, declining spirits, madness, and mania, and, incredibly to modern audiences, he illustrates on stage what was the standard treatment for excessive passion: bleeding the patient until he or she loses consciousness, although the goal of Orgilus's therapy is death rather than recovery.

Within a culture in which melancholiacs were immediately recognizable by their loss of appetite and resulting thinness (like the excessively lean figure decorating the title page of Burton's *Anatomy of Melancholy*), Penthea's starvation—unlike the many more ambiguous signs of melancholia—was vividly symptomatic. In the physiology of early modern theorists, love melancholy cooled and dried out the body, with negative repercussions for both appetite and digestion. Penthea is torn by the conflict between her emotional dedication to Orgilus, to whom she was betrothed, and her legal dedication to Bassanes, whom her brother has forced her to wed. In her version, her very blood is shamed by this conflict:

> *But since her blood was seasoned by the forfeit*
> *Of noble shame, with mixtures of pollution,*
> *Her blood——'tis just——be henceforth never heightened*
> *With taste of sustenance. Starve. . . . (4.2.149–52)*

The link she draws between blood and sustenance seems remote to modern readers, but seventeenth-century audiences would understand the humoral physiology Penthea appeals to here: blood, according to the standard models, was produced from food, in a three-step process. The theory was firmly enough established to prevail in popular understanding even after Harvey's demonstration in 1628 that the amount of blood in the human body cannot be accounted for through the conversion of food alone.[39]

Penthea, furthermore, offers the surprisingly specific information that her menstrual periods have ceased as a result of her starvation: "But 'tis too late for me to marry now, / I am past child-bearing" (4.2.93–94). Within the terms of humoral physiology, menstruation resulted from women's physical inability to create men's more perfect seed and the hotter blood that coursed in their superior bodies; menstrual blood was, in Paster's phrase, "doubly excremental," discarded in the process of producing seed and then discarded by the body altogether.[40] By the logic of humoralism, the cessation of menses would seem to establish control of the excessive fluidity that was one indication of women's inferiority. Penthea's self-control would be demonstrated explicitly in her refusal to eat and also implicitly in her moving "past child-bearing." Yet it is a measure of the limitation of women's possibilities that in "correcting" her feminine appetitiveness and excessive fluidity, Penthea destroys herself. The classical treatment for amenorrhea—bleeding the patient from her ankle—displays a similar paradox: although feminine bleeding is bad, not bleeding is worse. Modern understandings of anorexia help us to recognize Penthea's quest for autonomy and control. Also helpful is Merleau-Ponty's understanding of anorexia as an actualized "refusal of the future."[41] However overgeneralized, this perception, together with the humoral context, reminds us that Penthea's starvation resonates in multiple, complex ways and need not be confined to a pathology of madness or a romanticized narrative.[42] Her death offers a complex meditation on the phenomenology of selfhood.

Humoral theories typically exhibit a tautological aspect, rendering the therapies based on humoral physiology immune from what we consider scientific logic. Robert Burton explains that, "as the distraction of the minde, amongst other outward causes and perturbations, alters the temperature of the body, so the distraction and distemper of the Body will cause a distemperature of the Soule, and 'tis hard to decide which of these two doe more harme to the other. . . . as anger, feare, sorrow, obtrectation, emulation, etc. . . . cause grievous diseases in the Body, so bodily diseases affect the Soule by consent." In Wright's pithy phrase, "Passions ingender Humors, and Humors breede Passions."[43] Accordingly, a patient might be melancholy because of bad blood but also produce bad blood because of his melancholy. With the psychological and the physiological aspects so nearly coterminous, points of therapeutic intervention were many and varied. The understanding of whether and when a particular therapy worked, much less *why* it was effective, no doubt had at least as much to do with the surgeon's or physician's authority and influence as with anything else.

Privileging the social psychology of healing can help us understand the extent to which phlebotomy was practiced. As a dramatic technique of intervention, phlebotomy was rather like exorcism and could sometimes "work" for similar reasons. That it frequently caused harm by weakening the patient or introducing infection, or actually resulted in death when the bleeding went unchecked, did not, to the early modern mind, prove the dangers of phlebotomy per se, but of the maladies for which it was indicated. Not only would the processes and vocabulary of therapeutic bloodletting be familiar to a seventeenth-century audience, but the idea of bleeding as a cure for excessive passion would have been generally accepted. Nicholas Gyer recommends phlebotomy in such cases because it "maketh glad those that are pensive," "appeaseth such as are angrie," and "preserveth love-sicke persons, from madnesse, by drawing humors from the head to the lower partes, and so expelling the same."[44] Timothy Bright explains to his melancholic patient that "The humour requireth evacuation, and emptying: and because your body is not only melancholicke under the ribbes but the whole masse of your blood is chaunged therewith: it shall be first necessarye to open a vaine: that both thereby you may be disburthened in parte of that heavy load, and nature having lesse of that kinde to deale withall, may alter the remnant into a more milde and pleasant juice." Bright recommends drawing at least "nine or ten ownces" of the "thicke and grosse" melancholic blood.[45] While Burton is not an advocate of phlebotomy as a treatment for melancholy—he notes its dangers and generally prefers more holistic approaches—he nevertheless acknowledges ancient authorities, including Avicenna, who recommend bloodletting "as a principall remedy" for love-melancholy. The French physician Jacques Ferrand recommends a program including specific forms of diet, baths, and purging, but at the center is the "surgical" cure of drawing blood "from the hepatic vein in the right arm, according to the state of his disease and the complexion of his body, and in keeping with his physical tolerances."[46] Burton, Ferrand, and other writers on phlebotomy detail the significances of how the blood appears; Gyer devotes a chapter of *The English Phlebotomy* to the process of examining the blood for its color, quantity, viscosity, and even taste. With phlebotomy so firmly established as a medical procedure that Gyer found it necessary to inveigh against those "vagabund Horseleaches, & travailing Tinkers" who were misusing it,[47] we can reasonably conclude that many people in a typical viewing audience would have experienced it, whether for melancholy or some other malady (some people used it regularly as a preventive technique),[48] and that virtually everyone would consider bleeding, sometimes until the patient fainted, to be a standard treatment for erotic melancholy.

What a modern audience will view as an especially gruesome form of suicide—Orgilus's opening a vein and instructing his assistant to open a second—would thus have a more complex, if no less gruesome, context for seventeenth-century viewers.[49] Being familiar with the technical processes Orgilus details in clinical terms—"Bind fast This arm, that so the pipes may from their conduits Convey a full stream" (5.2.101–3)—they would be well prepared to feel on their pulses the actual memory of bloodletting. Bassanes, as Orgilus's obliging assistant, helps to "fillet both these arms" and takes the role of diagnosing surgeon when he observes that the blood "sparkles like a lusty wine new broached; The vessel must be sound from which it issues. Grasp hard this other stick" (5.2.125–27). With his dying words, Orgilus makes no attempt to explain or memorialize himself; there is no final instruction to tell a lamentable tale, no effort to regain blighted heroism.

Orgilus instead comments on the physical effects and sensations of bleeding to death:

> *So falls the standards*
> *Of my prerogative in being a creature.*
> *A mist hangs o'er mine eyes; the sun's bright splendour*
> *Is clouded in an everlasting shadow.*
> *Welcome, thou ice that sitt'st about my heart;*
> *No heat can ever thaw thee.* (5.2.150–55)

Because early modern physiology understood the heart to be the hottest organ, Orgilus's description gives extra point to the physiological fact that severe blood loss causes body temperature to drop. Richard Madelaine, arguing that its thematic import saves this scene from charges of melodrama, believes that "the idea of moral purgation through the shedding of overheated blood is implicit."[50] But the ambiguity of Orgilus's character—lover, melancholiac, revenger—makes it difficult to locate a moral position from which to judge him and accordingly dilutes the thematic significance of his death. Rather than achieving moral distance or narrative closure, this grisly suicide is designed to enable viewers' horrified sympathy and involvement as they draw on their own experiences of phlebotomy.

Whereas, according to Paster, bleeding in general emblematized a bodily fragility and porousness associated with feminine weakness, viewers' knowledge that undergoing phlebotomy required a degree of self-mastery would make Orgilus's bleeding the inverse of uncontrolled "feminine" bleeding.[51] "Look upon my steadiness," he instructs his onstage audience, and when Armostes notes his "Desperate courage!" Orgilus corrects him with another oxymoron: "Honourable infamy" (5.2.118, 123). His paradoxically destructive self-control reiterates Penthea's: each crosses the terms of gender, so crucial for constructing subjectivity, and each undoes the self in the act of asserting it.

The scene of Calantha's climactic death by broken heart has been criticized, much as the rest of the play, for its restraint.[52] Like Cleopatra, she stages her own death, but where Cleopatra orchestrates spectacular visual effects—"I am again for Cydnus"—Calantha depends upon emotional shock: the scene turns from Calantha's expected coronation and marriage with Nearchus to her gothic contract with the dead Ithocles.[53] Although the

dance of 5.2 has seemed to promise, in generic terms, the communal celebration of comedy or masque, the outcome is subverted by the series of messengers who whisper in Calantha's ear the news that her father, Penthea, and
Ithocles, her betrothed, have died. By contrasting the outward celebration
with Calantha's private reception of distressing news, Ford calls attention to
interiorized emotional effects. The point is not, however, to emphasize
Calantha's or any other character's inviolable internal self. Instead, once
again, the terms within which selfhood might be constructed are put into
riddling relation. Calantha's "masculine spirit" and lack of "female pity"
(5.2.95) are noted; she herself will claim that a woman might possess suffi-
cient "masculine and stirring composition . . . to govern wisely Her own
demeanours, passions, and divisions" (5.3.7–9). Her announcement of her
death is usually understood to manifest an exquisitely orchestrated control,
holding off an emotional response until the chosen moment:

> *I but deceived your eyes with antic gesture,*
> *When one news straight came huddling on another,*
> *Of death, and death, and death. Still I danced forward;*
> *But it struck home, and here, and in an instant.*
> *But such mere women, who with shrieks and outcries*
> *Can vow a present end to all their sorrows,*
> *Yet live to vow new pleasures, and outlive them.*
> *They are the silent griefs which cut the heartstrings.*
> *Let me die smiling.* (5.3.68–76)

Nevertheless, it also and at the same time demonstrates an extremity of passion that surpasses that of either Penthea or Orgilus, whose deaths required
actively self-destructive devising. She figures herself as caught between the
terms of "masculine spirit" and "mere women," between "govern[ance]"
and "passions, and divisions." If there is to be resolution of these terms, it
must take place within the responses of viewers, who are called on themselves to imagine the extremity of pain that constitutes Calantha's "broken
heart." Ford may refrain from either verbal elaboration of Calantha's suffering or spectacular demonstration of it because he assumes that viewers will
at this point have accumulated practice in imagining the deaths of Penthea,
Ithocles, and Orgilus.

Each of these characters illustrates the tormented and divided subjectivity of the melancholic or passional self, especially as etched within a humoral economy. Burton's Democritus Junior says: "Lust harrowes us on the one side, Envy, Anger, ambition on the other. Wee are torne in pieces by our passions, as so many wild horses."[54] In a discursive text such as Burton's or Montaigne's, giving expression to a fractured or dissolving subjectivity can present a productive opportunity. But a conflict exists between this sort of subjectivity and the demands of more traditionally structured literary forms such as tragic drama: the artistic form requires a degree of balance, harmony, and closure that belies the dispersive energies of the represented self. Scarry is leery of literary descriptions of torture or pain for just this reason; she fears that the reality of experienced pain will be covered over by aesthetic order, allowing it to be appropriated for political purposes.[55] Despite Ford's reference in the Prologue of *The Broken Heart* to a historical basis for the story ("What may be here thought a fiction, when time's youth / Wanted some riper years, was known *A Truth*" [Prol. 15-16]), the play has usually been understood as fiction (perhaps based on the life of Penelope Devereux) and has been called to account for its failures of characterological wholeness and formal order, rather than for any Scarry-like betrayal of the truth of suffering. So, for instance, Hopkins, having adeptly revealed in Ford's characters a pattern of linguistic and semiotic instability whereby various parts of the body (blood, heart, tears, sweat) are capable of speaking for the self, laments their failed search for completion. She notes "the terrifying nature of Ford's vision of personality as being so fragmented and disintegrated that the problem for his characters seems to be only secondarily one of self-expression, their primary difficulty being all too often the establishing, indeed the actual physical locating, of a self to be expressed."[56]

Where Hopkins finds a disturbing failure on Ford's part to achieve moral or imaginative coherence in his characters, I suggest that his play be understood as highlighting problematic questions concerning subjectivity, embodiedness, and perception. Rather than seeing his characters as fragmented in a way that precludes a convincing impression of their subjectivity, I think we can and should see Penthea, Orgilus, and Calantha as experiencing dispersion and as constituted as subjects through that very process.

Ford has also used effects of doubling and division to raise questions about subjectivity and embodiedness by structural means. Penthea, as we have observed, feels split between her love for Orgilus and her marriage to Bassanes. For her, this is not a matter of giving her body to one man and her soul to another: it is instead "a rape done on my truth" (2.3.79). She accuses her brother of making her, with the enforced marriage to Bassanes, "a faith-breaker, A spotted whore" (3.2.69–70). Feeling both body and soul to be shamed, she refuses solace with Orgilus.[57] Orgilus himself creates a form of self-doubling by disguising himself in the early scenes of the play; his disguise, like his false announcement to his father in 1.1 that he is leaving Sparta, serves no obvious or important function in the plot; it seems instead a means of complicating the action while subtly furthering the inquiry into the seat and stability of personal identity. Likewise, no obvious reason exists for Penthea and Ithocles to be twins. As her brother, Ithocles holds the legal right to dispose of her in marriage, and this is not Illyria—there is no *Twelfth Night*–esque pretence that they look alike, and no suggestion of a particularly close bond between the two. The twin motif exists solely to complicate the questions about the boundaries of personal autonomy.[58] Finally, the doubling of Penthea's situation in Orgilus's threatened response to *his* sister's proposed marriage is strongly overdetermined, as his scarcely motivated change of heart illustrates. These structural devices further the epistemological and ontological questions about the boundaries of unstable selves and the terms within which they can be known.

As I have suggested, it is primarily through the staging of prolonged suicides that Ford illustrates fracturing of the self. In suicide, the noncoincidence of self and body is illustrated phenomenologically; the suicide's body is simultaneously the object being destroyed and the subject enacting the destruction. Theatrical representation of suicide introduces particularly interesting questions about the location of the suffering body and the expiring self, since the actor's body on display in a staged suicide is not literally dying, except in the way we all are every minute. The staging of suicide heightens viewers' awareness of bodies even more than the staging of pain, a situation that "challenges the stability (and the separability) of representational levels," indicating "the body's representational volatility," as Stanton Garner Jr. observes.[59] Penthea may appear to fade away from starvation, grief, and sleeplessness, and Orgilus may appear to bleed to death, but on stage these will be moments of prolonged fakery, requiring the imaginative participation of viewers. If the scenes are successful in compelling belief, they do so phenomenologically, by encouraging viewers to imagine or (as I have suggested) to recall the physical sensations being mimed. Theatrical involvement here requires, more than tragedy ordinarily does, for viewers to surrender in ways that might be felt physically. Submission to the represented fiction is a matter of yielding bodily, analogously to the spiritual submission described in religious texts. The play uses the familiarity of the physical sensations it represents to establish viewers' sense of involvement but effectively tortures them, in a theatrical sense, by dramatically exceeding the bounds of ordinary experience (not just hunger but starving to death, not just bloodletting but bleeding to death).

If it is true that *The Broken Heart* works phenomenologically, requiring not only that its viewers submit to the contemplation of physical, mental, and emotional pain (the normal stuff of tragedy), but also that they involve themselves with suicidal, heartbroken characters in their actions of self-eradication, then what sort of reward or pleasure can exist in this experience? All tragedy, of course, proceeds across the paradoxical terrain of pain for pleasure's sake, but ordinarily we have been taught to expect an achieved narrative or thematic closure to afford some satisfactory moral or aesthetic distance, so that the experience can seem, in retrospect at least, worthwhile. When such closure and distance are not achieved, we typically call the tragedy flawed or failed—unless we are willing to allow that certain works actively pursue the effect of holding pain, violence, and victimization in irresolvable tension with whatever delight or lesson is delivered. It is commonly observed that Renaissance audiences, like those of our own era, had a taste for violent entertainments; this play adds to the evidence that we should understand this point in the strongest sense possible instead of dismissing these effects as accessories to a greater moral or aesthetic good. Accordingly, I would extend Anne Barton's description of *The Broken Heart* as fundamentally oxymoronic far past the formal grounds in which she traces her claim and argue that the play achieves its most characteristic effects by activating the masochistic involvement of viewers.[60]

I mean to use masochism in Bersani's sense, to name an aesthetic pleasure derived from the "shattering" of the constructed self. I am not suggesting a link between the play and a specific culture (modern or early modern) of sadomasochistic sexual practices or defining it in terms of the casual usage of masochism as "self-punishment." Masochism figures here as part of a dy-

namic relationship between viewers and the staged fiction—that is, it motivates and appears within both formal structures and phenomenological interactions. Rather than purging its viewers of disruptive passions in order to
leave them clean and whole, as in the classically normative understanding of
theatrical catharsis, the play encourages temporary eradication or purging of
the bounds of self. Thus, *purge* carries here a less literal and specific meaning
than it does for Paster when she traces the erotic associations of the alimen-
tary purge.[61] Nevertheless, from a psychological perspective the issues of
mastery and control associated with anal eroticism coincide at the level of
infantile ego formation with those of subjective autonomy. Bruce Smith has
linked spectacles of cutting and bleeding on stage with both phlebotomy
and catharsis; his understanding of how rupture and rapture occur within/
on/between viewers similarly extends and complicates the meaning of a
pleasurable purgation.[62] I propose that the pressures of mastery and control
that are purged in this case can be understood as socially and historically exerted—that theater viewers in the tense years leading up to the civil war,
faced with altered religious, scientific, economic, and political landscapes,
may have had particular reason to enjoy indulgence in the sensational emo-
tionalism offered by plays like *The Broken Heart.*

As we have seen, Ford's play initiates its viewers into imagined heartbreak and then reiterates the experience, offering characters who achieve a
kind of mastery through submission to suffering. *The Broken Heart* is peculiarly structured to postpone an emotional climax; the four separate death
scenes seem designed instead to prolong and perpetuate horrific effects. In
this deferral of closure, the play corresponds to Gilles Deleuze's paradigm
of literary masochism, as it does in its reliance on contractual logic and language. Most strikingly, as a series of tableaux of suffering, in which melo-
dramatic theatricality matters more than a vitally active plot, it resembles
the "frozen" scenes that Deleuze identifies as the essence of masochism in
Venus in Furs.[63] But as I have indicated above, Deleuze argues against the
mutuality of roles named by sadomasochism, which he terms "a semiological howler" (*Coldness*, 134). His attempted separation of the two strands
is not borne out in the case of *The Broken Heart*'s dynamic interplay of real,
mimed, imagined, and introverted subject positions, given the way theatrical phenomenology breaks down a stable sense of identity. By establishing
emotional interactions that work toward the subjective dissolution of the

viewer, the play corresponds to Freud's (sometime) sense of sadism as a vicissitude of masochism.

With its reiterated efforts at formal closure subverted by thematic senselessness, *The Broken Heart* strikes many critics as nihilistic or decadent; they complain of "numbness" in response.[64] A more affirmative view is taken by those who find in the play a complex inquiry into issues of autonomy, self-governance, passion, and social requirements. Interestingly, these debates about the worth of *The Broken Heart* closely parallel those about masochism, likewise criticized as morally decadent but also engaged analytically for its exposure of questions about subjectivity, power, and embodiment and seen as a complex reiteration of social tensions and inequities.[65] As Dave Hickey remarks in a different context, "the rituals of 'aesthetic' submission in our culture speak a language so closely analogous to those of sexual and spiritual submission that they are all but indistinguishable."[66] For seventeenth-century viewers of Ford's play, prepared by discourses of religious imagery and humoral psychology, an emotional response would be located in the body, where submission might be literally felt as a broken heart.

) (

Conclusion

THE REVIVED POPULARITY OF *Titus Andronicus* in the contemporary theater has occasioned an instructive renegotiation of established terms for considering violent texts. Traditionally, works that exhibit excessive, prurient violence "for its own sake" have been cordoned off from those including violence in appropriately contextualized and morally contained episodes. That Shakespeare himself might belong in the former camp rather than the latter has prompted a rethinking of the categories. One conclusion is the recognition that we need to ask more subtle questions about textual violence, about its provenance and purpose as well as its form and extent. In this book I have attempted to contribute an added dimension to such considerations by demonstrating how deeply the appeal of violence infuses our literary traditions and by accounting for its centrality in numerous and various texts from the English Renaissance period. All accounts of our relationship to the past and to past texts depend on a historical narrative of some sort, and mine is no exception. Where the dominant (though sometimes unacknowledged) paradigm of recent cultural historicist work has put forward an only slightly revised and ironized version of Burckhardt's tale of the emergence of the dominant individual, I have traced a more deeply recursive path. Looking back to the way violent literary forms characterized the Renaissance moment, I have probed the connection between emergent structures of identity and a desire for imaginative shattering of the self. Basically this has involved an extended analogy between the psychoanalytic account of the development of the conscious individual and the historical narrative of subjective emergence. The growing consolidation of a sense of autonomy as the defining characteristic of self-experience occasioned a corresponding development of textual and aesthetic modes capable of dispatching the markers of individuality, temporarily undoing the ego's structuring bonds. Thus, arising in conjunction with codes for understanding the self through the discourses of religion, erotic love, political agency, and ethical conduct were texts that turned demands from each arena toward the production of pleasure. I have used various terms to consider the dissolution of identity proffered by these textual interactions: jouissance, catharsis, masochism. In each case, the contemplation of described or enacted violence works both phenomenologically and psychologically on readers or viewers, displacing the ordinary structuring bonds of selfhood to effect a radical emotional response.

The psychoanalytic terms of Freud and Lacan help us understand why the installation within the emergent subject of a drive toward its own destruction occurs: not because people are innately cruel or aggressive but because the ego imposes an alienating unity that fails to contain all aspects or levels of the subject's experience and knowledge. In light of the evident failure of emerging codes of moral and political subjectivity to encompass the wider expanse of emotional, physical, and religious experiences documented in the early modern period, the notion of a misfit or misalliance between the ego and subjective experience takes on great resonance. People accustomed to considering themselves fluid in their emotions and dispersive in their energies no doubt found ways to benefit from stringent ethical codes and to exercise agency in available channels. But they seem also to have sought out occasions to engage with texts that allowed temporary reversion to a psychically disunified, emotionally shattered self-experience. The power of these texts helps us appreciate the misfit between the humanistic self or ego and the dehiscent sense of something Lacan calls the Real that refuses to match up with the self in its official versions.

In his reading of Lacan, Richard Boothby proposes that the "death drive operates on two levels, imaginary and symbolic," and this distinction proves helpful in considering the implications of an aesthetics of masochism. Within the Imaginary (in Lacanian terms the level of ordinary existence), the death drive or primary masochism produces actual violence, either in active form or mimetically through images of literal violence, while the Symbolic allows a mediation or sublimation of literal violence. "In either case, the death drive attempts to have its way with the imaginary ego, seeking to deconstruct its false unity."[1] Complex manipulations of the death drive that encourage symbolic mediation have an obvious advantage over the simple reiteration of images of literal violence. Confronting the centrality of violence in English Renaissance literature might enable us to see the potential benefit of promoting textual interactions that exercise destructive urges in complex and creative ways. Given the link between structures of self and the appeal of violence, we might also contemplate the possibility of fostering flexible self-definitions that would not necessitate reiterated shattering.

)(

Notes

When quoting early texts, I have in some instances silently normalized u/v and i/j. Works frequently cited are indicated in the text and notes by the following abbreviations:

BPP   Sigmund Freud. "Beyond the Pleasure Principle." *SE*, vol. 18.

Child   Sigmund Freud. "A Child Is Being Beaten." *SE*, vol. 17.

Civilization   Sigmund Freud. *Civilization and Its Discontents. SE*, vol. 21.

Coldness   Gilles Deleuze. "Coldness and Cruelty." *Masochism*. New York: Zone, 1989.

Écrits   Jacques Lacan. *Écrits: A Selection,* trans. Alan Sheridan. New York: Norton, 1977.

EPM   Sigmund Freud. "The Economic Problem of Masochism." *SE,* vol. 19.

Four Concepts   Jacques Lacan. *The Four Fundamental Concepts of Psycho-analysis,* ed. Jacques-Alain Miller, trans. Alan Sheridan. New York: Norton, 1978.

Freudian Body   Leo Bersani. *The Freudian Body: Psychoanalysis and Art.* New York: Columbia Univ. Press, 1986.

Freudian Subject   Mikkel Borch-Jacobsen. *The Freudian Subject,* trans. Catherine Porter. Stanford: Stanford Univ. Press, 1988.

Instincts   Sigmund Freud. "Instincts and Their Vicissitudes." *SE,* vol. 14.

Life and Death   Jean Laplanche. *Life and Death in Psychoanalysis,* trans. Jeffrey Mehlman. Baltimore: Johns Hopkins Univ. Press, 1976.

Norton   William Shakespeare. *The Norton Shakespeare: Based on the Oxford*

	Edition, ed. Stephen Greenblatt et al. New York: Norton, 1997. Quotations from Shakespeare's works follow this edition except where otherwise noted.
SE	Sigmund Freud. *The Standard Edition of the Complete Psychological Works of Sigmund Freud,* trans. James Strachey. 24 vols. London: Hogarth Press and the Institute of Psychoanalysis, 1953–74.
Seminar I	Jacques Lacan. *The Seminar of Jacques Lacan. Book I: Freud's Papers on Technique, 1953–1954,* ed. Jacques-Alain Miller, trans. John Forrester. New York: Norton, 1991.
Seminar II	Jacques Lacan. *The Seminar of Jacques Lacan. Book II: The Ego in Freud's Theory and in the Technique of Psychoanalysis, 1954–1955,* ed. Jacques-Alain Miller, trans. Sylvana Tomaselli. New York: Norton, 1991.
Seminar VII	Jacques Lacan. *The Seminar of Jacques Lacan. Book VII: The Ethics of Psychoanalysis, 1959–1960,* ed. Jacques-Alain Miller, trans. Dennis Porter. New York: Norton, 1992.
Seminar XX	Jacques Lacan. *The Seminar of Jacques Lacan. Book XX: Encore, 1972–1973, On Feminine Sexuality, The Limits of Love and Knowledge,* ed. Jacques-Alain Miller, trans. Bruce Fink. New York: Norton, 1998.
Three Essays	Sigmund Freud. "Three Essays on the Theory of Sexuality." *SE,* vol. 7.

Introduction

1. Stephen Booth, *King Lear, Macbeth, Indefinition, and Tragedy* (New Haven: Yale Univ. Press, 1983), 5; Michael Goldman, *Shakespeare and the Energies of Drama* (Princeton: Princeton Univ. Press, 1972), 94–108, and *Acting and Action in Shakespearean Tragedy* (Princeton: Princeton Univ. Press, 1985), 71–93.

2. Frank Kermode, *The Sense of an Ending: Studies in the Theory of Fiction* (New York: Oxford Univ. Press, 1967), 67–89. See also Kermode's Introduction to *King Lear* in *The Riverside Shakespeare,* ed. G. Blakemore Evans et al. (Boston: Houghton Mifflin, 1974), 1249–54.

3. Quotations from *Lear* follow the text of *The Tragedy of King Lear* in *Norton.*

4. For an example of how ahistorical formalism glosses over violence, we might note C. S. Lewis's comments on Christopher Marlowe's "Hero and Leander." Of the moment when Leander makes his way into Hero's bedroom with a love "not ful of pittie ... But deaffe and cruell," so that Hero "trembling strove" with (or against) him, Lewis comments that the poem's lack of tenderness serves to "dehumanize"

and thus "disinfect" its eroticism (Christopher Marlowe, "Hero and Leander," in *Elizabethan Minor Epics,* ed. Elizabeth Story Donno [New York: Columbia Univ. Press, 1963], 2:287–88, 291 [p. 68]; C. S. Lewis, *English Literature in the Sixteenth Century, Excluding Drama* [New York: Oxford, 1954], 487).

5. Because my focus is on the experience of the reader or viewer, I will not be arguing that individual authors or characters exhibit a wish for self-negation. For a recent example of character analysis in terms of sadomasochism, see Roberto Speziale-Bagliacca, *The King and the Adulteress: A Psychoanalytic and Literary Reinterpretation of* Madame Bovary *and* King Lear, ed. Colin Rice (Durham: Duke Univ. Press, 1998).

6. Slavoj Žižek, *The Metastases of Enjoyment: Six Essays on Women and Causality* (London: Verso, 1994), 89.

7. Joel Fineman, *Shakespeare's Perjured Eye: The Invention of Poetic Subjectivity in the Sonnets* (Berkeley and Los Angeles: Univ. of California Press, 1986), 46.

8. John K. Noyes, *The Mastery of Submission: Inventions of Masochism* (Ithaca: Cornell Univ. Press, 1997), 4.

9. Roy F. Baumeister, *Masochism and the Self* (Hillsdale, N.J.: Erlbaum, 1989), 53, cited in Noyes, *The Mastery of Submission,* 9.

10. Joan Copjec, *Read My Desire: Lacan against the Historicists* (Cambridge: MIT Press, 1994), 6, 14.

11. Leo Bersani, *The Culture of Redemption* (Cambridge: Harvard Univ. Press, 1990), 40.

12. Linda Williams has argued for the multiple and shifting identifications experienced by viewers of pornographic films in *Hard Core: Power, Pleasure, and the "Frenzy of the Visible"* (Berkeley and Los Angeles: Univ. of California Press, 1989), 195–228.

13. Mark Edmundson, *Nightmare on Main Street: Angels, Sadomasochism, and the Culture of Gothic* (Cambridge: Harvard Univ. Press, 1997), 125. For a carefully reasoned consideration of violence in contemporary culture, see Sissela Bok, *Mayhem: Violence as Public Entertainment* (Reading, Mass.: Addison-Wesley, 1998).

14. Ted Hughes, "On Ovid's 'Metamorphoses,'" *New York Review of Books,* 17 July 1997, 18.

Chapter 1. Violence, Subjectivity, and Paradoxes of Pleasure

1. Catherine Belsey, *The Subject of Tragedy* (London: Methuen, 1985); Francis Barker, *The Tremulous Private Body: Essays on Subjection* (London: Methuen, 1984); Jonathan Dollimore, *Radical Tragedy* (Brighton: Harvester, 1984; Chicago: Univ. of Chicago Press, 1989).

2. David Aers, "A Whisper in the Ear of Early Modernists; or, Reflections on Literary Critics Writing the 'History of the Subject,'" in *Culture and History, 1350–*

1600: Essays on English Communities, Identities, and Writing, ed. David Aers (Detroit: Wayne State Univ. Press, 1992), 177–202; Lee Patterson, "On the Margin: Postmodernism, Ironic History, and Medieval Studies," *Speculum* 65 (1990): 87–108.

3. Charles Taylor, *Sources of the Self: The Making of the Modern Identity* (Cambridge: Harvard Univ. Press, 1989), 199.

4. Gail Kern Paster, *The Body Embarrassed: Drama and the Disciplines of Shame in Early Modern England* (Ithaca: Cornell Univ. Press, 1993).

5. Timothy Bright, *A Treatise of Melancholie* (London: Thomas Vautrollier, 1586; reprint, New York: Columbia Univ. Press, 1940), 4, 33–34.

6. N[icholas] Coeffeteau, *A Table of Humane Passions,* trans. Edw[ard] Grimeston ([London]: Nicholas Okes, 1621), 4–5, 16–17.

7. Ibid., 7, 253–54.

8. Thomas Wright, *The Passions of the Minde in Generall* (London: Printed by Valentine Simmes for Walter Burre, 1604), 69–71.

9. Ibid., 201; Robert Burton, *The Anatomy of Melancholy,* 1620, ed. Thomas C. Faulkner, Nicolas K. Kiessling, Rhonda L. Blair, 6 vols. (Oxford: Clarendon, 1989–2000), Democritus to the Reader, 1.1.1.3; 1:56, 130; Edward Reynoldes, *A Treatise of the Passions and Faculties of the Soule of Man* (London: Printed by R. H. for Robert Bostock, 1640), 53.

10. Laura Levine, *Men in Women's Clothing: Anti-theatricality and Effeminization, 1579–1642* (New York: Cambridge Univ. Press, 1994), 15; Stephen Gosson, *Schoole of Abuse,* 1579 (reprint, New York: Johnson, 1973), Sig. B3, B6v; William Prynne, *Histriomastix: The Players Scourge, or, Actors Tragedie* (1633; reprint, New York: Johnson, 1974), 197.

11. William Rankins, *A Mirrour of Monsters* (1587; reprint, New York: Garland, 1973); Phillip Stubbes, *The Anatomie of Abuses* (1583; reprint, New York: Garland, 1973), A Preface to the Reader; Stephen Gosson, *Plays Confuted in Five Actions* (1582; reprint, New York: Garland, 1972), Sig. G4, Sig. F; Gosson, *Schoole of Abuse,* Sig. B7; [Anthony Munday], *A Second and third blast of retrait from plaies and theaters,* by Salvianus and 'Anglo-phile Eutheo' (1580; reprint, New York: Garland, 1972), 3–4.

12. Prynne, *Histriomastix,* 796.

13. John Rainoldes, *Th'overthrow of Stage-plays, by the way of controversy between D. Gager and D. Rainolds* (1599; reprint, New York: Garland, 1974), 118–19.

14. See Leeds Barroll, *Politics, Plague, and Shakespeare's Theater: The Stuart Years* (Ithaca: Cornell Univ. Press, 1991).

15. Prynne, *Histriomastix,* 560–61.

16. Gosson, *Plays Confuted,* A4v–A6; Rankins, *A Mirrour of Monsters,* fol. 24; Rainoldes, *Th'overthrow of Stage-plays,* 111–12.

17. Reynoldes, *A Treatise of the Passions,* 81; Peter [Pierre] de la Primaudaye, *The French Academie,* 1579, trans. [Thomas Bowes] (London: Edmund Bollifant, 1586), 19–

20; Coeffeteau, *A Table of Humane Passions*, 352–53; Jonathan Sawday, "Self and Self-hood in the Seventeenth Century," in *Rewriting the Self: Histories from the Renaissance to the Present*, ed. Roy Porter (New York: Routledge, 1997), 30.

18. John Donne, "Holy Sonnet 14," "Good Friday, 1613. Riding Westward," in *The Poems of John Donne*, ed. Herbert J. C. Grierson (Oxford: Clarendon, 1912), 328, 336–37; "Discipline," in *The English Poems of George Herbert*, ed. C. A. Patrides (Totowa, N.J.: Rowman & Littlefield, 1974), 183.

19. Religion has recently returned as a topic of critical interest, as evidenced by, e.g., Richard Rambuss, *Closet Devotions* (Durham: Duke Univ. Press, 1998); Huston Diehl, *Staging Reform, Reforming the Stage: Protestantism and Popular Theater in Early Modern England* (Ithaca: Cornell Univ. Press, 1997); and Ramie Targoff, *Common Prayer: The Language of Public Devotion in Early Modern England* (Chicago: Univ. of Chicago Press, 2001).

20. I am indebted here to Catherine Belling's paper, "Hamlet's Heart, Looking Back," circulated in the Historical Phenomenology section at the meeting of the Shakespeare Association of America, San Francisco, April 1999.

21. That Claudius is so moved to reveal his guilt is partial testimony to the relevance of a theory of catharsis to Renaissance drama, as Stephen Orgel observes. See his "The Play of Conscience," in *Performativity and Performance*, ed. Andrew Parker and Eve Kosofsky Sedgwick (New York: Routledge, 1995), 146–47.

22. Levine observes specifically that Stephen Greenblatt "often replicates the very notion he himself considers a fallacy," advancing in practice the model of the embedded self he has supposedly refuted (Levine, *Men in Women's Clothing*, 11).

23. Aers, "A Whisper in the Ear," 192.

24. Stephen Greenblatt, *Shakespearean Negotiations: The Circulation of Social Energy in Renaissance England* (Berkeley and Los Angeles: Univ. of California Press, 1988), 1.

25. On this habit of partial reading, see also Mark Breitenberg, *Anxious Masculinity in Early Modern England* (Cambridge: Cambridge Univ. Press, 1996); Elizabeth Hanson, *Discovering the Subject in Renaissance England* (Cambridge: Cambridge Univ. Press, 1998); Levine, *Men in Women's Clothing*.

26. Elizabeth J. Bellamy, *Translations of Power: Narcissism and the Unconscious in Epic History* (Ithaca: Cornell Univ. Press, 1992), 1–3. Another powerful demonstration of this concept is found in Julia Reinhard Lupton and Kenneth Reinhard, *After Oedipus: Shakespeare in Psychoanalysis* (Ithaca: Cornell Univ. Press, 1993). See Sigmund Freud, "Remembering, Repeating and Working-Through," in *SE* 12:147–56.

27. Bellamy, *Translations of Power*, 46. She refers here to Lacan's essay, "The Function and Field of Speech and Language in Psychoanalysis."

28. Marshall Grossman, *The Story of All Things: Writing the Self in English Renaissance*

Narrative Poetry (Durham: Duke Univ. Press, 1998); Lynn Enterline, *The Tears of Narcissus: Melancholia and Masculinity in Early Modern Writing* (Stanford: Stanford Univ. Press, 1995), 16. Other explorations of contemporary theory's recursive relation to Renaissance texts include Lupton and Reinhard, *After Oedipus*; Julia Lupton, *Afterlives of the Saints: Hagiography, Typology, and Renaissance Literature* (Stanford: Stanford Univ. Press, 1996); Ned Lukacher, *Daemonic Figures: Shakespeare and the Question of Conscience* (Ithaca: Cornell Univ. Press, 1994); Christopher Pye, *The Vanishing: Shakepeare, the Subject, and Early Modern Culture* (Durham: Duke Univ. Press, 2000); Timothy Murray, "Translating Montaigne's Crypts: Melancholic Relations and the Sites of Altarbiography," in *Repossessions: Psychoanalysis and the Phantasms of Early Modern Culture*, ed. Timothy Murray and Alan K. Smith (Minneapolis: Univ. of Minnesota Press, 1998), 47–77; Barbara Freedman, *Staging the Gaze: Postmodernism, Psychoanalysis, and Shakespearean Comedy* (Ithaca: Cornell Univ. Press, 1991).

29. Bellamy, *Translations of Power*, 5.

30. Greenblatt notes "an increased self-consciousness about the fashioning of human identity as a manipulable, artful process" (*Renaissance Self-fashioning: From More to Shakespeare* [Chicago: Univ. of Chicago Press, 1980], 2). Further references to this work will be noted parenthetically.

31. Emerson counseled: "Leave your theory as Joseph his coat in the hand of the harlot, and flee" ("Self-reliance," in *The Collected Works of Ralph Waldo Emerson*, ed. Joseph Slater, Alfred R. Ferguson, and Jean Ferguson Carr [Cambridge: Harvard-Belknap, 1979], 2:33).

32. Greenblatt initiated this development by fusing personal and critical modes in *Renaissance Self-fashioning*, most famously in the book's Epilogue. We might also note comments on the dissolving borders between literature and society, for instance: "Self-fashioning derives its interest precisely from the fact that it functions without regard for a sharp distinction between literature and social life" (3), and "it is everywhere evident in this book that the questions I ask of my material and indeed the very nature of this material are shaped by the questions I ask of myself" (5).

33. See Aers, "A Whisper in the Ear"; Patterson, "On the Margin"; Levine, *Men in Women's Clothing*.

34. "In the Middle Ages. . . . man was conscious of himself only as a member of a race, people, party, family, or corporation—only through some general category. . . . [In Renaissance Italy] man became a spiritual *individual*, and recognized himself as such" (Jacob Burckhardt, *The Civilization of the Renaissance in Italy*, trans. S. G. C. Middlemore, 2 vols. [New York: Harper-Colophon, 1958], 1:143).

35. In Hugh Grady's words, "Burckhardt in effect canonized Hegel's view that a new or renewed sense of subjectivity and individuality constituted the modern

epoch," and "Greenblatt . . . called for something like a revival of Burckhardt's idea of Renaissance modernity" ("Renewing Modernity: Changing Contexts and Contents of a Nearly Invisible Concept," *Shakespeare Quarterly* 50, no. 3 [1999]: 268–84, 270, 272). See also Vincent P. Pecora, "The Limits of Local Knowledge," in *The New Historicism*, ed. H. Aram Veeser (New York: Routledge, 1989), 243–76, 267, and William Kerrigan and Gordon Braden, *The Idea of the Renaissance* (Baltimore: Johns Hopkins Univ. Press, 1989), 223n. 27.

36. Levine, *Men in Women's Clothing*, 11.

37. Burckhardt, *The Civilization of the Renaissance*, 2:437.

38. Stephen Greenblatt, "Psychoanalysis and Renaissance Culture," in *Literary Theory / Renaissance Texts*, ed. Patricia Parker and David Quint (Baltimore: Johns Hopkins Univ. Press, 1986), 210–24, 221. On the impoverishment resulting from historicism's rejection of psychoanalytic theory, see Tracey Sedinger, "Historicism and Renaissance Culture," in *Discontinuities: New Essays on Renaissance Literature and Culture* (Toronto: Univ. of Toronto Press, 1998), 117–38.

39. Bellamy, *Translations of Power*, 6–7n. 17.

40. Jonathan Crewe comments on the "extraordinary intransigence" of Greenblatt's discussion of the Bower of Bliss: "The fashioning of the self requires the *destruction* of the other" (*Hidden Designs: The Critical Profession and Renaissance Literature* [New York: Methuen, 1986], 167n. 3).

41. *Civilization*, 105. Appended to the passage is a long footnote on the "bisexual disposition" and the difficulty of understanding sexuality from a psychological viewpoint.

42. Suzanne R. Stewart notes how the work has frequently been misread or oversimplified. Her own reading allegorizes the text or, more precisely, Freud's economy of the superego as a recuperation of paternal function; in her view, the installation of the superego creates masochism by moving the oedipal father inside the subject. Stewart equates the ego with the subject, repeating the familiar move of assuming a preconstituted subject, in this case one destined to be in thrall to the father/superego (*Sublime Surrender: Male Masochism at the Fin-de-Siècle* [Ithaca: Cornell Univ. Press, 1998], 144–58).

43. Cf. *Freudian Body*, 41: "In order to account for the mystery of sadistic sexuality—that is, how we can be sexually aroused by the suffering of others, as distinct from the easier question of why we wish to exercise power over others—Freud is led to suggest that the spectacle of pain in others stimulates a mimetic representation which shatters the subject into sexual excitement."

44. In the introduction to *Renaissance Self-fashioning*, Greenblatt outlines a tripartite notion of literature's function—to manifest the author's behavior, to express

"the [social] codes by which behavior is shaped," or to "[reflect] upon those [shaping] codes"—that leaves little space for slippage from or resistance to social codes and little for the dimension of literary pleasure (4).

45. David Scott Kastan observes that Greenblatt's argument became more subtle as it developed, shifting from a view of culture "structured by a Foucauldian notion of power inhabiting all social relations to one shaped by 'the circulation of social energy' (the subtitle of *Shakespearean Negotiations*)" and more and more emphasizing cultural "stresses and conflicts," although without fully embracing the possibility of real subversion or resistance (*Shakespeare after Theory* [New York: Routledge, 1999], 239n, 240n).

46. Jacques Lacan, "The Function and Field of Speech and Language in Psychoanalysis," in *Écrits*, 71. See also Teresa Brennan, *History after Lacan* (New York: Routledge, 1993), 26–75.

47. Carla Mazzio and Douglas Trevor, "Dreams of History: An Introduction," in *Historicism, Psychoanalysis, and Early Modern Culture*, ed. Carla Mazzio and Douglas Trevor (New York: Routledge, 2000), 1.

48. Greenblatt, "Psychoanalysis and Renaissance Culture," 210, 217.

49. See Valeria Finucci and Regina Schwartz, eds., *Desire in the Renaissance: Psychoanalysis and Literature* (Princeton: Princeton Univ. Press, 1994); Freedman, *Staging the Gaze*; Mazzio and Trevor, *Historicism, Psychoanalysis, and Early Modern Culture*; Carol Thomas Neely, "'Documents in Madness:' Reading Madness and Gender in Shakespeare's Tragedies and Early Modern Culture," *Shakespeare Quarterly* 42, no. 3 (1991): 315–38; Paster, *The Body Embarrassed*; Pye, *The Vanishing*; Meredith Skura, "Understanding the Living and Talking to the Dead: The Historicity of Psychoanalysis," *Modern Language Quarterly* 54, no. 1 (1993): 77–89; Valerie Traub, *Desire and Anxiety: Circulations of Sexuality in Shakespearean Drama* (New York: Routledge, 1992).

50. The claim that "the unconscious of the Renaissance *is* language" (Regina Schwartz with Valeria Finucci, "Introduction," in Finucci and Schwartz, *Desire in the Renaissance*, 10) seems to echo Joel Fineman's influential claim in *Shakespeare's Perjured Eye: The Invention of Poetic Subjectivity in the Sonnets* (Berkeley and Los Angeles: Univ. of California Press, 1986).

51. See Michael P. Clark, ed., *Revenge of the Aesthetic: The Place of Literature in Theory Today* (Berkeley and Los Angeles: Univ. of California Press, 2000); Graham L. Hammill, *Sexuality and Form: Caravaggio, Marlowe, and Bacon* (Chicago: Univ. of Chicago Press, 2000); Dympna Callaghan, "Body Problems," *Shakespeare Studies* 29 (2001): 68–71. As early as 1986, Jonathan Crewe diagnosed the "disappearance of the literary" as a consequence of historicism (*Hidden Designs*, 16).

52. Michael P. Clark, "Introduction," *Revenge of the Aesthetic*, 4, 5–6, 10.

53. Sedinger, "Historicism and Renaissance Culture," 135, 130–31, 135; Elizabeth J.

Bellamy, "Discourses of Impossibility: Can Psychoanalysis Be Political?" *diacritics* 23, no. 1 (1993): 35, 25.

54. Freud, "The Moses of Michelangelo," *SE* 13:214, 216; "Leondardo Da Vinci and a Memory of His Childhood," *SE* 11:63n. 2. Bellamy also notes Freud's references to Burckhardt (*Translations of Power*, 1–2).

55. Burckhardt, *The Civilization of the Renaissance*, 2:442.

56. Noyes, *The Mastery of Submission*, 141.

57. *Life and Death*, 87–92. See also Noyes, *The Mastery of Submission*, 158–59, for a somewhat different treatment.

58. Noyes, *The Mastery of Submission*, 152. See also J. Laplanche and J.-B. Pontalis, *The Language of Psycho-analysis*, trans. Donald Nicholson-Smith (New York: Norton, 1973), 245.

59. Gaylyn Studlar, *In the Realm of Pleasure: Von Sternberg, Dietrich, and the Masochistic Aesthetic* (New York: Columbia Univ. Press, 1988), 42.

60. *BPP*, 54–55, 62. Jean Laplanche sees Freud's articulations of the death drive as "profoundly contradictory," since the speculative endorsement of primary masochism in *Beyond the Pleasure Principle* (1920) is followed by the claim in *New Introductory Lectures* (1933) of a "special aggressive and destructive instinct" (*The Unconscious and the Id* [London: Rebus, 1999], 192). Presumably the *Lectures*, prepared for a generalist audience, intentionally domesticate the theory, blunting its subversive edge.

61. *Life and Death*, 23; emphasis in original. See also Noyes, *The Mastery of Submission*, 154.

62. Leo Bersani, *The Culture of Redemption* (Cambridge: Harvard Univ. Press, 1990), 38, 40; emphasis in original.

63. *Freudian Body*, 107. One might compare Julia Kristeva's theory of the semiotic in relation to art. In *Black Sun: Depression and Melancholia*, trans. Leon S. Roudiez (New York: Columbia Univ. Press, 1989), for instance, she claims that artists succeed in giving formal expression to their experience of melancholia, whereas ordinary people simply suffer its symptoms.

64. Kaja Silverman, *Male Subjectivity at the Margins* (New York: Routledge, 1992), 213; Stewart, *Sublime Surrender*, 9, 1–15.

65. Tim Dean, Hal Foster, and Kaja Silverman, "A Conversation with Leo Bersani," *October* 82 (fall 1997): 3–16, 6, 15.

66. Leo Bersani, *Homos* (Cambridge: Harvard Univ. Press, 1995), 90–99.

67. Stewart, *Sublime Surrender*, 53–54.

68. Studlar, *In the Realm of Pleasure*, 185–86.

69. A similar crux occurs in Julia Kristeva's theory of the preoedipal origins of the semiotic, which is frequently understood to essentialize women's maternal role, although the identities involved (mother, infant) are necessarily produced recur-

sively, after the passage into the symbolic order. See Cynthia Marshall, review of Lynn Enterline's *Tears of Narcissus: Melancholia and Masculinity in Early Modern England* and John Russell's *Hamlet and Narcissus, Shakespeare Quarterly* 49, no. 1 (1998): 112.

70. Bersani, *Homos,* 101.

71. *Life and Death,* 104; emphasis in original. Stewart, following Deleuze, understands the Freudian psychomachia as an internal theater of sadomasochism, with sadistic superego punishing masochistic ego (*Sublime Surrender,* 29–30, 155), an allegorizing formulation that grants more autonomous status to the constituent parts of the subject than Freud's theory supports.

72. *Life and Death,* 19, quoting *Three Essays.* See Lynn Enterline's excellent discussion of Ovid's *Metamorphoses* as tales of "passion . . . *without* object" and sometimes in excess of the subject as well (*The Rhetoric of the Body from Ovid to Shakespeare* [Cambridge: Cambridge Univ. Press, 2000], 85–86).

73. *Life and Death,* 20; emphasis in original. See also Enterline, *Tears of Narcissus,* 29–34.

74. *Life and Death,* 122; emphasis in original; Pye, *The Vanishing,* 94.

75. Laplanche and Pontalis, *The Language of Psycho-analysis,* 317.

76. Ibid., 318; Linda Williams, *Hard Care: Power, Pleasure, and the 'Frenzy of the Visible'* (Berkeley and Los Angeles: Univ. of California Press, 1989), 195–228. Williams also argues against Deleuze's division of sadism from masochism; her critique mainly concerns Deleuze's avoidance of female readers and characters (210–17).

77. Leopold von Sacher-Masoch, "Venus in Furs," in *Masochism* (New York: Zone, 1989), 271.

78. Cf. Lacan's comment: "What Freud's primary masochism teaches us is that, when life has been dispossessed of its speech, its final word can only be the final malediction expressed at the end of *Oedipus at Colonnus.* Life doesn't want to be healed" (*Seminar II,* 232–33).

79. Aristotle, *Poetics,* 1448b, quoted in Jody Enders, *The Medieval Theater of Cruelty: Rhetoric, Memory, Violence* (Ithaca: Cornell Univ. Press, 1999), 7.

80. James W. Earl, "Identification and Catharsis," in *Pragmatism's Freud: The Moral Disposition of Psychoanalysis,* ed. Joseph H. Smith and William Kerrigan (Baltimore: Johns Hopkins Univ. Press, 1986), 79–92, 81.

81. Orgel, "The Play of Conscience," 138.

82. Earl, "Identification and Catharsis," 91, 90.

83. Orgel, "The Play of Conscience," 143.

84. A. D. Nuttall, *Why Does Tragedy Give Pleasure?* (Oxford: Clarendon, 1996), 78, 77, 76, 78, 77.

85. Ibid., 74. Nuttall cites *Civilization and Its Discontents,* trans. Joan Rivière (Lon-

don: Hogarth Press, 1963), esp. 59. He also calls the Freudian unconscious the "dark side of the mind," imposing a moral reading on a structural frame (57). Laplanche calls this sort of emphasis on aggressivity a "watered down" version of the death drive (*The Unconscious and the Id*, 197).

86. Nuttall, *Why Does Tragedy Give Pleasure?* 104.

87. Studlar reads the *Fort/Da* in relation to the ambivalence of infantile desire, locating an "obsessive return to the moment of separation from the oral mother" (*In the Realm of Pleasure*, 124).

88. This paragraph is taken, in slightly revised form, from my essay "The Doubled Jacques and Constructions of Negation in *As You Like It*," *Shakespeare Quarterly* 49, no. 4 (1998): 382–83.

89. Richard Boothby, *Death and Desire: Psychoanalytic Theory in Lacan's Return to Freud* (New York: Routledge, 1991), 136.

90. *Seminar II*, 90, also quoted in Boothby, *Death and Desire*, 136.

91. *Life and Death*, 89–102. See also Studlar, *In the Realm of Pleasure*, 26–27.

Chapter 2. "To Speak of Love" in the Language of Petrarchanism

1. N[icholas] Coeffeteau, *A Table of Humane Passions*, trans. Edw[ard] Grimeston ([London]: Nicholas Okes, 1621), 157, 166; "The Life of Marcus Antonius," in *Shakespeare's Plutarch*, trans. Thomas North, ed. T. J. B. Spencer (New York: Penguin, 1964), 258; Coeffeteau, *A Table of Humane Passions*, 169; Robert Burton, *Anatomy of Melancholy*, 1620, ed. Thomas C. Faulkner, Nicolas K. Kiessling, and Rhonda L. Blair, 6 vols. (Oxford: Clarendon, 1989–2000), 3.2.4.1; 3:199.

2. As William Kerrigan and Gordon Braden point out, the connection was inscribed from the start: "In the great pun that spreads throughout [Petrarch's] lyrics, Laura, the object of his all-consuming desire, can be indistinguishable from *lauro*, the laurel of poetic achievement" (*The Idea of the Renaissance* [Baltimore: Johns Hopkins Univ. Press, 1989], 161).

3. Kaja Silverman attempts to rehabilitate love as a politically useful term in *The Threshold of the Visible World* (New York: Routledge, 1996).

4. [Thomas Lodge], *Phillis: Honoured with Pastorall Sonnets, Elegies, and amorous delights* (London: John Busbie, 1593), sonnet 18.

5. John Freccero, "The Fig Tree and the Laurel: Petrarach's Poetics," in *Literary Theory / Renaissance Texts*, ed. Patricia Parker and David Quint (Baltimore: Johns Hopkins Univ. Press, 1986), 21.

6. Giuseppe Mazzotta, "The *Canzoniere* and the Language of the Self," *Studies in Philology* 75 (1978): 273; Lynn Enterline, *The Rhetoric of the Body from Ovid to Shakespeare* (Cambridge: Cambridge Univ. Press, 2000), 91–124.

7. Joel Fineman, *Shakespeare's Perjured Eye: The Invention of Poetic Subjectivity in the Sonnets* (Berkeley and Los Angeles: Univ. of California Press, 1986), 25, 26.

8. Fineman wrote that Shakespeare's sonnets were written "after or against, rather than in, the context of such sonnet sequences as *Astrophil and Stella*, Daniel's *Delia*, Spenser's *Amoretti*, Constable's *Diana*, Lodge's *Phillis*, Barnes's *Parthenophil and Parthenophe*, Fletcher's *Licia*, among many others, all published by 1595" (*Shakespeare's Perjured Eye*, 318n. 3); see also 27.

9. Hallett Smith, *Elizabethan Poetry* (Ann Arbor: Univ. of Michigan Press, 1952), 147.

10. Kerrigan and Braden write that "one thing the Petrarchan poet has, in compensation for his anguish, is poems" (*The Idea of the Renaissance*, 172). Jonathan Dollimore, describing Shakespeare's sonnets, calls verse a "compensation for disappointment in love" (*Death, Desire, and Loss in Western Culture* [New York: Routledge, 1998], 106). On poetry as a "substitute" satisfaction, see Carol Thomas Neely, "The Structure of English Renaissance Sonnet Sequences," *ELH* 45 (1978): 359–89, 366.

11. C. S. Lewis, *English Literature in the Sixteenth Century, Excluding Drama* (New York: Oxford Univ. Press, 1954), 490–91.

12. Slavoj Žižek, *The Metastases of Enjoyment: Six Essays on Women and Causality* (London: Verso, 1994), 187; Slavoj Žižek, *The Sublime Object of Ideology* (New York: Verso, 1989), 32.

13. Correcting a common misreading of Lacanian mirror stage theory, Richard Boothby explains, "What is alienating is not the relation of the nascent ego to another ego, but of the inchoate subject to its own ego" (*Death and Desire: Psychoanalytic Theory in Lacan's Return to Freud* [New York: Routledge, 1991], 45).

14. As Scott Wilson puts it, the "metaphorical torment of the Petrarchan lover is [grotesquely] literalized by Elizabethan sonnet makers" ("Racked on the Tyrant's Bed: The Politics of Pleasure and Pain and the Elizabethan Sonnet Sequences," *Textual Practice* 3 [1989]: 234).

15. Barbara L. Estrin, *Laura: Uncovering Gender and Genre in Wyatt, Donne, and Marvell* (Durham: Duke Univ. Press, 1994), 12.

16. Roland Greene, *Post-Petrarchism: Origins and Innovations of the Western Lyric Sequence* (Princeton: Princeton Univ. Press, 1991); Heather Dubrow, *Echoes of Desire: English Petrarchism and Its Counterdiscourses* (Ithaca: Cornell Univ. Press, 1995).

17. Burton, *Anatomy of Melancholy*, 3.1.2.1; 3:16.

18. Ibid., "Democritus Junior to the Reader," 1:6; 3.2.3.1; 3:195–96.

19. [William Percy], *Sonnets to the Fairest Coelia* (London: Printed by Adam Islip, 1594), sonnet 20.

20. See Julia Kristeva, "The System and the Speaking Subject," in *The Kristeva Reader*, ed. Toril Moi (New York: Columbia Univ. Press, 1986), 24–33.

21. *Zepheria* (London: Printed by the Widdowe Orwin, for N.L. and John Busbie,

1594), canzon 40. In the Folger Shakespeare Library copy, initial letters of several lines are missing. For a Lacanian reading of this sequence focusing on its politics of looking, see Andrew Stott, "From *Voi Che* to *Che Vuoi?* The Gaze, Desire, and the Law in the *Zepheria* Sonnet Sequence," *Criticism* 36, no. 3 (1994): 329–58.

22. See Julia Kristeva, "Stabat Mater," in *The Kristeva Reader*, ed. Toril Moi (New York: Columbia Univ. Press, 1986), 160–86.

23. Burton, *Anatomy of Melancholy*, 3.2.3.1; 3:169.

24. [Samuel Daniel], *Delia: Contayning certayne Sonnets: with the complaint of Rosamond* (London: Printed by I.C. for Simon Waterson, 1592), sonnet 3.

25. Burton, *Anatomy of Melancholy*, 3.2.3.1; 3:195.

26. Žižek, *The Sublime Object*, 74.

27. Julia Kristeva, *Black Sun: Depression and Melancholia*, trans. Leon S. Roudiez (New York: Columbia Univ. Press, 1989).

28. Daniel, *Delia*, sonnet 6, lines 13–14; Bruce Fink, *The Lacanian Subject: Between Language and Jouissance* (Princeton: Princeton Univ. Press, 1995), 60.

29. *Shakespeare's Sonnets*, ed. Stephen Booth (New Haven: Yale Univ. Press, 1977), 127.

30. Dollimore, *Death, Desire, and Loss*, 103, 104, 186.

31. Margreta de Grazia, "1590s: Fin-de-Siècle Renaissance England," *Fins de Siècle: English Poetry in 1590, 1690, 1790, 1890, 1990*, ed. Elaine Scarry (Baltimore: Johns Hopkins Univ. Press, 1995), 42; Dubrow, *Echoes of Desire*, 37.

32. Marshall Grossman, *The Story of All Things: Writing the Self in English Renaissance Narrative Poetry* (Durham: Duke Univ. Press, 1998), 103.

33. William Smith, *Chloris, or The Complaint of the passionate despised Shepheard* (London: Edm. Bollifant, 1596), sonnet 29.

34. Daniel, *Delia*, sonnet 14.

35. Michael Drayton, *Idea. In Sixtie Three Sonnets*, in *Poems* (London: John Smethwicke, 1619), sonnet 50. Wilson also discusses this sonnet in "Racked on the tyrant's bed" as an example of the interplay between discourses of torture and Petrarchanism (245–46).

36. *Zepheria*, canzon 4. Some initial line letters are missing.

37. See Tilottama Rajan's claim that Donne refuses to confuse "representation with reality" and writes frequently in his sonnets "of the beloved's absence and of the literary act as an attempt to re-present that which is absent" ("'Nothing Sooner Broke': Donne's *Songs and Sonets* as Self-consuming Artifact," *ELH* 49 [1982]: 805–28, 828n. 21).

38. Sir Philip Sidney, "Astrophil and Stella," sonnet 60, in *The Poems of Sir Philip Sidney*, ed. William A. Ringler Jr. (Oxford: Clarendon, 1962), 195.

39. Enterline, *The Rhetoric of the Body*, 97; Nancy J. Vickers, "Diana Described: Scat-

tered Woman and Scattered Rhyme," *Critical Inquiry* 8, no. 2 (1981): 265–79, 275; Enterline, *The Rhetoric of the Body*, 105.

40. Barnabe Barnes, *Parthenophil and Parthenophe*, ed. Victor A. Doyno (Carbondale: Southern Illinois Univ. Press, 1971), 39, sonnet 63.

41. Dubrow, *Echoes of Desire*, 250.

42. Gordon Braden, "Love and Fame: The Petrarchan Career," in *Pragmatism's Freud: The Moral Disposition of Psychoanalysis*, ed. Joseph H. Smith and William Kerrigan (Baltimore: Johns Hopkins Univ. Press, 1986), 126–58, 127.

43. Barnes, *Parthenophil and Parthenophe*, 20, sonnet 31.

44. "The aim of my teaching . . . is to dissociate *a* and A by reducing the first to what is related to the imaginary and the other to what is related to the symbolic" (Lacan, *Seminar XX*, 83).

45. On thematic similarities in the writings of Renaissance sonneteers and Sacher-Masoch, see Carol Siegel, *Male Masochism: Modern Revisions of the Story of Love* (Bloomington: Indiana Univ. Press, 1995), 8–9; Lisa S. Starks, "'Like the Lover's pinch, which hurts and is desired': The Libidinal Economy of Male Masochism and Shakespeare's *Antony and Cleopatra*," *Literature and Psychology* 45, no. 4 (1999): 58–73; and "'Won with thy words and conquered with thy looks': Sadism, Masochism, and the Masochistic Gaze in *I Tamburlaine*," in *Marlowe, History, and Sexuality: New Critical Essays on Christopher Marlowe*, ed. Paul Whitfield White (New York: AMS Press, 1998), 179–93, 180.

46. Leo Bersani, *Homos* (Cambridge: Harvard Univ. Press, 1995), 195n. 25.

47. In an interesting look at the "dissemination of Petrarchan codes," Jonathan Crewe suggests that the episode of Serena among the savages in book 6 of Spenser's *Faerie Queene* illustrates the blazon's link with cannibalism and ultimately anticipates "a consumer economy in which the woman will be both the object of unsatisfied consumption and the prototype of everything to be consumed" ("Spenser's Saluage Petrarchanism: *Pensées Sauvages* in *The Faerie Queene*," *Bucknell Review* 35, no. 2 [1992]: 89, 100).

48. Lacan denies that he is attempting "to reduce mysticism to questions of cum (*affaires de foutre*)" as nineteenth-century psychological theorists did (*Seminar XX*, 77).

49. On Lacanian jouissance in relation to gender, see Amy Hollywood, *Sensible Ecstasy: Mysticism, Sexual Difference, and the Demands of History* (Chicago: Univ. of Chicago Press, 2002). On conjunctions of the sexual with religious devotion, see Richard Rambuss, *Closet Devotions* (Durham: Duke Univ. Press, 1998).

50. Burton, *Anatomy of Melancholy*, 3.4.1.1; 3:330.

51. On Other jouissance, see Fink, *The Lacanian Subject*, 120. Fink is a reliable guide, although at one point he associates Other jouissance with women and debars it from

men (107), reproducing a standard error among readers of Lacan by equating those who speak from a feminine position with women per se. Lacan explicitly indicates that mystical jouissance is not limited to women (*Seminar XX*, 76).

52. See Dubrow, *Echoes of Desire*; Estrin, *Laura*; Vickers, "Diana Described."

53. Michael Drayton, *Ideas Mirrour. Amours in Quatorzains* (London: Printed by James Roberts, 1594), amour 15.

54. Smith, *Chloris*, sonnet 11.

Chapter 3. Foxe and the Jouissance of Martyrology

1. John Foxe, *The First Volume of the Ecclesiasticall history contayning the Actes and Monumentes of . . . the sufferyng of martyrs* (London: John Day, 1570, 1576, 1583). When quoting from Foxe, I provide the page number in the 1570 edition or the later edition in which the material first appeared, followed by the corresponding page reference to the Cattley-Townsend (CT) edition (*The Acts and Monuments of John Foxe*, ed. Stephen R. Cattley and George Townsend, 8 vols. [1837–41; reprint, New York: AMS, 1965]). Cattley's text was based on the 1583 edition but occasionally includes parts of other editions. Until the appearance of the complete critical edition currently being prepared with support of the British Academy, the Cattley-Townsend reprint remains the only generally available text of the *Acts and Monuments*. References are cited parenthetically.

2. D. R. Woolf considers the problem of generic classification in "The Rhetoric of Martyrdom: Generic Contradiction and Narrative Strategy in John Foxe's *Acts and Monuments*," in *The Rhetorics of Life-Writing in Early Modern Europe*, ed. Thomas F. Mayer and D. R. Woolf (Ann Arbor: Univ. of Michigan Press, 1995), 243–82. See also, on ecclesiastical history, J. F. Mozeley, *John Foxe and His Book* (1940; reprint, London: Society for Promoting Christian Knowledge, 1970); on nationalism, William Haller, *The Elect Nation: The Meaning and Relevance of Foxe's* Book of Martyrs (New York: Harper & Row, 1963), and Richard Helgerson, *Forms of Nationhood: The Elizabethan Writing of England* (Chicago: Univ. of Chicago Press, 1992); on hagiography, Ross Bartlett, "John Foxe as Hagiographer: The Question Revisited," *Sixteenth Century Journal* 26 (1995): 771–89; on martyrology, John R. Knott, "John Foxe and the Joy of Suffering," *Sixteenth Century Journal* 27 (1996): 721–34, and *Discourses of Martyrdom in English Literature, 1563–1694* (New York: Cambridge Univ. Press, 1993); on apocalyptic, Tom Betteridge, "From Prophetic to Apocalyptic: John Foxe and the Writing of History," in *John Foxe and the English Reformation*, ed. David Loades (Aldershot, Hants, U.K.: Scolar Press, 1997), 210–32.

3. See, e.g., Susan Felch, "Shaping the Reader in the *Acts and Monuments*," in Loades, *John Foxe*, 52–65; Damian Nussbaum, "Appropriating Martyrdom: Fears of

Renewed Persecution and the 1632 Edition of *Acts and Monuments*," in Loades, *John Foxe*, 178–91; and Jesse Lander, "'Foxe's' *Books of Martyrs*: Printing and Popularizing the *Acts and Monuments*," in *Religion and Culture in Renaissance England*, ed. Claire McEachern and Debora Shuger (New York: Cambridge Univ. Press, 1997), 69–92.

4. Betteridge, "From Prophetic to Apocalyptic."

5. See Knott, *Discourses of Martyrdom*, 3, and Mark Breitenberg, "The Flesh Made Word: Foxe's *Acts and Monuments*," *Renaissance and Reformation/Renaissance et Réforme* 25, no. 4 (1989): 381–407, 385. Cathedral churches were required to have copies of *Acts and Monuments*, and many parish churches reportedly owned copies as well.

6. David Loades, "Introduction: John Foxe and the Editors," in *John Foxe*, 4.

7. See Nussbaum, "Appropriating Martyrdom," for an account of how the 1632 edition of the *Acts and Monuments* left open the possibility of resistance to the Church of England. Helgerson lists Baptists, Methodists, Quakers, and American Congregationalists as among those who eventually adapted *Acts and Monuments* to their purposes (*Forms of Nationhood*, 284). See also Loades, *John Foxe*, 5.

8. Margaret Aston, quoted in Eirwen Nicholson, "Eighteenth-Century Foxe: Evidence for the Impact of the *Acts and Monuments* in the 'Long' Eighteenth Century," in Loades, *John Foxe*, 157.

9. The illustrations accompanying Foxe's text are acknowledged as fascinating for readers; see Margaret Aston and Elizabeth Ingram, "The Iconography of the *Acts and Monuments*," in Loades, *John Foxe*, 66–142. By contrast, Felch's essay on "Shaping the Reader in the *Acts and Monuments*" examines the way Foxe's editorial material works to create "morally sensitive and adequately informed readers" (58).

10. George Eliot, *The Mill on the Floss* (New York: Penguin, 1979), 79; Nicholson, "Eighteenth-Century Foxe," 151–52.

11. I include within the category of "readers" those among the illiterate or semiliterate who heard the text or portions of it read aloud.

12. On public executions as spectacles of cruelty, see Mitchell B. Merback, *The Thief, the Cross, and the Wheel: Pain and the Spectacle of Punishment in Medieval and Renaissance Europe* (Chicago: Univ. of Chicago Press, 1998).

13. I am drawing on Barthes's *The Pleasure of the Text*, trans. Richard Miller (New York: Farrar, Straus & Giroux, 1975), and "From Work to Text," in *Textual Strategies: Perspectives in Post-structuralist Criticism*, ed. Josué V. Harari (Ithaca: Cornell Univ. Press, 1979), 73–81. In his analysis of Sade as a "founde[r] of language," Barthes writes that "the text is an object of pleasure" (*Sade / Fourier / Loyola*, trans. Richard Miller [Baltimore: Johns Hopkins Univ. Press, 1976], 3, 7.

14. For a related argument about the logic whereby juridicial torture was practiced in England in the late sixteenth century, see Elizabeth Hanson, "Torture and

Truth," in her *Discovery of the Subject in Renaissance England* (New York: Cambridge Univ. Press, 1998), 24–54.

15. "And do not fear them which kill the body, but are not able to kill the soul: but rather fear him which is able to destroy both soul and body in hell" (Mt. 10.28; KJV).

16. Janel M. Mueller, "Pain, Persecution, and the Construction of Selfhood in Foxe's *Acts and Monuments*," in *Religion and Culture in Renaissance England*, ed. Claire McEachern and Debora Shuger (New York: Cambridge Univ. Press, 1997), 171.

17. Cf. D. R. Woolf's comment: "What strikes the reader most about the many successive accounts of persecutions, trials, and martyrdoms is how little they differ from one another: it is almost literally true that if you have heard one martyr's death, you've read them all" ("The Rhetoric of Martyrdom," 258).

18. In "John Foxe and the Joy of Suffering," Knott also examines Foxe's presentation of troubling details; in his view these serve to provide dramatic power. Knott considers it Foxe's "task, as martyrologist, to persuade his readers that his 'saints' did indeed die mildly, with spiritual rejoicing" (722), but acknowledges that the details of suffering sometimes overwhelm this narrative purpose.

19. Knott similarly wonders if at least some of the martyrs' stylized gestures, such as washing the hands in flames, might have "evolved from efforts to alleviate the actual pain of burning" (*Discourses of Martyrdom*, 80).

20. Mueller, "Pain, Persecution," 166, 162. See also Knott, *Discourses of Martyrdom*, 9.

21. Mueller, "Pain, Persecution," 173.

22. For review of historical debates, see Betteridge, "From Prophetic to Apocalyptic," 211–13, and Breitenberg, "The Flesh Made Word," 382–83. On theatricality, see David Nicholls, "The Theatre of Martyrdom in the French Reformation," *Past and Present* 121 (1988): 49–73; Daryl W. Palmer, "Histories of Violence and the Writer's Hand: Foxe's *Actes and Monuments* and Shakespeare's *Titus Andronicus*," in *Reading and Writing in Shakespeare*, ed. David M. Bergeron (Newark: Univ. of Delaware Press, 1996), 82–115; and Huston Diehl, *Staging Reform, Reforming the Stage: Protestantism and Popular Theater in Early Modern England* (Ithaca: Cornell Univ. Press, 1997), 9–53, 185–93.

23. Foxe, quoted in Haller, *The Elect Nation*, 111.

24. Caroline Walker Bynum, *The Resurrection of the Body in Western Christianity, 200–1336* (New York: Columbia Univ. Press, 1995), 310.

25. Interestingly, modern knowledge of physiology supports the possibility that martyrs would not necessarily have suffered greatly; medical professionals suggest that the state of hypoxia (inadequate oxygen in the bodily tissues) produced by, for instance, smoke inhalation, can sometimes be experienced as mildly pleasurable.

26. "Black hole" is Slavoj Žižek's phrase in *The Metastases of Enjoyment: Six Essays on Women and Causality* (London: Verso, 1994), 96; Bruce Fink, *The Lacanian Subject: Between Language and Jouissance* (Princeton: Princeton Univ. Press, 1995), 95; emphasis in original.

27. Cf. Roland Barthes's distinction between texts of pleasure and those of bliss (jouissance): "Text of pleasure: the text that contents, fills, grants euphoria; the text that comes from culture and does not break with it, is linked to a *comfortable* practice of reading. Text of bliss: the text that imposes a state of loss, the text that discomforts (perhaps to the point of a certain boredom), unsettles the reader's historical, cultural, psychological assumptions, the consistency of his tastes, values, memories, brings to a crisis his relation with language" (*The Pleasure of the Text*, 14).

28. In *Seminar XX*, see Lacan's diagram of the relation between Imaginary, Symbolic, and Real (90) and his explanation of it (90–100).

29. Jonathan Culler, *On Deconstruction: Theory and Criticism after Structuralism* (Ithaca: Cornell Univ. Press, 1982), 43–64.

30. Diehl, *Staging Reform*, 193.

31. This complexity was registered by the confused response of viewers to the opening scene of the film *Elizabeth I*, which showed a martyr being burned at the stake. The passion and horror of the scene made it nearly impossible to distinguish acts of mercy from those of torment or to clarify who sympathized with whom.

32. Georges Bataille, *Erotism: Death and Sensuality*, 1957, trans. Mary Dalwood [San Francisco: City Lights, 1986], 191. Bataille's inarticulate violence that resists symbolic logic corresponds to the Lacanian Real. See Jean Dragon, "The Work of Alterity: Bataille and Lacan," *diacritics* 26, no. 2 (1996): 31–48. Dragon sees the Lacanian Real as closer to communicability than Bataille's notion of the unsignifiable (47).

33. Žižek, *The Metastases of Enjoyment*, 82n. 2. Žižek is following Lacan, who saw the association of violent fantasies with the victim's position to constitute a return to Freud's position in "Instincts and Their Vicissitudes," where sadism is seen as disavowed masochism (*Four Concepts*, 186).

34. Slavoj Žižek, *The Sublime Object of Ideology* (New York: Verso, 1989), 135.

35. Michel Foucault, *The History of Sexuality*. Vol. 1: *An Introduction*, trans. Robert Hurley (New York: Random-Vintage, 1990), 105. See also Bersani and Dutoit's account of how Caravaggio works against "the reduction of the sensual to the sexual" (Leo Bersani and Ulysse Dutoit, *Caravaggio's Secrets* [Cambridge: MIT Press, 1998], 79).

36. The 120 *Days* is rife with outrages committed against the church and things associated with religion; a comparably mild instance is the statute specifying that "it

is strictly forbidden to relieve oneself anywhere save in the chapel" (Marquis de Sade [Donatien Alphonse François de Sade], *The 120 Days of Sodom and Other Writings*, trans. Austryn Wainhouse and Richard Seaver [New York: Grove Press, 1966], 242).

37. Leopold von Sacher-Masoch, "A Childhood Memory and Reflections on the Novel," in *Masochism* (New York: Zone, 1989), 274.

38. *The Works of Thomas Nashe*, ed. Ronald B. McKerrow, 2 vols. (Oxford: Basil Blackwell, 1958), 2:315–16.

39. In the Induction to *The Unfortunate Traveller*, Nashe ridicules the monumental status of the *Acts and Monuments*, offering his own book as "lawful for anie whatsoever to play with false dice in a corner on the cover of this foresayd Acts and Monuments" (*Nashe*, 2:208).

40. Bruce R. Smith writes that Nashe has identified "a curious kind of pleasure to be taken in imagining oneself as the *victim* of violence" and finds in the "fluid boundary between victim and victimizer . . . the psychological dynamics of sadomasochism" ("Rape, Rap, Rupture, Rapture: R-rated Futures on the Global Market," *Textual Practice* 9, no. 3 (1995): 421–44, 439). In "Nashe's Pornographic Travels in the 'Sodom of Italy,'" Barbara Baines finds *The Unfortunate Traveller* to be "consistent in its sadism"; she compares the text at one point to a snuff film (paper delivered at the South Atlantic Modern Language Association, Atlanta, Nov. 1997).

41. Smith, "Rape, Rap, Rupture, Rapture," 438.

42. Jonathan V. Crewe, *Unredeemed Rhetoric: Thomas Nashe and the Scandal of Authorship* (Baltimore: Johns Hopkins Univ. Press, 1982), 75.

Chapter 4. *The Pornographic Economy of* Titus Andronicus

1. *London Daily Express*, 24 October 1955, cited by Alan Hughes, Introduction to *Titus Andronicus*, ed. Alan Hughes (New York: Cambridge Univ. Press, 1994), 43.

2. D. J. Palmer, "The Unspeakable in Pursuit of the Uneatable: Language and Action in *Titus Andronicus*," *Critical Quarterly* 14 (1972): 330.

3. J. C. Maxwell calls *Titus* "the one play of Shakespeare which could have left an intelligent contemporary in some doubt whether the author's truest bent was for the stage" (Introduction, *Titus Andronicus*, ed. J. C. Maxwell, The Arden Shakespeare [New York: Methuen, 1953], xxxvii). Frank Kermode emphasizes the difference between the original audience of *Titus Andronicus* and the more refined viewers of *King Lear* (*Shakespeare's Language* [London: Allen Lane-Penguin, 2000], 268).

4. Keir Elam, "'In what chapter of his bosom?': Reading Shakespeare's Bodies," in *Alternative Shakespeares*, ed. Terence Hawkes (New York: Routledge, 1996), 2:140–63, 162.

5. Jonathan Bate, ed., *Titus Andronicus*, The Arden Shakespeare, Third Series (New York: Routledge, 1995). Quotations from the play follow this edition and are noted parenthetically.

6. Montaigne goes on to explain this erotic taste, drawing on "ancient philosophy": "since the legs and thighs of lame women, because of their imperfection, do not receive the food that is their due, the result is that the genital parts, which are above, are fuller, better nourished, and more vigorous. Or else that, since this defect prevents exercise, those who are tainted by it dissipate their strength less and come more entire to the sports of Venus." "Of Cripples," in *The Complete Essays of Montaigne*, trans. Donald M. Frame (Stanford: Stanford Univ. Press, 1976), 791.

7. Kaja Silverman, "*Histoire d'O:* The Construction of a Female Subject," in *Pleasure and Danger: Exploring Female Sexuality*, ed. Carole S. Vance (Boston: Routledge & Kegan Paul, 1984), 345.

8. John H. Astington makes reference to some seventeenth-century examples in "Three Shakespearean Prints," *Shakespeare Quarterly* 47, no. 2 (summer 1996): 178–89, 185.

9. Wendy Steiner, *The Scandal of Pleasure: Art in an Age of Fundamentalism* (Chicago: Univ. of Chicago Press, 1995), 43.

10. Lynda Nead, *The Female Nude: Art, Obscenity, and Sexuality* (New York: Routledge, 1992), 27.

11. Roland Barthes, *Camera Lucida: Reflections on Photography*, trans. Richard Howard (New York: Hill & Wang, 1981), 59.

12. Frances Ferguson, "Pornography: The Theory," *Critical Inquiry* 21 (spring 1995): 682, 677.

13. See Catharine MacKinnon, *Only Words* (Cambridge: Harvard Univ. Press, 1993). As Albert H. Tricomi notes, *Titus Andronicus* is distinguished by "the literalness of its central metaphors"; he maintains that the play "investigates the chasm between the spoken word and the actual fact" ("The Aesthetics of Mutilation in 'Titus Andronicus,'" *Shakespeare Survey* 27 [1974]: 11, 13). Katharine Eisaman Maus observes more generally that "the early Shakespeare seems characteristically to rehabilitate the conventional language of desire by unleashing its violent potential" ("Taking Tropes Seriously: Language and Violence in Shakespeare's *Rape of Lucrece*," *Shakespeare Quarterly* 37, no. 1 [1986]: 77–78).

14. Of course, theater in general flirts with the boundary between representation and reality by arousing emotional and visceral responses in its viewers. As Wendy Steiner observes, "Laughing, crying, screaming, and accelerated heartrate are all 'real' effects produced by art," so that, for her, "pornography ceases to be a special case" (68). Although I think Steiner moves too quickly to erase the distinction between

pornography and other forms of exciting material, given that the sexual charge can activate complex psychic effects, she is nevertheless right to see viewer responses of all types as collapsing the gap between staged fiction and experiential reality.

15. Thomas Heywood, *An Apology for Actors*, 1612 (reprint, New York: Garland, 1973), Sig. B3v–B4.

16. Judith Butler, *Excitable Speech: A Politics of the Performative* (New York: Routledge, 1997), 77–82. Further references will be noted parenthetically.

17. Lynda E. Boose relates the historical occurrence of the Bishops' Ban in 1599 to the distinctive qualities of Jacobean theater, suggesting that theater became more "Italianized, sexualized, politicized, spectacularized, and . . . radicalized" after 1599, when writers such as Middleton and Marston turned their interest in sexual and satirical violence from print to dramatic mediums ("The 1599 Bishops' Ban, Elizabethan Pornography, and the Sexualization of the Jacobean Stage," in *Enclosure Acts: Sexuality, Property, and Culture in Early Modern England*, ed. Richard Burt and John Michael Archer [Ithaca: Cornell Univ. Press, 1994], 198).

18. Bruce R. Smith, "Rape, Rap, Rupture, Rapture: R-rated Futures on the Global Market," *Textual Practice* 9, no. 3 (1995): 421–44, 422.

19. Walter Kendrick, *The Secret Museum: Pornography in Modern Culture* (Berkeley: Univ. of Calif. Press, 1987), xiii; Lynn Hunt, "Introduction," in *The Invention of Pornography: Obscenity and the Origins of Modernity, 1500–1800* (New York: Zone, 1993), 10.

20. Henr[y] Peacham, *Graphice, or The Most Auncient and Excellent Art of Drawing and Limming* (London, 1612), 9, 9–10.

21. Ibid., 10; David O. Frantz, *Festum Voluptatis: A Study of Renaissance Erotica* (Columbus: Ohio State Univ. Press, 1989), 141.

22. G. Vasari, *Le vits de'più eccellenti pittori ed architettori* (1568), ed. G. Milanesi, 9 vols. (Florence, 1878–85), 4:188, quoted in David Freedberg, *The Power of Images: Studies in the History and Theory of Response* (Chicago: Univ. of Chicago Press, 1989), 347.

23. Later the painting was sold to the king of France, confirming its status as "a work of art" rather than a devotional item (Freedberg, *The Power of Images*, 347).

24. Peter Webb, *The Erotic Arts* (New York: Farrar, Straus & Giroux, 1983), 125–26, 126.

25. T. J. B. Spencer, "Shakespeare and the Elizabethan Romans," *Shakespeare Survey* 10 (1957): 32.

26. Barbara Parker makes a similar claim about the Rome of Shakespeare's *Julius Caesar*. See her "The Whore of Babylon and Shakespeare's *Julius Caesar*," *Studies in English Literature 1500–1900* 35 (1995): 251–69. An even stronger example occurs in *Cymbeline*, where first-century Britons travel to what appears to be sixteenth-century Italy.

27. See Bate, *Titus Andronicus*, 17–20.

28. Leopold von Sacher-Masoch, "Appendix I: A Childhood Memory and Reflections on the Novel," in *Masochism* (New York: Zone, 1993), 274.

29. "The Interpretation of Dreams," *SE*, 4:262–66.

30. Central texts for Freud's development of the concept of identification are "The Ego and the Id," "Mourning and Melancholia," and "Group Psychology and the Analysis of the Ego."

31. See Sarah Kofman, *The Enigma of Woman: Woman in Freud's Writings*, trans. Catherine Porter (Ithaca: Cornell Univ. Press, 1985), and Madelon Sprengnether, *The Spectral Mother: Freud, Feminism, and Psychoanalysis* (Ithaca: Cornell Univ. Press, 1990).

32. Slavoj Žižek, *Looking Awry: An Introduction to Jacques Lacan through Popular Culture* (Cambridge: MIT Press, 1991).

33. Stanley Cavell, *Disowning Knowledge in Six Plays of Shakespeare* (New York: Cambridge Univ. Press, 1987), 3. Further references will be noted parenthetically.

34. Timothy Murray, Review of *Disowning Knowledge*, *Modern Language Notes* 105, no. 5 (Dec. 1990): 1083, 1085. Although Cavell himself acknowledges the "male inflection" of his essay on *King Lear* (Cavell, *Disowning Knowledge*, x), as well as the gendered working of skepticism, Murray's point about the masculinist bias of his readings is nevertheless a strong critique.

35. Cavell, *Disowning Knowledge*, 206. He structures his essay on *The Winter's Tale* around the fact that at its end "a dead five- or six-year-old boy remains unaccounted for" (193).

36. In a thoughtful response to an earlier version of this essay prepared for the World Shakespeare Congress in Los Angeles, April 1996, David Willbern described Lavinia as a "cartoon" who does not achieve full characterological status.

37. Albert H. Tricomi, "The Aesthetics of Mutilation in *Titus Andronicus*," *Shakespeare Survey* 27 (1974): 17.

38. E.g., William H. Desmonde connects the play's ritual actions with the Freudian concept of the primal crime ("The Ritual Origin of Shakespeare's *Titus Andronicus*," *International Journal of Psychoanalysis* 36 [1955]: 61–65; reprint, in M. D. Faber, *The Design Within: Psychoanalytic Approaches to Shakespeare* [New York: Science House, 1970], 23–31).

39. David Willbern, "Rape and Revenge in *Titus Andronicus*," *English Literary Renaissance* 8 (1978): 171, 175.

40. E.g., Mary Laughlin Fawcett considers Lavinia the "central emblem" of the play's meditation on language, calling her a text that the audience "must learn to read." Fawcett compares Lavinia's situation to that of the author, since the character "finds the language of the fathers (staff and hand) and recreates the image of writing

in her act of inscribing." In spite of her attention to Lavinia's voicelessness and to the phenomenology of language, Fawcett's speculations retain a classically Freudian framework: language is seen as an appropriation of castration; the severed hand carried in Lavinia's mouth becomes "an enlargement (almost an erection) of the tongue-root" ("Arms/Words/Tears: Language and the Body in *Titus Andronicus,*" *ELH* 50 [1983]: 265, 266, 262).

41. Žižek, *Looking Awry,* 120, 121.

42. Marion Wynne-Davies, "'The Swallowing Womb': Consumed and Consuming Women in *Titus Andronicus,*" in *The Matter of Difference: Materialist Feminist Criticism of Shakespeare,* ed. Valerie Wayne (Ithaca: Cornell Univ. Press, 1991), 134. Wynne-Davies is discussing both Lavinia and Tamora.

43. Sara Eaton, "Defacing the Feminine in Renaissance Tragedy," in Wayne, *The Matter of Difference,* 187, 189.

44. In "Visual Pleasure and Narrative Cinema," Mulvey famously neglected to theorize feminine response to classic cinema. See "Afterthoughts on 'Visual Pleasure and Narrative Cinema'; Inspired by King Vidor's *Duel in the Sun* (1946)," in Mulvey's *Visual and Other Pleasures* (Bloomington: Indiana Univ. Press, 1989), 29–38.

45. Kaja Silverman, *Male Subjectivity at the Margins* (New York: Routledge, 1992), 201–13.

46. Bate, *Titus Andronicus,* 2.

47. Nicholas Brooke, *Shakespeare's Early Tragedies* (London: Methuen, 1968), 16, cited in Bate, *Titus Andronicus,* 189n.

48. Bate, *Titus Andronicus,* 36.

49. Willbern, who identifies the "central force behind Lavinia's fate" as "sexual desire," also notes the buildup of sexual tension, although he sees it as displaced onto the symbolism of the pit: "Any unconscious expectation of Lavinia's ravishment, frustrated to an extent by its apparent enactment offstage, is satisfied by its symbolic substitute," the attack on Bassianus in 2.3 and the description of "the loathsome pit" (Willbern, "Rape and Revenge," 173, 170).

50. Jonathan Sawday connects the Renaissance poetic trope of the blazon with a male quest to dissect the female body, and he identifies a "scopic desire" in the anatomists' wish to see the hidden parts of women's bodies (*The Body Emblazoned: Dissection and the Human Body in Renaissance Culture* [New York: Routledge, 1995], 191, 211).

51. Willbern sees the wounded Lavinia as "a living symbol" for the pit, which itself has "over-determined symbolic significance as vagina, womb, tomb, and mouth" ("Rape and Revenge," 173, 169).

52. Stephanie H. Jed, *Chaste Thinking. The Rape of Lucretia and the Birth of Humanism* (Bloomington: Indiana Univ. Press, 1989), 10.

53. "Rape is not a crime of irrational, impulsive, uncontrollable lust, but is a deliberate, hostile, violent act of degradation and possession on the part of a would-be conqueror, designed to intimidate and inspire fear." Susan Brownmiller, *Against Our Will: Men, Women and Rape* (New York: Simon & Schuster, 1975), 391. On rape as property crime, see p. 18. For a critique of the liberal view of rape, see also Catharine A. MacKinnon, "Feminism, Marxism, Method, and the State: Toward Feminist Jurisprudence," *Signs: Journal of Women in Culture and Society* 8, no. 4 (1983): 635–58. The definition of rape is disputed in *Titus Andronicus* as well: see 1.1.408–13. See Sid Ray, "'Rape, I fear, was root of thy annoy': The Politics of Consent in *Titus Andronicus,*" *Shakespeare Quarterly* 49, no. 1 (1998): 22–39.

54. Bate, *Titus Andronicus,* 64–65, 63.

55. Linda Williams, *Hard Core: Power, Pleasure, and the 'Frenzy of the Visible'* (Berkeley and Los Angeles: Univ. of California Press, 1989), 227.

56. Alan C. Dessen, *Shakespeare in Performance:* Titus Andronicus (Manchester: Manchester Univ. Press; New York: St. Martin's, 1989), 60; Bate, *Titus Andronicus,* 62–63.

57. Žižek, *Looking Awry,* 110.

58. Willbern, "Rape and Revenge," 173.

59. Williams plots the shifting identifications of viewers of pornographic films (*Hard Core,* 195–228).

60. Smith, "Rape, Rap, Rupture, Rapture," 436, 437, 439.

Chapter 5. Form, Characters, Viewers, and Ford's The Broken Heart

1. M. L. Lyon and J. M. Barbalet, "Society's Body: Emotion and the 'Somatization' of Social Theory," in *Embodiment and Experience: The Existential Ground of Culture and Self,* ed. Thomas J. Csordas (New York: Cambridge Univ. Press, 1994), 48.

2. Stephen Orgel, "The Play of Conscience," in *Performativity and Performance,* ed. Andrew Parker and Eve Kosofsky Sedgwick (New York: Routledge, 1995), 136–37.

3. See A. D. Nuttall, *Why Does Tragedy Give Pleasure?* (Oxford: Clarendon, 1996), for a review of this argument. Nuttall himself understands the doctrine's relevance to the Renaissance in terms of a Stoic drive to eliminate passion: Emotions "are what is washed away, or purged. *They* are the obstacle, the dirt, the obscurity" (14).

4. Orgel, "The Play of Conscience," 144.

5. For the early moderns as well as for Aristotle, the emotions had their cognitive aspects. See Velvet Yates, "A Sexual Model of Catharsis," *Apeiron: A Journal for Ancient Philosophy and Science* 31, no. 1 (March 1998): 35–58, 50.

6. Gail Kern Paster, *The Body Embarrassed: Drama and the Disciplines of Shame in Early Modern England* (Ithaca: Cornell Univ. Press, 1993).

7. Quotations from Ford's plays refer to *'Tis Pity She's a Whore and Other Plays*, ed. Marion Lomax (New York: Oxford Univ. Press, 1995).

8. Michael Neill, "Ford's Unbroken Art: The Moral Design of 'The Broken Heart,'" *Modern Language Review* 75 (1980): 249–68, esp. 259.

9. See, e.g., Mark Stavig, *John Ford and the Traditional Moral Order* (Madison: Univ. of Wisconsin Press, 1968), and, in a more complex argument, Reed Barbour, "John Ford and Resolve," *Studies in Philology* 86, no. 3 (1989): 341–66.

10. Lyon and Barbalet, "Society's Body," 56.

11. See, e.g., H. J. Oliver, *The Problem of John Ford* (Melbourne: Melbourne Univ. Press, 1955), 2–3; Roger T. Burbridge, "The Moral Vision of Ford's *The Broken Heart*," *Studies in English Literature 1500–1900* 10 (1970): 397–407.

12. T. S. Eliot, *Selected Essays* (New York: Harcourt, 1964), 180; Robert B. Heilman, "The Perverse: An Aspect of Ford's Art," in *'Concord in Discord': The Plays of John Ford, 1586–1986*, ed. Donald K. Anderson Jr. (New York: AMS, 1986), 27–48; T. B. Tomlinson, *A Study of Elizabethan and Jacobean Tragedy* (Cambridge: Cambridge Univ. Press, 1964), 265.

13. Rowland Wymer, *Webster and Ford* (New York: St. Martin's, 1995), 86–87. As for the chronological basis for charges of decadence, Wymer understands "Ford's self-conscious reworkings of previous plays" as "part of a continuing struggle to achieve authentic emotional expression despite the suffocating pressure of the 'already written'" (91).

14. See Harriet Hawkins, "Mortality, Morality, and Modernity in *The Broken Heart*: Some Dramatic and Critical Counter-arguments," in *John Ford: Critical Re-visions*, ed. Michael Neill (New York: Cambridge Univ. Press, 1988), 129–52, and Ronald Huebert, *John Ford: Baroque English Dramatist* (Montreal: McGill-Queen's Univ. Press, 1977). For the argument that not only are Ford's tragedies meant to arouse emotional responses but such responses may involve a moral dimension, see Wymer, *Webster and Ford*, 10–15.

15. On the last point, see esp. Michael Neill, "Ending *The Broken Heart*," in his *Issues of Death: Mortality and Identity in English Renaissance Tragedy* (Oxford: Clarendon, 1997), 354–74.

16. Lomax, Introduction, in *'Tis Pity She's a Whore*, xiii; Hawkins, "Mortality, Morality, and Modernity," 135, 140.

17. Critics who comment on the tableau structure, associating it with the emblem tradition, include Lisa Hopkins, *John Ford's Political Theatre* (Manchester: Manchester Univ. Press, 1994), 81–82, 163; Stavig, *John Ford*, 145; Neill, "Ford's Unbroken Art," 250–51.

18. Maurice Merleau-Ponty, *Phenomenology of Perception*, trans. Colin Smith (London: Routledge & Kegan Paul, 1962), 146, 186.

19. See Jonathan Sawday, *The Body Emblazoned: Dissection and the Human Body in Renaissance Culture* (New York: Routledge, 1995), esp. 145–59; Scott Manning Stevens, "Sacred Heart and Secular Brain," in *The Body in Parts: Fantasies of Corporeality in Early Modern Europe*, ed. David Hillman and Carla Mazzio (New York: Routledge, 1997), 268–69; Roger Smith, "Self-reflection and the Self," in *Rewriting the Self: Histories from the Renaissance to the Present*, ed. Roy Porter (New York: Routledge, 1997), 49–57.

20. Merleau-Ponty, *Phenomenology of Perception*, 146.

21. Roger Smith points out that discussions of personhood by Descartes and Locke were understood in theological terms by their original audiences ("Self-reflection and the Self," 50).

22. Merleau-Ponty, *Phenomenology of Perception*, 164.

23. David Hillman, "Visceral Knowledge," in *The Body in Parts: Fantasies of Corporeality in Early Modern Europe*, ed. David Hillman and Carla Mazzio (New York: Routledge, 1997), 85.

24. Louis L. Martz, *The Poetry of Meditation* (New Haven: Yale Univ. Press, 1954), 75, 78.

25. Interestingly, the only surviving contemporary reference to Ford's art is a couplet by the Catholic poet Richard Crashaw: "Thou cheat'st us, Ford; mak'st one seem two by art: / What is Love's Sacrifice but The Broken Heart?" cited in Hopkins, *John Ford's Political Theatre*, 124.

26. Ibid., 123.

27. Ibid., 14.

28. *The English Poems of George Herbert*, ed. C. A. Patrides (London: Dent, 1974): "Sion," "The Dawning," "The Size," "The Discharge," "Longing," "Confession," "An Offering," "Grace," "Longing."

29. Stevens, "Sacred Heart and Secular Brain," 271. Even in secular discourse the heart was granted intellectual ability, as in Shakespeare's *Rape of Lucrece* (ll. 442–45).

30. Elaine Scarry, *The Body in Pain: The Making and Unmaking of the World* (New York: Oxford Univ. Press, 1985), 203–4.

31. *Freudian Body*, esp. 107. See also Bersani's *The Culture of Redemption* (Cambridge: Harvard Univ. Press, 1990), esp. 22, 37–38.

32. Gweneth Whitteridge, Introduction, *An Anatomical Disputation Concerning the Movement of the Heart and Blood in Living Creatures*, by William Harvey (Oxford: Blackwell Scientific Publications, 1976), lii.

33. John B. deC. M. Saunders and Charles Donald O'Malley, Introduction to *The Bloodletting Letter of 1539, by Andreas Vesalius* (New York: Henry Schuman, [1947]), 19–20. Charles Estienne first mentioned venous valves in 1539; Hieronymus Fabricus later claimed to have discovered them in 1574 (20, 33). Realdo Colombo [Columbus]

extended this knowledge with description, but not proof, of pulmonary transit based on the action of the heart's valves (*De re anatomica* [Venice, 1559], 175–80, cited in Robert G. Frank Jr. *Harvey and the Oxford Physiologists: Scientific Ideas and Social Interaction* [Berkeley and Los Angeles: Univ. of California Press, 1980], 10; Saunders and O'Malley, *The Bloodletting Letter*, 27).

34. Stevens attributes seventeenth-century insistence on the heart as the location of the soul to a Counter-Reformation response to scientific innovation ("Sacred Heart and Secular Brain," 271–72).

35. Owsei Temkin, *Galenism: Rise and Decline of a Medical Philosophy* (Ithaca: Cornell Univ. Press, 1973), 143.

36. Timothy Bright, *A Treatise of Melancholie* (London: Thomas Vautrollier, 1586; reprint, New York: Columbia Univ. Press, 1940), 66, 87; Helkiah Crooke, *Microcosmographia: A Description of the Body of Man* (London: Jaggard, 1618), 367.

37. Thomas Wright, *The Passions of the Minde in Generall* (London: Printed by Valentine Simmes for Walter Burre, 1604), 33, 33, 45.

38. S. Blaine Ewing, *Burtonian Melancholy in the Plays of John Ford* (Princeton: Princeton Univ. Press, 1940). Ewing, discovering in Ford's plays "a gallery of melancholy types" (92), offers a catalogue rather than an analysis.

39. Whitteridge, *An Anatomical Disputation*, xvii; see also Paster, *The Body Embarrassed*, 69–70.

40. Paster, *The Body Embarrassed*, 81.

41. Merleau-Ponty, *Phenomenology of Perception*, 164.

42. As when, for instance, Donald K. Anderson Jr. suggests that "she starves for lack of love" ("The Heart and the Banquet: Imagery in Ford's *Tis Pity* and *The Broken Heart*," *Studies in English Literature 1500–1900* 2 [1962]: 215).

43. Robert Burton, *The Anatomy of Melancholy*, 1620, ed. Thomas C. Faulkner, Nicolas K. Kiessling, and Rhonda L. Blair, 6 vols. (Oxford: Clarendon, 1989–2000), 1.2.5.1; 1:372; Wright, *The Passions of the Minde*, 64.

44. Nicholas Gyer, *The English Phlebotomy* (London: Andrew Mansell, 1592), 36.

45. Bright, *A Treatise of Melancholie*, 269, 271, 270.

46. Burton, *The Anatomy of Melancholy*, 3.2.5.1; 3:206; Jacques Ferrand, *A Treatise on Lovesickness*, trans. and ed. Donald A. Beecher and Massimo Ciavolella (Syracuse: Syracuse Univ. Press, 1990), 356.

47. Gyer, *The English Phlebotomy*, "A profitable observation of the blood extracted" (chap. 22) and "The Epistle Dedicotorie."

48. Lucinda McCray Beier, *Sufferers and Healers: The Experience of Illness in Seventeenth-Century England* (New York: Routledge & Kegan Paul, 1987), 62.

49. Huebert, who notes "the masochistic strain in Ford's tragedy," observes that

Orgilus "wishes to die slowly, so that he can savour each moment of this unique experience as long as possible" (*John Ford*, 48, 52).

50. Richard Madelaine, "'Sensationalism' and 'Melodrama' in Ford's Plays," in *John Ford: Critical Re-visions*, ed. Michael Neill (New York: Cambridge Univ. Press, 1988), 39.

51. "The sign of phlebotomy is menstruation's cultural inversion" (Paster, *The Body Embarrassed*, 83).

52. R. J. Kauffman, "Ford's 'Waste Land': *The Broken Heart*," *Renaissance Drama*, New Series III (1970): 167–87, esp. 184; Clifford Leech, *John Ford and the Drama of His Time* (London: Chatto & Windus, 1957), 13.

53. Neill also notes parallels with *Antony and Cleopatra* ("Ending *The Broken Heart*," 362–63, 367–68).

54. Burton, *Anatomy of Melancholy*, "Democritus Junior to the Reader"; 1:56.

55. See Scarry, *The Body in Pain*, 11–12.

56. Hopkins, *John Ford's Political Theatre*, 154.

57. Burbridge complains of Penthea's "morbid intensification" of her situation ("The Moral Vision," 403).

58. Along these lines, Wymer suggests that Penthea's self-destructiveness results from displaced anger toward Ithocles (*Webster and Ford*, 112–13).

59. Stanton B. Garner Jr., *Bodied Spaces: Phenomenology in Contemporary Performance* (Ithaca: Cornell Univ. Press, 1994), 44, 45.

60. Anne Barton, "Oxymoron and the Structure of Ford's 'The Broken Heart,'" *Essays & Studies*, n.s., 33 (1980): 70–94. See also Neill, "Ford's Unbroken Art" and "Ending *The Broken Heart*."

61. Paster, *The Body Embarrassed*, 132–41.

62. Bruce R. Smith, "Rape, Rap, Rupture, Rapture: R-rated Futures on the Global Market," *Textual Practice* 9, no. 3 (1995): 429, 435–36.

63. *Coldness*, 33–35. Deleuze's connection between narrative suspense and "physical suspension (the hero is hung up, crucified or suspended)" (33) also has relevance for Ithocles' being caught in the trick chair and Orgilus's insistence on performing his death rites while standing.

64. Burbridge, "The Moral Vision," 399.

65. For moral opposition, see Mark Edmundson, *Nightmare on Main Street: Angels, Sadomasochism, and the Culture of Gothic* (Cambridge: Harvard Univ. Press, 1997). For a more rigorous, but also ultimately moralistic, feminist critique of masochism, see Suzanne R. Stewart, *Sublime Surrender: Male Masochism at the Fin-de-Siècle* (Ithaca: Cornell Univ. Press, 1998). For a searching analysis of masochism as a reworking of social violence, see John K. Noyes, *The Mastery of Submission: Inventions of Masochism* (Ithaca:

Cornell Univ. Press, 1997). For an attempt to see sadomasochism as a performative displacement of violence, see Lynda Hart, *Between the Body and the Flesh: Performing Sadomasochism* (New York: Columbia Univ. Press, 1998).

66. Dave Hickey, *The Invisible Dragon: Four Essays on Beauty* (Los Angeles: Art Issues Press, 1993), 35.

Conclusion

1. Richard Boothby, *Death and Desire: Psychoanalytic Theory in Lacan's Return to Freud* (New York: Routledge, 1991), 177.

)(

Bibliography

Aers, David. "A Whisper in the Ear of Early Modernists; or, Reflections on Literary Critics Writing the 'History of the Subject.'" In *Culture and History, 1350–1600: Essays on English Communitites, Identities, and Writing*, edited by David Aers, 177–202. Detroit: Wayne State Univ. Press, 1992.

Anderson, Donald K., Jr. "The Heart and the Banquet: Imagery in Ford's *Tis Pity* and *The Broken Heart*." *Studies in English Literature 1500–1900* 2 (1962): 209–17.

Arnold, Martin. "Making Books." *New York Times*, 18 Feb. 1999.

Astington, John H. "Three Shakespearean Prints." *Shakespeare Quarterly* 47, no. 2 (1996): 178–89.

Aston, Margaret, and Elizabeth Ingram. "The Iconography of the *Acts and Monuments*." In *John Foxe and the English Reformation*, edited by David Loades, 66–142.

Baines, Barbara. "Nashe's Pornographic Travels in the 'Sodom' of Italy." Paper presented at the meeting of the South Atlantic Modern Language Association, Atlanta, November 1997.

Barbour, Reed. "John Ford and Resolve." *Studies in Philology* 86, no. 3 (1989): 341–66.

Barker, Francis. *The Culture of Violence: Essays on Tragedy and History*. Chicago: Univ. of Chicago Press, 1993.

———. *The Tremulous Private Body: Essays on Subjection*. London: Methuen, 1984.

Barnes, Barnabe. *Parthenophil and Parthenophe*, edited by Victor A. Doyno. Carbondale: Southern Illinois Univ. Press, 1971.

Barroll, Leeds. *Politics, Plague, and Shakespeare's Theater: The Stuart Years*. Ithaca: Cornell Univ. Press, 1991.

Bartlett, Ross. "John Foxe as Hagiographer: The Question Revisited." *Sixteenth Century Journal* 26 (1995): 771–89.

Barthes, Roland. *Camera Lucida: Reflections on Photography*, translated by Richard Howard. New York: Hill & Wang, 1981.

———. "From Work to Text." *Textual Strategies: Perspectives in Post-structuralist Criticism*, edited by Josué V. Harari, 73–81. Ithaca: Cornell Univ. Press, 1979.

———. *The Pleasure of the Text*, translated by Richard Miller. New York: Farrar,
Straus & Giroux, 1975.

———. *Sade / Fourier / Loyola*, translated by Richard Miller. Baltimore: Johns
Hopkins Univ. Press, 1976.

Barton, Anne. "Oxymoron and the Structure of Ford's 'The Broken Heart.'" *Essays
& Studies*, n.s., 33 (1980): 70–94.

Bataille, Georges. *Erotism: Death and Sensuality*, 1957, translated by Mary Dalwood. San
Francisco: City Lights, 1986.

Baumeister, Roy F. *Masochism and the Self.* Hillsdale, N.J.: Erlbaum, 1989.

Beauvoir, Simone de. "Must We Burn Sade?" translated by Annette Michelson. In *The
120 Days of Sodom and Other Writings*, by Marquis de Sade, translated by Austryn
Wainhouse and Richard Seaver, 3–64. New York: Grove Press, 1966.

Beier, Lucinda McCray. *Sufferers and Healers: The Experience of Illness in Seventeenth-Century
England.* New York: Routledge & Kegan Paul, 1987.

Bellamy, Elizabeth J. "Discourses of Impossibility: Can Psychoanalysis Be Political?" *diacritics* 23, no. 1 (1993): 24–38.

———. *Translations of Power: Narcissism and the Unconscious in Epic History.* Ithaca: Cornell Univ. Press, 1992.

Belling, Catherine. "Hamlet's Heart, Looking Back." Paper circulated in the Historical Phenomenology section at the meeting of the Shakespeare Association
of America, San Francisco, April 1999.

Belsey, Catherine. *The Subject of Tragedy.* London: Methuen, 1985.

Bersani, Leo. *The Culture of Redemption.* Cambridge: Harvard Univ. Press, 1990.

———. *The Freudian Body: Psychoanalysis and Art.* New York: Columbia Univ. Press,
1986.

———. *Homos.* Cambridge: Harvard Univ. Press, 1995.

Bersani, Leo, and Ulysse Dutoit. *Caravaggio's Secrets.* Cambridge: MIT Press, 1998.

Betteridge, Tom. "From Prophetic to Apocalyptic: John Foxe and the Writing of
History." In *John Foxe and the English Reformation*, edited by David Loades,
210–32.

Bok, Sissela. *Mayhem: Violence as Public Entertainment.* Reading, Mass.: Addison-Wesley,
1998.

Boose, Lynda E. "The 1599 Bishops' Ban, Elizabethan Pornography, and the Sexualization of the Jacobean Stage." In *Enclosure Acts: Sexuality, Property, and Culture*

in Early Modern England, edited by Richard Burt and John Michael Archer, 185–200. Ithaca: Cornell Univ. Press, 1994.

Booth, Stephen. King Lear, Macbeth, *Indefinition, and Tragedy.* New Haven: Yale Univ. Press, 1983.

Boothby, Richard. *Death and Desire: Psychoanalytic Theory in Lacan's Return to Freud.* New York: Routledge, 1991.

Borch-Jacobsen, Michel. *The Freudian Subject,* translated by Catherine Porter. Stanford: Stanford Univ. Press, 1988.

Braden, Gordon. "Love and Fame: The Petrarchan Career." In *Pragmatism's Freud: The Moral Disposition of Psychoanalysis,* edited by Joseph H. Smith and William Kerrigan, 126–58. Baltimore: Johns Hopkins Univ. Press, 1986.

Breitenberg, Mark. *Anxious Masculinity in Early Modern England.* Cambridge: Cambridge Univ. Press, 1996.

———. "The Flesh Made Word: Foxe's *Acts and Monuments.*" *Renaissance and Reformation / Renaissance et Réforme* 25, no. 4 (1989): 381–407.

Brennan, Teresa. *History after Lacan.* New York: Routledge, 1993.

Bright, Timothy. *A Treatise of Melancholie.* London: Thomas Vautrollier, 1586. Reprint, New York: Columbia Univ. Press, 1940.

Brooke, Nicholas. *Shakespeare's Early Tragedies.* London: Methuen, 1968.

Brownmiller, Susan. *Against Our Will: Men, Women, and Rape.* New York: Simon & Schuster, 1975.

Burbridge, Roger T. "The Moral Vision of Ford's *The Broken Heart.*" *Studies in English Literature 1500–1900* 10 (1970): 397–407.

Burckhardt, Jacob. *The Civilization of the Renaissance in Italy,* translated by S. G. C. Middlemore, 2 vols. New York: Harper-Colophon, 1958.

Burton, Robert. *The Anatomy of Melancholy,* 1620, edited by Thomas C. Faulkner, Nicolas K. Kiessling, and Rhonda L. Blair. 6 vols. Oxford: Clarendon, 1989–2000.

Butler, Judith. *Excitable Speech: A Politics of the Performative.* New York: Routledge, 1997.

Bynum, Caroline Walker. *The Resurrection of the Body in Western Christianity, 200–1336.* New York: Columbia Univ. Press, 1995.

Callaghan, Dympna. "Body Problems." *Shakespeare Studies* 29 (2001): 68–71.

Cavell, Stanley. *Disowning Knowledge in Six Plays of Shakespeare.* New York: Cambridge Univ. Press, 1987.

Clark, Michael P., ed. *Revenge of the Aesthetic: The Place of Literature in Theory Today.* Berkeley and Los Angeles: Univ. of California Press, 2000.

Coeffeteau, N[icholas]. *A Table of Humane Passions,* translated by Edw[ard] Grimeston. [London]: Nicholas Okes, 1621.

Cohen, Derek. *Shakespeare's Culture of Violence.* New York: St. Martin's, 1993.

Colombo [Columbus], Realdo. *De re anatomica.* Venice, 1559.

Copjec, Joan. *Read My Desire: Lacan against the Historicists.* Cambridge: MIT Press, 1994.

Crewe, Jonathan V. *Hidden Designs: The Critical Profession and Renaissance Literature.* New York: Methuen, 1986.

————. "Spenser's Saluage Petrarchanism: *Pensées Sauvages* in *The Faerie Queene.*" *Bucknell Review* 35, no. 2 (1992): 89–103.

————. *Unredeemed Rhetoric: Thomas Nashe and the Scandal of Authorship.* Baltimore: Johns Hopkins Univ. Press, 1982.

Crooke, Helkiah. *Microcosmographia: A Description of the Body of Man.* London: Jaggard, 1618.

Culler, Jonathan. *On Deconstruction: Theory and Criticism after Structuralism.* Ithaca: Cornell Univ. Press, 1982.

Daniel, Samuel. *Delia: Contayning certayne Sonnets: with the complaint of Rosamond.* London: Printed by I.C. for Simon Waterson, 1592.

Dean, Carolyn. *The Self and Its Pleasures: Bataille, Lacan, and the History of the Decentered Subject.* Ithaca: Cornell Univ. Press, 1992.

Dean, Tim, Hal Foster, and Kaja Silverman. "A Conversation with Leo Bersani." *October* 82 (fall 1997): 3–16.

De Grazia, Margreta. "1590s: Fin-de-Siècle Renaissance England." *Fins de Siècle: English Poetry in 1590, 1690, 1790, 1890, 1990,* edited by Elaine Scarry. Baltimore: Johns Hopkins Univ. Press, 1995.

Deleuze, Gilles. "Coldness and Cruelty." In *Masochism.* New York: Zone, 1991.

Desmonde, William H. "The Ritual Origin of Shakespeare's *Titus Andronicus.*" *International Journal of Psychoanalysis* 36 (1955): 61–65. Reprint in *The Design Within: Psychoanalytic Approaches to Shakespeare,* edited by M. D. Faber, 23–31. New York: Science House, 1970.

Dessen, Alan C. *Shakespeare in Performance:* Titus Andronicus. Manchester: Manchester Univ. Press; New York: St. Martin's Press, 1989.

Diehl, Huston. *Staging Reform, Reforming the Stage: Protestantism and Popular Theater in Early Modern England.* Ithaca: Cornell Univ. Press, 1997.

Dollimore, Jonathan. *Death, Desire, and Loss in Western Culture.* New York: Routledge, 1998.

————. *Radical Tragedy.* Brighton: Harvester, 1984; Chicago: Univ. of Chicago Press, 1989.

Donne, John. *The Poems of John Donne,* edited by Herbert J. C. Grierson. Oxford: Clarendon, 1912.

Dragon, Jean. "The Work of Alterity: Bataille and Lacan." *diacritics* 26, no. 2 (1996): 31–48.

Drayton, Michael. *Idea. In Sixtie Three Sonnets,* in his *Poems.* London: John Smethwicke, 1619.

————. *Ideas Mirrour. Amours in Quatorzains.* London: Printed by James Roberts, 1594.

Dubrow, Heather. *Echoes of Desire: English Petrarchism and Its Counterdiscourses.* Ithaca: Cornell Univ. Press, 1995.

Earl, James W. "Identification and Catharsis." *Pragmatism's Freud: The Moral Disposition of Psychoanalysis,* edited by Joseph H. Smith and William Kerrigan, 79–92. Baltimore: Johns Hopkins Univ. Press, 1986.

Eaton, Sara. "Defacing the Feminine in Renaissance Tragedy." In *The Matter of Difference: Materialist Feminist Criticism of Shakespeare,* edited by Valerie Wayne, 181–98. Ithaca: Cornell Univ. Press, 1991.

Edmundson, Mark. *Nightmare on Main Street: Angels, Sadomasochism, and the Culture of Gothic.* Cambridge: Harvard Univ. Press, 1997.

Elam, Keir. "'In what chapter of his bosom?': Reading Shakespeare's Bodies." In *Alternative Shakespeares,* edited by Terence Hawkes, 2:140–63. New York: Routledge, 1996.

Eliot, George. *The Mill on the Floss.* New York: Penguin, 1979.

Eliot, T. S. *Selected Essays.* New York: Harcourt, 1964.

Emerson, Ralph Waldo. *The Collected Works of Ralph Waldo Emerson,* edited by Joseph Slater, Alfred R. Ferguson, and Jean Ferguson Carr. Cambridge: Harvard-Belknap, 1979.

Enders, Jody. *The Medieval Theater of Cruelty: Rhetoric, Memory, Violence.* Ithaca: Cornell Univ. Press, 1999.

Enterline, Lynn. *The Rhetoric of the Body from Ovid to Shakespeare.* Cambridge: Cambridge Univ. Press, 2000.

————. *The Tears of Narcissus: Melancholia and Masculinity in Early Modern Writing.* Stanford: Stanford Univ. Press, 1995.

Estrin, Barbara L. *Laura: Uncovering Gender and Genre in Wyatt, Donne, and Marvell.* Durham: Duke Univ. Press, 1994.

Ewing, S. Blaine. *Burtonian Melancholy in the Plays of John Ford.* Princeton: Princeton Univ. Press, 1940.

Fawcett, Mary Laughlin. "Arms/Words/Tears: Language and the Body in *Titus Andronicus.*" *ELH* 50 (1983): 261–77.

Felch, Susan. "Shaping the Reader in the *Acts and Monuments.*" In *John Foxe and the English Reformation,* edited by David Loades, 52–65.

Ferguson, Frances. "Pornography: The Theory." *Critical Inquiry* 21 (spring 1995): 670–95.

Ferrand, Jacques. *A Treatise on Lovesickness,* translated and edited by Donald A. Beecher and Massimo Ciavolella. Syracuse: Syracuse Univ. Press, 1990.

Fineman, Joel. *Shakespeare's Perjured Eye: The Invention of Poetic Subjectivity in the Sonnets.* Berkeley and Los Angeles: Univ. of California Press, 1986.

Fink, Bruce. *The Lacanian Subject: Between Language and Jouissance.* Princeton: Princeton Univ. Press, 1995.

Finucci, Valeria, and Regina Schwartz, eds. *Desire in the Renaissance: Psychoanalysis and Literature.* Princeton: Princeton Univ. Press, 1994.

Ford, John. *'Tis Pity She's a Whore and Other Plays,* edited by Marion Lomax. New York: Oxford Univ. Press, 1995.

Foucault, Michel. *Discipline and Punish: The Birth of the Prison,* translated by Alan Sheridan. New York: Vintage, 1979.

———. *The History of Sexuality. Volume 1: An Introduction,* translated by Robert Hurley. New York: Random-Vintage, 1990.

Foxe, John. *The First Volume of the Ecclesiasticall history contayning the Actes and Monumentes of . . . the sufferyng of martyrs.* London: John Day, 1570, 1576, 1583.

———. *The Acts and Monuments of John Foxe,* edited by Stephen R. Cattley and George Townsend, 8 vols., 1837–41. Reprint, New York: AMS, 1965.

Frank, Robert G., Jr. *Harvey and the Oxford Physiologists: Scientific Ideas and Social Interaction.* Berkeley and Los Angeles: Univ. of California Press, 1980.

Frantz, David O. *Festum Voluptatis: A Study of Renaissance Erotica.* Columbus: Ohio State Univ. Press, 1989.

Freccero, John. "The Fig Tree and the Laurel: Petrarch's Poetics." *Literary Theory / Renaissance Texts,* edited by Patricia Parker and David Quint, 20–32. Baltimore: Johns Hopkins Univ. Press, 1986.

Freedberg, David. *The Power of Images: Studies in the History and Theory of Response.* Chicago: Univ. of Chicago Press, 1989.

Freedman, Barbara. *Staging the Gaze: Postmodernism, Psychoanalysis, and Shakespearean Comedy.* Ithaca: Cornell Univ. Press, 1991.

Freud, Sigmund. "Beyond the Pleasure Principle." In *Standard Edition,* vol. 18.

———. "A Child Is Being Beaten." In *Standard Edition,* vol. 17.

———. *Civilization and Its Discontents.* In *Standard Edition,* vol. 21.

———. "The Economic Problem of Masochism." In *Standard Edition,* vol. 19.

———. "Instincts and Their Vicissitudes." In *Standard Edition,* vol. 14.

———. "The Interpretation of Dreams." In *Standard Edition,* vol. 4.

———. "Leonardo Da Vinci and a Memory of His Childhood." In *Standard Edition,* vol. 11.

———. "The Moses of Michelangelo." In *Standard Edition,* vol. 13.

———. "Remembering, Repeating and Working-Through." In *Standard Edition,* vol. 12.

―――. *The Standard Edition of the Complete Psychological Works,* translated by James Strachey, 24 vols. London: Hogarth Press & Institute of Psychoanalysis, 1953–74.

―――. "Three Essays on the Theory of Sexuality." In *Standard Edition,* vol. 7.

Garner, Stanton B., Jr. *Bodied Spaces: Phenomenology in Contemporary Performance.* Ithaca: Cornell Univ. Press, 1994.

Girard, Rene. *Violence and the Sacred,* translated by Patrick Gregory. Baltimore: Johns Hopkins Univ. Press, 1977.

Goldman, Michael. *Acting and Action in Shakespearean Tragedy.* Princeton: Princeton Univ. Press, 1985.

―――. *Shakespeare and the Energies of Drama.* Princeton: Princeton Univ. Press, 1972.

Gosson, Stephen. *Plays Confuted in Five Actions,* 1582. Reprint, New York: Garland, 1972.

―――. *Schoole of Abuse,* 1579. Reprint, New York: Johnson, 1973.

Grady, Hugh. "Renewing Modernity: Changing Contexts and Contents of a Nearly Invisible Concept." *Shakespeare Quarterly* 50, no. 3 (1999): 268–84.

Greenblatt, Stephen. "Psychoanalysis and Renaissance Culture." In *Literary Theory / Renaissance Texts,* edited by Patricia Parker and David Quint, 210–24. Baltimore: Johns Hopkins Univ. Press, 1986.

―――. *Renaissance Self-fashioning: From More to Shakespeare.* Chicago: Univ. of Chicago Press, 1980.

―――. *Shakespearean Negotiations: The Circulation of Social Energy in Renaissance England.* Berkeley and Los Angeles: Univ. of California Press, 1988.

Greene, Roland. *Post-Petrarchism: Origins and Innovations of the Western Lyric Sequence.* Princeton: Princeton Univ. Press, 1991.

Grossman, Marshall. *The Story of All Things: Writing the Self in English Renaissance Narrative Poetry.* Durham: Duke Univ. Press, 1998.

Gyer, Nicholas. *The English Phlebotomy.* London: Andrew Mansell, 1592.

Haidu, Peter. *The Subject of Violence: The Song of Roland and the Birth of the State.* Bloomington: Indiana Univ. Press, 1993.

Haller, William. *The Elect Nation: The Meaning and Relevance of Foxe's* Book of Martyrs. New York: Harper & Row, 1963.

Hamacher, Werner. "One 2 Many Multiculturalisms," translated by Dana Hollander. In *Violence, Identity, and Self-determination,* edited by Hent de Vries and Samuel Weber, 284–325. Stanford: Stanford Univ. Press, 1997.

Hammill, Graham L. *Sexuality and Form: Caravaggio, Marlowe, and Bacon.* Chicago: Univ. of Chicago Press, 2000.

Hanson, Elizabeth. *Discovering the Subject in Renaissance England.* Cambridge: Cambridge Univ. Press, 1998.

Hart, Lynda. *Between the Body and the Flesh: Performing Sadomasochism.* New York: Columbia Univ. Press, 1998.

Hawkins, Harriet. "Mortality, Morality, and Modernity in *The Broken Heart:* Some Dramatic and Critical Counter-arguments." In *John Ford: Critical Re-visions,* edited by Michael Neill. New York: Cambridge Univ. Press, 1988.

Heilman, Robert B. "The Perverse: An Aspect of Ford's Art." In *'Concord in Discord': The Plays of John Ford, 1586–1986,* edited by Donald K. Anderson Jr., 27–48. New York: AMS, 1986.

Helgerson, Richard. *Forms of Nationhood: The Elizabethan Writing of England.* Chicago: Univ. of Chicago Press, 1992.

Herbert, George. *The English Poems of George Herbert,* edited by C. A. Patrides. Totowa, N.J.: Rowman & Littlefield, 1974.

Heywood, Thomas. *An Apology for Actors,* 1612. Reprint, New York: Garland, 1973.

Hickey, Dave. *The Invisible Dragon: Four Essays on Beauty.* Los Angeles: Art Issues Press, 1993.

Hillman, David. "Visceral Knowledge." *The Body in Parts: Fantasies of Corporeality in Early Modern Europe,* edited by David Hillman and Carla Mazzio, 80–105. New York: Routledge, 1997.

Holland, Norman N. *Psychoanalysis and Shakespeare.* New York: McGraw-Hill, 1966.

Hollywood, Amy. *Sensible Ecstasy: Mysticism, Sexual Difference, and the Demands of History.* Chicago: Univ. of Chicago Press, 2002.

Hopkins, Lisa. *John Ford's Political Theatre.* Manchester: Manchester Univ. Press, 1994.

Huebert, Ronald. *John Ford: Baroque English Dramatist.* Montreal: McGill Queen's Univ. Press, 1977.

Hughes, Alan. Introduction to *Titus Andronicus,* by William Shakespeare, edited by Alan Hughes. New York: Cambridge Univ. Press, 1994.

Hughes, Ted. "On Ovid's 'Metamorphoses.'" *New York Review of Books,* 17 July 1997.

Hunt, Lynn. *The Invention of Pornography: Obscenity and the Origins of Modernity, 1500–1800.* New York: Zone, 1993.

Jed, Stephanie H. *Chaste Thinking: The Rape of Lucretia and the Birth of Humanism.* Bloomington: Indiana Univ. Press, 1989.

Kastan, David Scott. *Shakespeare after Theory.* New York: Routledge, 1999.

Kauffman, R. J. "Ford's 'Waste Land': *The Broken Heart." Renaissance Drama,* New Series III (1970): 167–87.

Kendrick, Walter. *The Secret Museum: Pornography in Modern Culture.* Berkeley and Los Angeles: Univ. of California Press, 1987.

Kermode, Frank. Introduction to *King Lear.* In *The Riverside Shakespeare,* edited by G. Blakemore Evans et al., 1249–54. Boston: Houghton Mifflin, 1974.

————. *The Sense of an Ending: Studies in the Theory of Fiction.* New York: Oxford Univ. Press, 1967.

————. *Shakespeare's Language.* London: Allen Lane-Penguin, 2000.

Kerrigan, William, and Gordon Braden. *The Idea of the Renaissance.* Baltimore: Johns Hopkins Univ. Press, 1989.

Knott, John. *Discourses of Martyrdom in English Literature, 1563–1694.* New York: Cambridge Univ. Press, 1993.

————. "John Foxe and the Joy of Suffering." *Sixteenth Century Journal* 27 (1996): 721–34.

Kofman, Sarah. *The Enigma of Woman: Woman in Freud's Writings,* translated by Catherine Porter. Ithaca: Cornell Univ. Press, 1985.

Kolin, Philip C. "*Titus Andronicus* and the Critical Legacy." In Titus Andronicus: *Critical Essays,* edited by Philip C. Kolin. New York: Garland, 1995.

Kristeva, Julia. *Black Sun: Depression and Melancholia,* translated by Leon S. Roudiez. New York: Columbia Univ. Press, 1989.

————. "Stabat Mater." In *The Kristeva Reader,* edited by Toril Moi, 160–86. New York: Columbia Univ. Press, 1986.

————. "The System and the Speaking Subject." In *The Kristeva Reader,* edited by Toril Moi, 24–33. New York: Columbia Univ. Press, 1986.

Lacan, Jacques. *Écrits: A Selection,* translated by Alan Sheridan. New York: Norton, 1977.

————. *The Four Fundamental Concepts of Psycho-analysis,* edited by Jacques-Alain Miller, translated by Alan Sheridan. New York: Norton, 1978.

————. *The Seminar of Jacques Lacan. Book I: Freud's Papers on Technique, 1953–1954,* edited by Jacques-Alain Miller, translated by John Forrester. New York: Norton, 1991.

————. *The Seminar of Jacques Lacan. Book II: The Ego in Freud's Theory and in the Technique of Psychoanalysis, 1954–1955,* edited by Jacques-Alain Miller, translated by Sylvana Tomaselli. New York: Norton, 1991.

————. *The Seminar of Jacques Lacan. Book III: The Psychoses, 1955–1956,* edited by Jacques-Alain Miller, translated by Russell Grigg. New York: Norton, 1993.

————. *The Seminar of Jacques Lacan. Book VII: The Ethics of Psychoanalysis, 1959–1960,* edited by Jacques-Alain Miller, translated by Dennis Porter. New York: Norton, 1992.

————. *The Seminar of Jacques Lacan. Book XX: Encore 1972–1973, On Feminine Sexuality, The Limits of Love and Knowledge,* edited by Jacques-Alain Miller, translated by Bruce Fink. New York: Norton, 1998.

Lander, Jesse. "'Foxe's' *Books of Martyrs:* Printing and Popularizing the *Acts and Monu-*

ments." In *Religion and Culture in Renaissance England,* edited by Claire Mc-
Eachern and Debora Shuger, 69–92. New York: Cambridge Univ. Press,
1997.

Laplanche, Jean. *Life and Death in Psychoanalysis,* translated by Jeffrey Mehlman. Baltimore: Johns Hopkins Univ. Press, 1976.

———. *The Unconscious and the Id,* translated by Luke Thurson with Lindsay Wat-
son. London: Rebus, 1999.

Laplanche, Jean, and J.-B. Pontalis. *The Language of Psycho-analysis,* translated by Donald Nicholson-Smith. New York: Norton, 1973.

La Primaudaye, Peter [Pierre] de. *The French Academie,* 1579, translated by [Thomas
Bowes]. London: Edmund Bollifant, 1586.

Leech, Clifford. *John Ford and the Drama of His Time.* London: Chatto & Windus, 1957.

Levine, Laura. *Men in Women's Clothing: Anti-theatricality and Effeminization, 1579–1642.*
New York: Cambridge Univ. Press, 1994.

Lewis, C. S. *English Literature in the Sixteenth Century, Excluding Drama.* New York: Oxford, 1954.

Loades, David, ed. *John Foxe and the English Reformation.* Aldershot, Hants, U.K.: Scolar
Press, 1997.

Lodge, Thomas. *Phillis: Honoured with Pastorall Sonnets, Elegies, and amorous delights.* London: John Busbie, 1593.

Lomax, Marion. Introduction to *'Tis Pity She's a Whore and Other Plays,* by John Ford.

Lukacher, Ned. *Daemonic Figures: Shakespeare and the Question of Conscience.* Ithaca: Cornell
Univ. Press, 1994.

Lupton, Julia Reinhard. *Afterlives of the Saints: Hagiography, Typology, and Renaissance Literature.* Stanford: Stanford Univ. Press, 1996.

Lupton, Julia Reinhard, and Kenneth Reinhard. *After Oedipus: Shakespeare in Psychoanalysis.* Ithaca: Cornell Univ. Press, 1993.

Lyon, M. L., and J. M. Barbalet. "Society's Body: Emotion and the 'Somatization' of
Social Theory." In *Embodiment and Experience: The Existential Ground of Culture
and Self,* edited by Thomas J. Csordas, 48–66. New York: Cambridge Univ.
Press, 1994.

MacKinnon, Catharine A. "Feminism, Marxism, Method, and the State: Toward
Feminist Jurisprudence." *Signs: Journal of Women in Culture and Society* 8, no. 4
(1983): 635–58.

———. *Only Words.* Cambridge: Harvard Univ. Press, 1993.

Madelaine, Richard. "'Sensationalism' and 'Melodrama' in Ford's Plays." In *John
Ford: Critical Re-visions,* edited by Michael Neill. New York: Cambridge
Univ. Press, 1988.

Marlowe, Christopher. "Hero and Leander." In *Elizabethan Minor Epics,* edited by Elizabeth Story Donno. New York: Columbia Univ. Press, 1963.

Marshall, Cynthia. "The Doubled Jacques and Constructions of Negation in *As You Like It." Shakespeare Quarterly* 49, no. 4 (1998): 375–92.

———. Review of Lynn Enterline's *Tears of Narcissus: Melancholia and Masculinity in Early Modern England* and John Russell's *Hamlet and Narcissus. Shakespeare Quarterly* 49, no. 1 (1998): 110–13.

Martz, Louis L. *The Poetry of Meditation.* New Haven: Yale Univ. Press, 1954.

Maus, Katharine Eisaman. Introduction to *Julius Caesar.* In *The Norton Shakespeare.*

———. "Taking Tropes Seriously: Language and Violence in Shakespeare's *Rape of Lucrece." Shakespeare Quarterly* 37, no. 1 (1986): 66–82.

Maxwell, J. C. Introduction to *Titus Andronicus,* by William Shakespeare, edited by J. C. Maxwell. The Arden Shakespeare. New York: Methuen, 1953.

Mazzio, Carla, and Douglas Trevor. "Dreams of History: An Introduction." In *Historicism, Psychoanalysis, and Early Modern Culture,* edited by Carla Mazzio and Douglas Trevor, 1–18. New York: Routledge, 2000.

Mazzotta, Giuseppe. "The *Canzoniere* and the Language of the Self." *Studies in Philology* 75 (1978): 271–96.

Merback, Mitchell B. *The Thief, the Cross, and the Wheel: Pain and the Spectacle of Punishment in Medieval and Renaissance Europe.* Chicago: Univ. of Chicago Press, 1998.

Merleau-Ponty, Maurice. *Phenomenology of Perception,* translated by Colin Smith. London: Routledge & Kegan Paul, 1962.

Montaigne, Michel de. *The Complete Essays of Montaigne,* translated by Donald M. Frame. Stanford: Stanford Univ. Press, 1976.

Mozeley, J. F. *John Foxe and His Book,* 1940. Reprint, London: Society for Promoting Christian Knowledge, 1970.

Mueller, Janel M. "Pain, Persecution, and the Construction of Selfhood in Foxe's *Acts and Monuments.*" In *Religion and Culture in Renaissance England,* edited by Claire McEachern and Debora Shuger, 161–87. New York: Cambridge Univ. Press, 1997.

Mulvey, Laura. "Afterthoughts on 'Visual Pleasure and Narrative Cinema'; Inspired by King Vidor's *Duel in the Sun* (1946)." In *Visual and Other Pleasures,* 29–38. Bloomington: Indiana Univ. Press, 1989.

[Munday, Anthony]. *A Second and third blast of retrait from plaies and theaters,* by Salvianus and 'Anglo-phile Eutheo,' 1580. Reprint, New York: Garland, 1972.

Murray, Timothy. Review of *Disowning Knowledge,* by Stanley Cavell. *Modern Language Notes* 105, no. 5 (Dec. 1990): 1080–85.

———. "Translating Montaigne's Crypts: Melancholic Relations and the Sites of

Altarbiography." *Repossessions: Psychoanalysis and the Phantasms of Early Modern Culture*, edited by Timothy Murray and Alan K. Smith, 47–77. Minneapolis: Univ. of Minnesota Press, 1998.

Nashe, Thomas. *The Works of Thomas Nashe*, edited by Ronald B. McKerrow, 2 vols. Oxford: Basil Blackwell, 1958.

Nead, Lynda. *The Female Nude: Art, Obscenity, and Sexuality.* New York: Routledge, 1992.

Neely, Carol Thomas. "'Documents in Madness': Reading Madness and Gender in Shakespeare's Tragedies and Early Modern Culture." *Shakespeare Quarterly* 42,no. 3 (1991): 315–38.

———. "The Structure of English Renaissance Sonnet Sequences." *ELH* 45 (1978): 359–89.

Neill, Michael. "Ending *The Broken Heart.*" In *Issues of Death: Mortality and Identity in English Renaissance Tragedy.* Oxford: Clarendon, 1997.

———. "Ford's Unbroken Art: The Moral Design of 'The Broken Heart.'" *Modern Language Review* 75 (1980): 249–68.

Nicholls, David. "Theatre of Martyrdom in the French Reformation." *Past and Present* 121 (1988): 49–73.

Nicholson, Eirwen. "Eighteenth-Century Foxe: Evidence for the Impact of the *Acts and Monuments* in the 'Long' Eighteenth Century." In *John Foxe and the English Reformation*, edited by David Loades, 143–77.

Noyes, John K. *The Mastery of Submission: Inventions of Masochism.* Ithaca: Cornell Univ. Press, 1997.

Nussbaum, Damian. "Appropriating Martyrdom: Fears of Renewed Persecution and the 1632 Edition of *Acts and Monuments.*" In *John Foxe and the English Reformation*, edited by David Loades, 178–91.

Nuttall, A. D. *Why Does Tragedy Give Pleasure?* Oxford: Clarendon, 1996.

Oliver, H. J. *The Problem of John Ford.* Melbourne: Melbourne Univ. Press, 1955.

Orgel, Stephen. "The Play of Conscience." In *Performativity and Performance*, edited by Andrew Parker and Eve Kosofsky Sedgwick, 133–51. New York: Routledge, 1995.

Palmer, D. J. "The Unspeakable in Pursuit of the Uneatable: Language and Action in *Titus Andronicus.*" *Critical Quarterly* 14 (1972): 320–39.

Palmer, Daryl W. "Histories of Violence and the Writer's Hand: Foxe's *Actes and Monuments* and Shakespeare's *Titus Andronicus.*" In *Reading and Writing in Shakespeare*, edited by David M. Bergeron, 82–115. Newark: Univ. of Delaware Press, 1996.

Parker, Barbara. "The Whore of Babylon and Shakespeare's *Julius Caesar.*" *Studies in English Literature 1500–1900* 35 (1995): 251–69.

Paster, Gail Kern. *The Body Embarrassed: Drama and the Disciplines of Shame in Early Modern England.* Ithaca: Cornell Univ. Press, 1993.

Patterson, Lee. "On the Margin: Postmodernism, Ironic History, and Medieval Studies." *Speculum* 65 (1990): 87–108.

Peacham, Henr[y]. *Graphice, or The Most Auncient and Excellent Art of Drawing and Limming.* London, 1612.

Pecora, Vincent P. "The Limits of Local Knowledge." In *The New Historicism*, edited by H. Aram Veeser, 243–76. New York: Routledge, 1989.

[Percy, William]. *Sonnets to the Fairest Coelia.* London: Printed by Adam Islip, 1594.

Plutarch. "The Life of Marcus Antonius." In *Shakespeare's Plutarch*, translated by Thomas North, edited by T. J. B. Spencer. New York: Penguin, 1964.

Prynne, William. *Histriomastix: The Players Scourge, or, Actors Tragedie*, 1633. Reprint, New York: Johnson, 1974.

Pye, Christopher. *The Vanishing: Shakespeare, the Subject, and Early Modern Culture.* Durham: Duke Univ. Press, 2000.

Rainoldes, John. *Th'overthrow of Stage-plays, by the way of controversy between D. Gager and D. Rainolds*, 1599. Reprint, New York: Garland, 1974.

Rajan, Tilottama. "'Nothing Sooner Broke': Donne's *Songs and Sonets* as Self-consuming Artifact." *ELH* 49 (1982): 805–28.

Rambuss, Richard. *Closet Devotions.* Durham: Duke Univ. Press, 1998.

Rankins, William. *A Mirrour of Monsters*, 1587. Reprint, New York: Garland, 1973.

Ray, Sid. "'Rape, I fear, was root of thy annoy': The Politics of Consent in *Titus Andronicus*." *Shakespeare Quarterly* 49, no. 1 (1998): 22–39.

Reynoldes, Edward. *A Treatise of the Passions and Faculties of the Soule of Man.* London: Printed by R. H. for Robert Bostock, 1640.

Sacher-Masoch, Leopold von. "Appendix I: Childhood Memory and Reflections on the Novel." In *Masochism.* New York: Zone, 1989.

———. "Venus in Furs." In *Masochism.* New York: Zone, 1989.

Sade, Marquis de [Donatien Alphonse Francois.] *The 120 Days of Sodom and Other Writings*, translated by Austryn Wainhouse and Richard Seaver. New York: Grove Press, 1966.

Saunders, John B. deC. M., and Charles Donald O'Malley. Introduction to *The Bloodletting Letter of 1539, by Andreas Vesalius.* New York: Henry Schuman, [1947].

Sawday, Jonathan. *The Body Emblazoned: Dissection and the Human Body in Renaissance Culture.* New York: Routledge, 1995.

———. "Self and Selfhood in the Seventeenth Century." In *Rewriting the Self: Histories from the Renaissance to the Present*, edited by Roy Porter, 29–48. New York: Routledge, 1997.

Scarry, Elaine. *The Body in Pain: Making and Unmaking the World.* New York: Oxford Univ. Press, 1985.

Sedinger, Tracey. "Historicism and Renaissance Culture." In *Discontinuities: New Essays on Renaissance Literature and Culture,* 117–38. Toronto: Univ. of Toronto Press, 1998.

Shakespeare, William. *The Norton Shakespeare: Based on the Oxford Edition,* edited by Stephen Greenblatt et al. New York: Norton, 1997.

———. *Shakespeare's Sonnets,* edited by Stephen Booth. New Haven: Yale Univ. Press, 1977.

———. *Titus Andronicus,* edited by Jonathan Bate. The Arden Shakespeare, Third Series. New York: Routledge, 1995.

Sidney, Philip. "Astrophil and Stella." In *The Poems of Sir Philip Sidney,* edited by William A. Ringler Jr. Oxford: Clarendon, 1962.

Siegel, Carol. *Male Masochism: Modern Revisions of the Story of Love.* Bloomington: Indiana Univ. Press, 1995.

Silverman, Kaja. *"Histoire d'O:* The Construction of a Female Subject." *Pleasure and Danger: Exploring Female Sexuality,* edited by Carole S. Vance, 320–49. Boston: Routledge & Kegan Paul, 1984.

———. *Male Subjectivity at the Margins.* New York: Routledge, 1992.

———. *The Threshold of the Visible World.* New York: Routledge, 1996.

Skura, Meredith. "Understanding the Living and Talking to the Dead: The Historicity of Psychoanalysis." *Modern Language Quarterly* 54, no. 1 (1993): 77–89.

Smith, Bruce R. "Rape, Rap, Rupture, Rapture: R-rated Futures on the Global Market." *Textual Practice* 9, no. 3 (1995): 421–44.

Smith, Hallett. *Elizabethan Poetry.* Ann Arbor: Univ. of Michigan Press, 1952.

Smith, Roger. "Self-reflection and the Self." In *Rewriting the Self: Histories from the Renaissance to the Present,* edited by Roy Porter, 49–57. New York: Routledge, 1997.

Smith, William. *Chloris, or The Complaint of the passionate despised Shepheard.* London: Edm. Bollifant, 1596.

Spencer, T. J. B. "Shakespeare and the Elizabethan Romans." *Shakespeare Survey* 10 (1957): 27–38.

Speziale-Bagliacca, Roberto. *The King and the Adulteress: A Psychoanalytic and Literary Reinterpretation of Madame Bovary and King Lear,* edited by Colin Rice. Durham: Duke Univ. Press, 1998.

Sprengnether, Madelon. *The Spectral Mother: Freud, Feminism, and Psychoanalysis.* Ithaca: Cornell Univ. Press, 1990.

Starks, Lisa S. "'Like the Lover's pinch, which hurts and is desired': The Libidinal Economy of Male Masochism and Shakespeare's *Antony and Cleopatra.*" *Literature and Psychology* 45, no. 4 (1999): 58–73.

———. "'Won with thy words and conquered with thy looks': Sadism, Masochism, and the Masochistic Gaze in *I Tamburlaine*." In *Marlowe, History, and Sexuality: New Critical Essays on Christopher Marlowe*, edited by Paul Whitfield White, 179–93. New York: AMS Press, 1998.

Stavig, Mark. *John Ford and the Traditional Moral Order*. Madison: Univ. of Wisconsin Press, 1968.

Steiner, Wendy. *The Scandal of Pleasure: Art in an Age of Fundamentalism*. Chicago: Univ. of Chicago Press, 1995.

Stevens, Scott Manning. "Sacred Heart and Secular Brain." In *The Body in Parts: Fantasies of Corporeality in Early Modern Europe*, edited by David Hillman and Carla Mazzio, 263–84. New York: Routledge, 1997.

Stewart, Suzanne R. *Sublime Surrender: Male Masochism at the Fin-de-Siècle*. Ithaca: Cornell Univ. Press, 1998.

Stott, Andrew. "From *Voi Che* to *Che Vuoi?* Gaze, Desire, and the Law in the *Zepheria* Sonnet Sequence." *Criticism* 36, no. 3 (1994): 329–58.

Stubbes, Phillip. *The Anatomie of Abuses*, 1583. Reprint, New York: Garland, 1973.

Studlar, Gaylyn. *In the Realm of Pleasure: Von Sternberg, Dietrich, and the Masochistic Aesthetic*. New York: Columbia Univ. Press, 1988.

Targoff, Ramie. *Common Prayer: The Language of Public Devotion in Early Modern England*. Chicago: Univ. of Chicago Press, 2001.

Taylor, Charles. *Sources of the Self: The Making of the Modern Identity*. Cambridge: Harvard Univ. Press, 1989.

Temkin, Owsei. *Galenism: Rise and Decline of a Medical Philosophy*. Ithaca: Cornell Univ. Press, 1973.

Tomlinson, T. B. *A Study of Elizabethan and Jacobean Tragedy*. Cambridge: Cambridge Univ. Press, 1964.

Traub, Valerie. *Desire and Anxiety: Circulations of Sexuality in Shakespearean Drama*. New York: Routledge, 1992.

Tricomi, Albert H. "The Aesthetics of Mutilation in *Titus Andronicus*." *Shakespeare Survey* 27 (1974): 11–19.

Vasari, G. *Le vits de'più eccellenti pittori ed architettori*, 1568, edited by G. Milanesi, 9 vols. Florence, 1878–85.

Vickers, Nancy J. "Diana Described: Scattered Woman and Scattered Rhyme." *Critical Inquiry* 8, no. 2 (1981): 265–79.

Wainhouse, Austryn, and Richard Seaver. Introductory comments to *The 120 Days of Sodom and Other Writings*, by Marquis de Sade, 183–87. New York: Grove Press, 1966.

Webb, Peter. *The Erotic Arts*. New York: Farrar, Straus & Giroux, 1983.

Whitteridge, Gweneth. Introduction to *An Anatomical Disputation Concerning the Move-*

ment of the Heart and Blood in Living Creatures, by William Harvey. Oxford: Blackwell Scientific Publications, 1976.

Willbern, David. "Rape and Revenge in *Titus Andronicus.*" *English Literary Renaissance* 8 (1978): 159–82.

Williams, Linda. *Hard Core: Power, Pleasure, and the 'Frenzy of the Visible.'* Berkeley and Los Angeles: Univ. of California Press, 1989.

Wilson, Scott. "Racked on the tyrant's bed: The Politics of Pleasure and Pain and the Elizabethan Sonnet Sequences." *Textual Practice* 3 (1989): 234–49.

Woolf, D. R. "The Rhetoric of Martyrdom: Generic Contradiction and Narrative Strategy in John Foxe's *Acts and Monuments.*" In *The Rhetorics of Life-Writing in Early Modern Europe,* edited by Thomas F. Mayer and D. R. Woolf, 243–82. Ann Arbor: Univ. of Michigan Press, 1995.

Wright, Thomas. *The Passions of the Minde in Generall.* London: Printed by Valentine Simmes for Walter Burre, 1604.

Wymer, Rowland. *Webster and Ford.* New York: St. Martin's, 1995.

Wynne-Davies, Marion. "'The Swallowing Womb': Consumed and Consuming Women in *Titus Andronicus.*" In *The Matter of Difference: Materialist Feminist Criticism of Shakespeare,* edited by Valerie Wayne, 129–51. Ithaca: Cornell Univ. Press, 1991.

Yates, Velvet. "A Sexual Model of Catharsis." *Apeiron: A Journal for Ancient Philosophy and Science* 31, no. 1 (March 1998): 35–58.

Zepheria. London: Printed by the Widdowe Orwin, for N.I. and John Busbie, 1594.

Žižek, Slavoj. *Looking Awry: An Introduction to Jacques Lacan through Popular Culture.* Cambridge: MIT Press, 1991.

———. *The Metastases of Enjoyment: Six Essays on Women and Causality.* London: Verso, 1994.

———. *The Sublime Object of Ideology.* New York: Verso, 1989.

) (

Index

Aers, David, 23, 165–66n. 2, 168n. 33
Anderson, Donald K., Jr., 187n. 12,
    189n. 42
antitheatricalism, 17–20, 22, 24, 38, 43,
    48, 139
Astington, John H., 182n. 8
Aston, Margaret, 178n. 8
audience response, 1–5, 7, 47–50, 106–15,
    121–44, 152, 156–58; and closure, 153;
    and contagion, 17–19; contradictions,
    19–20; identification, 50, 133–36; to
    staged suicide, 155; submission, 146.
    See also phenomenology

Baines, Barbara, 181n. 40
Barbalet, J. M., 138, 140, 186n. 1
Barbour, Reed, 187n. 9
Barker, Francis, 165n. 1
Barnes, Barnabe, 11, 76–81, 174n. 8,
    176n. 40
Barroll, Leeds, 166n. 14
Barthes, Roland, 111, 178n. 13, 180n. 27,
    182n. 11
Bartlett, Ross, 177n. 2
Barton, Anne, 156, 190n. 60
Bataille, Georges, 101, 180n. 32

Baumeister, Roy F., 8, 165n. 9
Beier, Lucinda McCray, 189n. 48
Bellamy, Elizabeth J., 25–28, 34, 167nn.
    26, 27, 170–71n. 53
Belling, Catherine, 167n. 20
Belsey, Catherine, 165n. 1
Bersani, Leo, 10, 37, 41–43, 51, 146, 156–
    57, 165n. 11, 171nn. 62, 66, 180n. 35,
    188n. 31
Betteridge, Tom, 87, 177n. 2, 179n. 22
blazon, 75–76, 80
body: critical discourse, 108–10; frag-
    mented, 32, 75, 82, 108, 113, 118, 145,
    154; and humoral theory, 2–4, 9,
    14–21, 48, 137–44, 147–51, 154, 158;
    language of, 21, 62–66, 75, 144–45;
    religious views of, 20–21, 81, 91–94,
    102–3, 121, 137, 143–46, 158
body-ego, 124
Bok, Sissela, 165n. 13
Boose, Lynda E., 183n. 17
Booth, Stephen, 1, 164n. 1
Boothby, Richard, 160–61, 173n. 89,
    174n. 13, 191n. 1
Borch-Jacobsen, Michel, 32–33, 122–24,
    126

Braden, Gordon, 169n. 35, 173n. 2, 174n. 10, 176n. 42

Breitenberg, Mark, 167n. 25, 178n. 5, 179n. 22

Brennan, Teresa, 170n. 46

Bright, Timothy, 14, 15, 147, 150, 151, 166n. 5

Brownmiller, Susan, 186n. 53

Burbridge, Roger T., 187n. 11, 190n. 57

Burckhardt, Jacob, 9–10, 26–29, 34–35, 159, 168–69n. 34, 169n. 35, 171n. 54

Burton, Robert, 16–17, 56–57, 63, 65, 67, 81, 148, 150, 151, 154, 166n. 9

Butler, Judith, 113–15, 136, 183n. 16

Bynum, Caroline Walker, 97, 179n. 24

Callaghan, Dympna, 170n. 51

canonicity, 5–7, 113, 136

castration, 75, 109, 128, 134

catharsis, 2–4, 8, 47–49, 54, 138–41, 157, 160, 167n. 21

Cavell, Stanley, 125–130, 134, 184nn. 33, 34, 35

censorship, 113–14, 136

closure, 3, 70–71, 87, 140, 152, 154, 156–58

Coeffeteau, Nicholas, 15–16, 18, 20, 56, 57, 166n. 6, 173n. 1

Colombo (Columbus), Realdo, 188–89n. 33

Copjec, Joan, 165n. 10

Crewe, Jonathan V., 105, 169n. 40, 170n. 51, 176n. 47, 181n. 42

Crooke, Helkiah, 147, 189n. 36

Culler, Jonathan, 100, 180n. 29

Daniel, Samuel, 11, 66–68, 72, 79, 174n. 8, 175n. 24

De Grazia, Margreta, 70, 175n. 31

Deleuze, Gilles, 42, 46–47, 75–76, 80, 130–31, 157–58, 172nn. 71, 76, 190n. 63

Desmonde, William H., 184n. 38

Dessen, Alan C., 133–34, 186n. 56

Diehl, Huston, 100–101, 167n. 19, 179n. 22

dismemberment, 5, 75–78, 95, 107, 109, 112–13, 128, 131, 136

Dollimore, Jonathan, 69–70, 165n. 1, 174n. 10

Donne, John, 21, 167n. 18, 175n. 37

Dragon, Jean, 180n. 32

Drayton, Michael, 11, 72–73, 82–83, 175n. 35, 177n. 53

dualism, mind-body, 15, 91, 102, 139, 143

Dubrow, Heather, 63, 70, 77–78, 174n. 16

Earl, James W., 172n. 80

Eaton, Sara, 129, 185n. 43

Edmundson, Mark, 165n. 13, 190n. 65

ego psychology, 7

Elam, Keir, 108, 110, 181n. 4

Eliot, George, 88, 178n. 10

Emerson, Ralph Waldo, 12, 26, 168n. 31

Enterline, Lynn, 25, 59, 75, 167–68n. 28, 172nn. 72, 73, 173n. 6

Estrin, Barbara L., 174n. 15

Ewing, S. Blaine, 148, 189n. 38

fantasy, 24, 34, 45; of annihilation, 30; in drama, 107, 128, 135; Freud on, 38–39, 66, 122–23, 126, 135–36; Lacan on, 61, 102; and masochism, 38–39, 42, 45–46, 53, 62, 80; modes of identification, 65, 123–24, 135; and Nashe, 104; Petrarchanist, 61, 68, 73, 75–76, 78; rape, 78, 80; and sadism, 104; and writing, 46–47, 95, 104

Fawcett, Mary Laughlin, 184–85n. 40
Felch, Susan, 177n. 3, 178n. 9
feminism, 42–43, 82–83, 108–9, 114, 124, 126–33
Ferguson, Frances, 111, 182n. 12
Ferrand, Jacques, 151, 189n. 46
Fineman, Joel, 7–8, 24, 54, 59, 165nn. 7, 8, 170n. 50, 174n. 7
Fink, Bruce, 68, 99, 175n. 28, 176–77n. 51, 180n. 26
Finucci, Valeria, and Regina Schwartz, 170nn. 49, 50
Ford, John, 11, 12, 55, 137–58; *The Broken Heart*, 6, 11, 43, 54, 55, 105, 138–58, 187nn. 13, 14, 188n. 25, 189n. 38, 189–90n. 49
formalism, 5, 24, 140–41
Foucault, Michel, 102, 170n. 45, 180n. 35
Foxe, John, 2, 11, 20–21, 43, 55, 66, 84–105, 121, 179n. 18; *Acts and Monuments*, 5–6, 11, 79, 84, 85–105, 118; as propagandist, 91; and sadism, 101–3; use of rhetoric, 87, 89, 94–95, 101
Frank, Robert G., Jr., 189n. 33
Frantz, David O., 116, 183n. 21
Freccero, John, 59, 173n. 5
Freedberg, David, 183nn. 22, 23
Freedman, Barbara, 168n. 28
Freud, Sigmund, 7, 27–29, 47, 124, 135, 158, 160, 169nn. 42, 43, 172n. 71; "Beyond the Pleasure Principle," 39–40, 49–51, 70–71, 75, 99, 171n. 60; compared to Burckhardt, 34–35; "A Child Is Being Beaten," 38–39, 65–66, 106, 122–23, 126, 128, 135–36; *Civilization and Its Discontents*, 28–29, 35, 49; death instinct, 39–40, 49–51, 69–71, 99, 171n. 60, 173n. 85; "The Economic Problem of Masochism," 39–40, 74;

fantasy, 38–39, 66, 122–23, 126, 135–36; *Fort/Da*, 50–51, 70–71; and humanism, 40; identification, 122–23, 184n. 30; "Instincts and Their Vicissitudes," 37–39, 43–44; "The Interpretation of Dreams," 184n. 29; "Leonardo Da Vinci and a Memory of His Childhood," 34; masochism, 10, 35–44, 46, 52, 74, 172nn. 71, 78; "The Moses of Michelangelo," 34; "Remembering, Repeating and Working-Through," 167n. 26; sadism, 36–38, 40; "Three Essays on the Theory of Sexuality," 36–37, 44; the unconscious, 173n. 85

Garner, Stanton B., Jr., 155, 190n. 59
Goldman, Michael, 1, 164n. 1
Gosson, Stephen, 17, 19, 21, 166nn. 10, 11
Grady, Hugh, 168–69n. 35
Greenblatt, Stephen, 2, 12, 23, 25–35, 40–41, 105, 167nn. 22, 24, 168nn. 30, 32, 168–69n. 35, 169nn. 38, 40, 169–70n. 44, 170n. 45
Greene, Roland, 62–63, 174n. 16
Grossman, Marshall, 25, 71, 167–68n. 28, 175n. 32
Gyer, Nicholas, 150, 151, 189n. 44

Haller, William, 177n. 2
Hammill, Graham L., 170n. 51
Hanson, Elizabeth, 167n. 25, 178–79n. 14
Hart, Lynda, 191n. 65
Hawkins, Harriet, 141, 187n. 14
heart: heartbreak, 8, 36, 139, 140–45, 152–53, 157, 158; physiological function of, 15–17, 145–48, 152; shattering of, 21

Heilman, Robert B., 187n. 12

Helgerson, Richard, 177n. 2, 178n. 7

Herbert, George, 21, 144–46, 167n. 18, 188n. 28

Heywood, Thomas, 112, 183n. 15

Hickey, Dave, 158, 191n. 66

Hillman, David, 144, 188nn. 19, 23

historicism, 2, 4–5, 8, 9, 13, 159; and humanism, 24–32; as methodology, 23–32, 47; and psychoanalytic theory, 27–33

historiography, 23–24, 32

Hollywood, Amy, 176n. 49

Hopkins, Lisa, 144, 145, 154, 187n. 17

Huebert, Ronald, 187n. 14, 189–90n. 49

Hughes, Alan, 181n. 1

Hughes, Ted, 12, 165n. 14

humanism: and Christianity, 60; conception of romantic love, 57; and masochism, 35, 44, 137; model of subjectivity, 10, 26, 35, 160; narrative of rape, 127–29, 133; narrative of the subject's emergence, 2, 10, 26, 32, 34–35; response to violence, 136–37

humoral theory, 4, 9, 14–17, 20, 21, 48, 137, 139, 142, 147–54, 158; blood, 149–50; and body, 2, 3, 141, 143–44, 149–50; heart, 147–48, 152; melancholy, 148; phlebotomy, 150–53

Hunt, Lynn, 115, 183n. 19

identification, 17–19, 45–46, 50, 57, 107, 115, 126, 129, 184n. 30; blind spots, 122–25, 133; modalities of, 121–22; with victims, 89–90, 100, 105, 135–37; viewers of theater and film, 101, 106–7, 121–22, 165n. 12, 186n. 59

individualism, 2, 9, 14, 34, 160; and Freud, 40–41; and Hegel, 168–69n.

35; and Lacan, 9; and martyrdom, 93–95, 102

Jed, Stephanie H., 131, 185n. 52

Johnson, Samuel, 1

Jonson, Ben, 6

jouissance, 8, 11, 36, 52, 54, 58–59, 66, 79–83, 94, 98–100, 105, 121, 137, 160; changing meaning of, 74; and language, 59–62, 68; "other" jouissance, 81–82; and transgression, 90, 102–3

Kastan, David Scott, 30, 170n. 45

Kauffman, R. J., 190n. 52

Kendrick, Walter, 115, 183n. 19

Kermode, Frank, 3, 164n. 2, 181n. 3

Kerrigan, William, and Gordon Braden, 169n. 35, 173n. 2, 174n. 10

Knott, John, 177n. 2, 178n. 5, 179nn. 18, 19

Kofman, Sarah, 184n. 31

Kristeva, Julia, 32, 64–65, 67, 171n. 63, 171–72n. 69, 174n. 20, 175nn. 22, 27

La Primaudaye, Peter [Pierre] de, 20, 21, 166–67n. 17

Lacan, Jacques, 27, 63, 122, 136, 167n. 27; death instinct, 51–52, 61, 160–61; desire, 74, 123–25; *Écrits*, 61–62, 108, 170n. 46; ethics, 9, 102; *Fort/Da*, 51, 75; *The Four Fundamental Concepts of Psycho-analysis*, 98–99, 180n. 33; historical awareness, 31; jouissance, 62, 68, 90, 102, 176n. 49; jouissance and pleasure, 99, 100; on language, 32–33, 59–62; masochism, 10, 51–52; mirror stage, 108, 174n. 13; "other"

Index

jouissance, 81–82; *point de capiton*, 97; the Real, 79, 82, 108, 160, 180n. 32; on Sade, 11, 28, 101–3; *Seminar I*, 51–52, 61, 75, 124–25; *Seminar II*, 172n. 78; *Seminar VII*, 9, 77, 83, 98–103; *Seminar XX*, 68, 77–81, 99, 176nn. 44, 48, 177n. 51, 180n. 28; specular ego, 124; theory of Imaginary, Symbolic, and Real, 60–61, 67, 97–98, 123; the Thing, 62, 99

Lander, Jesse, 178n. 3

Laplanche, Jean, 10, 32, 38, 43–47, 51, 171nn. 58, 60, 173n. 85; on fantasy, 33, 45–46; on subject formation, 44–45, 146

Leech, Clifford, 190n. 52

Levine, Laura, 17, 23, 27, 166n. 10, 167n. 22

Lewis, C. S., 60, 164–65n. 4, 174n. 11

Loades, David, 177n. 2, 177–78n. 3

Lodge, Thomas, 58, 173n. 4, 174n. 8

Lomax, Marion, 141, 187n. 16

Lovesickness: in early modern England, 11, 56–58, 63; and linguistic failure, 63–69; masochism of, 36, 57–59, 61–62, 71–73, 79–81; and neurotic symptom, 67–68; in Petrarchan poetry, 2, 54–55, 56–84, 100; and the Real, 62, 79; and religion, 81

Lukacher, Ned, 168n. 28

Lupton, Julia Reinhard, 168n. 28; and Kenneth Reinhard, 167n. 26, 168n. 28

Lyon, M. L., and J. M. Barbalet, 138, 140, 186n. 1

MacKinnon, Catherine A., 111–14, 136, 182n. 13, 186n. 53

Madelaine, Richard, 152, 190n. 50

Marlowe, Christopher, 164–65n. 4

Marshall, Cynthia, 172n. 69, 173n. 88

martyrdom: and the body, 91–94; and eroticism, 110, 114, 116–18, 121, 137; in Foxe, 85–103, 179n. 18; images of, 86, 117, 118, 119, 120, 132; and jouissance, 58, 79, 90, 94–100, 137; political aspects, 55, 87–91, 94; staging of, 3, 11, 55, 101, 105, 110, 137; and transubstantiation, 92–93

martyrology, 11, 20–21, 58, 66, 85–105, 136–37

Martz, Louis L., 188n. 24

masochism, 7–8, 35–47, 49, 121, 169n. 42, 189n. 49; aesthetics of, 10, 43–44, 47–50, 146–47, 156–57, 160–61; economy of, 39, 74; and fantasy, 38–39, 42, 44–47, 122, 136, 180n. 33; and gender, 39–43, 79–83, 135; *Hamlet*, 22; and jouissance, 52, 68, 83, 98–99; and language, 10, 50–53, 59–62; and Petrarchan ideology, 57–84; political dimensions, 8–9, 41–43, 80–81; political responses, 158, 190n. 65; primary, 39–41, 44–46, 51–53, 160, 171n. 60, 172n. 78; and reading, 89, 95, 98–105; theatricality, 73, 130, 157–58, 172n. 71; viewers', 133, 135. *See also* sadomasochism

Maus, Katharine Eisaman, 182n. 13

Maxwell, J. C., 181n. 3

Mazzio, Carla, and Douglas Trevor, 31, 170nn. 47, 49, 188nn. 19, 23

Mazzotta, Giuseppe, 59, 173n. 6

Merback, Mitchell B., 178n. 12

Merleau-Ponty, Maurice, 142–45, 149–50, 187n. 18

Montaigne, Michel de, 109, 154, 182n. 6

Mozeley, J. F., 177n. 2
Mueller, Janel M., 92–95, 179n. 16
Mulvey, Laura, 129, 185n. 44
Munday, Anthony, 18, 166n. 11
Murray, Timothy, 126, 168n. 28, 184n. 34
mutilation, 85, 92, 131; fetishized, 109–10; staging of, 3, 108, 111–13, 121, 127, 130–31, 134–36

Nashe, Thomas, 104–5, 181nn. 38, 40
Nead, Lynda, 182n. 10
Neely, Carol Thomas, 170n. 49, 174n. 10
Neill, Michael, 187nn. 8, 15, 17, 190nn. 53, 60
Nicholls, David, 179n. 22
Nicholson, Eirwen, 88, 178n. 8
normativity, 48, 136, 157
Noyes, John K., 39, 46, 165n. 8, 171n. 57, 190–91n. 65
Nussbaum, Damian, 177–78n. 3, 178n. 7
Nuttall, A. D., 48–50, 172n. 84, 172–73n. 85, 186n. 3

objectivity, 23, 113, 125–28, 135–36
Oliver, H. J., 187n. 11
O'Malley, Charles Donald, 188–89n. 33
Orgel, Stephen, 138, 167n. 21, 186n. 2
Ovid, 12, 129–31, 172n. 72

Palmer, D. J., 106, 107, 181n. 2
Parker, Barbara, 183n. 26
Paster, Gail Kern, 14, 139, 149, 152, 157, 166n. 4, 170n. 49, 186n. 6, 190n. 51
Patterson, Lee, 166n. 2
Peacham, Henry, 6, 115, 116, 121, 183n. 20
Pecora, Vincent P., 169n. 35
Percy, William, 11, 64, 65, 80, 174n. 19

Petrarch, 75
Petrarchan poetry, 45, 57–84, 100, 141
Petrarchanism, 5–6, 11, 54, 56–84, 174nn. 10, 14, 175n. 35, 176n. 47; and gender, 77–83; and interpretive closure, 70–73; language, 52, 59–60; and martyrdom, 58; masochism, 57–84; sadism, 65–66; symbolic gaps, 78
phenomenology, 1, 3, 7, 31–32, 92, 108, 112, 140, 142–46, 150; and staged suicide, 155–57
phlebotomy, 142, 150–52, 157
Plutarch, 56, 118
pornography, 11, 76, 91, 109–16; economic motive, 137; and eroticism, 127, 130, 134; history of, 115–21; and phenomenology, 112; theory of, 110–15, 133–37
Prynne, William, 17–19, 166n. 10
psychoanalytic theory: and ethics, 9, 102–3; and historicism, 7–9, 24–34, 36–37; and political critique, 8–9, 33
Pye, Christopher, 45, 168n. 28

Rainoldes, John, 18–20, 166n. 13
Rajan, Tilottama, 175n. 37
Rambuss, Richard, 167n. 19
Rankins, William, 17, 19, 166n. 11
rape, 78, 109–10, 121, 127–28, 130–34, 136, 186n. 53; and humanism, 131
Ray, Sid, 186n. 53
readers, 66–67; displacement of affect, 96–98; double consciousness, 103; and identification, 105; as individuals, 88–91, 93; and jouissance, 98–100; and masochism, 95, 99–105. *See also* textuality
Reformation, 7, 13, 28, 53, 87, 92, 103, 121

Reinhard, Kenneth, 167n. 26, 168n. 28
Reynoldes, Edward, 16, 70, 166n. 9

Sacher-Masoch, Leopold von, 46, 80,
   103, 121, 172n. 77, 176n. 45, 181n. 37,
   184n. 28
Sade, Marquis de [Donatien Alphonse
   François], 9, 11, 28, 46–47, 80, 95,
   101–5, 178n. 13
sadomasochism, 7, 10, 12, 36, 40, 42,
   46–47, 53, 68, 73, 82–83, 110, 125, 135–
   36, 156, 157–58; historical dimensions
   of, 8, 53, 103–5, 137. *See also*
   masochism
Saunders, John B. deC. M., and Charles
   Donald O'Malley, 188–89n. 33
Sawday, Jonathan, 20, 167n. 17, 185n. 50,
   188n. 19
Scarry, Elaine, 95, 129, 145–46, 154,
   188n. 30
Schwartz, Regina, 170nn. 49, 50
Sedinger, Tracey, 33, 34, 169n. 38, 170n.
   53
self and selfhood, 2, 4, 6, 14, 54, 94, 153,
   160; negation, 2, 30–31, 76;
   theological view of, 20–21. *See also*
   subjectivity
self-fashioning, 2, 12, 24–31, 168nn. 30,
   32, 169n. 40
semiotics, 5, 63–65, 108, 154, 171nn. 63, 69
Shakespeare, William: *Antony and
   Cleopatra*, 8–9, 190n. 53; *As You Like It*,
   63; *Cymbeline*, 111, 183n. 26; *Hamlet*,
   22–23, 122; *Henry V*, 85; *King Lear*, 1,
   3, 6, 50, 125–26, 129–30, 181n. 3, 184n.
   34; *Macbeth*, 50; *Measure for Measure*,
   8–9; sonnets, 174nn. 8, 10, *Titus
   Andronicus*, 6, 11, 43, 50, 54, 55, 105,
   106–37, 139, 159, 181n. 3, 182n. 13,

184nn. 36, 38, 40, 185nn. 42, 49, 51,
   186n. 53; *Twelfth Night*, 47, 63, 155;
   Winter's Tale, 118, 126, 184n. 35
Sidney, Philip, 75, 76, 145, 175n. 38
Siegel, Carol, 176n. 45
Silverman, Kaja, 41, 110–11, 129, 171nn.
   64, 65, 173n. 3, 182n. 7, 185n. 45
skepticism, 125–27, 184n. 34
Skura, Meredith, 170n. 49
Smith, Bruce R., 114, 135, 157, 181n. 40,
   183n. 18
Smith, Hallett, 59–60, 174n. 9
Smith, Roger, 188nn. 19, 21
Smith, William, 11, 71–72, 74, 83, 175n. 33
Spencer, T. J. B., 118, 183n. 25
Speziale-Bagliacca, Roberto, 165n. 5
Sprengnether, Madelon, 184n. 31
Starks, Lisa S., 176n. 45
Stavig, Mark, 187n. 9
Steiner, Wendy, 182n. 9, 182–83n. 14
Stevens, Scott Manning, 145, 188nn. 19,
   29, 189n. 34
Stewart, Suzanne R., 41–42, 169n. 42,
   172n. 71, 190n. 65
Stott, Andrew, 175n. 21
Stubbes, Phillip, 17, 166n. 11
Studlar, Gaylyn, 171n. 59, 173n. 87
subjectivity, 18, 20, 108, 122, 140, 142,
   143; and fantasy, 45–46; female
   characters and, 127–36; historical
   emergence of, 2, 3–5, 7, 13–14, 18–24,
   34, 53–55, 69; humanist model of, 9–
   10; humoral view of, 14–17, 154–55;
   and individualism, 26–27; and
   language, 52–53; mutable, 18;
   paradoxical basis, 7–9, 40–41; and
   postmodern culture, 12; reflexivity,
   43–44; and religious discourse, 21.
   See also self and selfhood

Taylor, Charles, 13, 166n. 3

Temkin, Owsei, 189n. 35

textuality, 7, 9, 31, 34, 79, 98, 102–5, 136; aesthetic dimension, 2, 33; and pleasure, 5, 53, 88–91, 94; and Protestantism, 95–96, 100, 103. *See also* readers

Tomlinson, T. B., 187n. 12

torture, 56, 89, 90, 94–95, 101, 118, 129, 175n. 35, 178n. 14

Traub, Valerie, 170n. 49

Trevor, Douglas, 31, 170nn. 47, 49, 188nn. 19, 23

Tricomi, Albert H., 128, 182n. 13, 184n. 37

Vasari, G., 116, 183n. 22

Vickers, Nancy J., 75, 76, 175–76n. 39

violence: and aesthetics, 12, 29–30, in entertainment, 55; entry into language, 101. *See also* dismemberment, mutilation, rape, torture

Webb, Peter, 116, 118, 183n. 24

Whitteridge, Gweneth, 188n. 32

Willbern, David, 128, 134–35, 184nn. 36, 39, 185nn. 49, 51

Williams, Linda, 46, 133, 165n. 12, 172n. 76, 186nn. 55, 59

Wilson, Scott, 174n. 14, 175n. 35

Woolf, D. R., 177n. 2, 179n. 17

Wright, Thomas, 16, 148, 150, 166n. 8

Wymer, Rowland, 140, 187nn. 13, 14, 190n. 58

Wynne-Davies, Marion, 129, 185n. 42

Yates, Velvet, 186n. 5

Zepheria, 11, 64–66, 73–74, 80, 174–75n. 21

Žižek, Slavoj, 6, 32–33, 61, 77, 101, 102, 124, 128, 134, 165n. 6, 174n. 12, 180nn. 33, 34, 184n. 32